Country Sports II

Country Sports II

More Rabid Pursuits of a Redneck
Environmentalist

By M. H. Dutch Salmon

Acknowledgments

Most of these essays appeared previously in different form in the Las Cruces (New Mexico) *Sun-News*; others in the Silver City (New Mexico) *Daily Press, Fur-Fish-Game, The Rabbit Hunter, The Fox & Coyote Hunter, New Mexico Wildlife* and the New Mexico Wildlife Federation *Outdoor Reporter*. The author also acknowledges the contributions of fishing buddy Steve Siegfried, aka Stephen O'Day – good fisherman, good writer, good editor.

High-Lonesome Books
P.O. Box 878
Silver City, New Mexico 88062

www.High-LonesomeBooks.com
info@High-LonesomeBooks.com

Dedication

This one is for my son, John Pomeroy "Bud" Salmon II –
always my best companion afield.
He was a great kid; now he's a fine man.

Table of Contents

Photo by Dan Gauss © Shot On Site Photography.

Introduction

It sounds funny to say so, because I'm sixty-five, but sometimes I think I'd like to be Dutch Salmon when I grow up. It is not so odd, really. M. H. Salmon is not only the model of the modern sporting writer, but I have been following his tracks for over thirty years now.

Dutch was born in the northeast, in upstate New York. He left there as a young adult, and went to southern Texas and northwestern Minnesota, and finally New Mexico, chasing jackrabbits and coyotes, catfish and dreams. I first encountered him around 1979 or 80 when I was an editor at *Gray's Sporting Journal*, and a publisher came to me with a remarkable manuscript. Titled "Home With the Hounds" it was an account of hunting with coursing longdogs of various breeds. I was a falconer, and it seemed to me that this was a kind of falconry on the ground.

Ed Gray thought the material was a little too esoteric for *Gray's*, but I became a correspondent with Dutch. Soon, I found myself in southwestern New Mexico, where he was a close neighbor, about a hundred miles away. I soon acquired a couple of hounds from him, and longdog crosses and salukis became a permanent part of my life.

If longdogs and the State of New Mexico had been the only things that I had gotten from Dutch, I would be in his debt forever. But they weren't. The unspoiled Gila Wilderness, chile as a natural part of one's diet, Aldo Leopold's legacy, and fishing for catfish are four rather random things that I took from our friendship, and there are doubtless a lot more ideas and attitudes I have picked up unconsciously.

Eventually, Dutch, frustrated with mainstream publishing, decided that if you can't get them to publish your work, you might as well start your own press and book business. Since that day High-Lonesome Books has become the premier house for Southwestern classics and environmentally conscious new books about hunting and fishing and Wilderness. He has published several stirring novels, including *Home is the River, Signal to Depart,* and *Forty Freedoms*; a couple of books on the Gila River; the definitive American coursing dog manual, now in what I believe is its second iteration; and a literary book on catfish. The last made my eccentric list of 100 best sporting books in *A Sportsman's Library*.

He has also written various newspaper and magazine pieces on every aspect of field sport and conservation, of which this is the second collection. And I do mean various. The latest volume includes a portrait of an Anglican priest who is a falconer, a tale of his son's first big wilderness buck, an elegy for the old cockfighters of New Mexico, and a nuanced appreciation of feral pigs.

Not content to defend wilderness, especially his beloved Gila, Dutch eventually made it to the New Mexico Game Commission, where he became one of its most outspoken, individual, non- partisan, and occasionally contrary voices. He had the respect of everyone I know, including some that disagreed with him on one matter or another. And I am among those who think that his utterly political firing was a disgrace. He never complained, but went back calmly to the field and his work of portraying it and defending it.

Lately, I have followed Dutch down some more difficult roads. Several years ago he was diagnosed with Parkinson's Disease. One would not know it, considering that he never left the field behind. But one of the weirdest coincidences on earth, I, another writer and long-dogger born in the east, was diagnosed a year later. I have a pretty funny picture of us in a field of thirty-somethings, all holding a very various pack of sighthounds on leashes. On it is my note bragging that two sixty-somethings with Parkinson's (and one woman of the same age, my wife Libby) elected to keep going, chasing the dogs, when the kids all called a halt for mid-day lunch break.

Parkinson's won't kill you, say the humorous – it will only make you wish you were dead. There is even a god-awful New-Agey whine: "Parkinson's isn't a *death* sentence; it is a *life* sentence." Gack! With time, unfortunately, it does get worse. But now there's a promising alternative, a surgery called Deep Brain Stimulation. Once again Dutch became my mentor, going under the knife a year ago at UNM Hospital. His improvement convinced me to do it too. And I'm very glad I did.

Dutch would doubtless blush at this and change the subject to flyfishing, or the Desert Hare Classic, the annual gathering of the sighthound clans in southern New Mexico. He continues to hunt and fish and write, most recently this book you are holding in your hands. Finally, I salute him as not only a friend who has been a pioneer in so many of my own pursuits, but as a pioneer conservationist, and a defender of all the Old Ways and things that we must hold on to, lest our civilization become too artificial to live. I'm going to raise a glass to him with the punchline of a shaggy dog story about making toasts on two sides of the border, which he told me when I first knew him and several time since. Dutch: "DOWN THE RATHOLE!" May you live to be 100!

Steve Bodio
Magdalena, New Mexico

Country Sports II

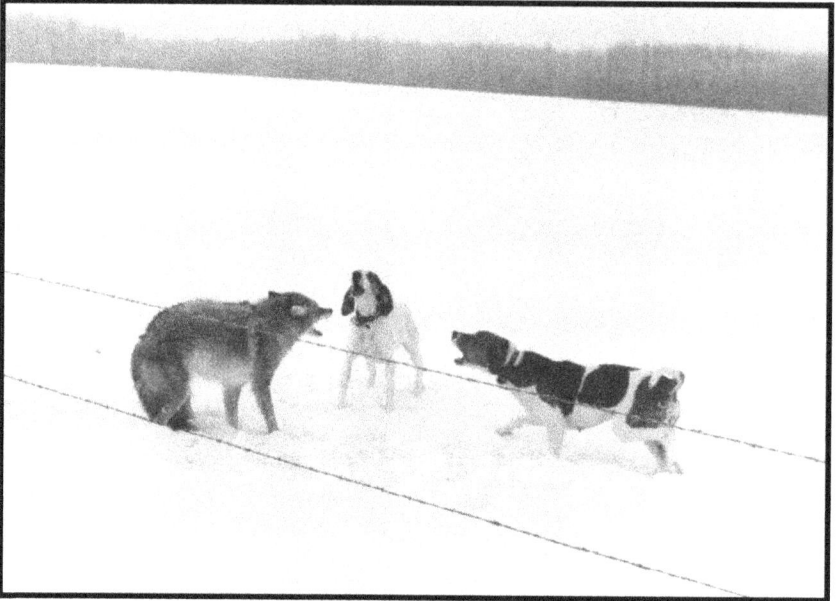

HUNTING

Wilderness Mule Deer Yields a Classic Hunt

In the West the mule deer hunt sets the standard for big game, the first critter you think of when somebody asks: "Did you draw a tag?" Elk are beyond the means of many, and the likes of Coues whitetail deer, antelope, bear, lion, oryx, ibex, *et al*, are all relatively esoteric pursuits. But most everyone out West has been on a mule deer hunt, if they hunt at all.

The mule deer hunt can take many forms. Ubiquitous in all but pure grasslands habitat, a great many mule deer are taken by hunters who drive to the kill, or nearly so, rarely hunting more than a half mile from a road. The classic mule deer hunt is quite different, its character immortalized time and again in articles that spanned four decades in *Outdoor Life* magazine and authored by the famed outdoor scribe, Jack O'Connor.

Usually leading his story off with something like, "One time in Sonora" (or Arizona, or New Mexico), O'Connor, a gifted expository writer as well as hunter, took the reader off-road, into the southwestern Wilderness, usually toting a scoped, bolt action .270 shooting a 130 grain bullet. The hunter was invariably challenged in finding the deer, stalking, making a long-distance shot, and getting the meat out in good shape.

This year son Bud, 16, drew a deer permit ascribed to a youth hunt. We looked at the map and picked out a range of rough hills in the Gila Wilderness where I had seen in recent years a fair number of deer while on fishing trips. That the hunt was limited to youth and would take place in some rough country well away from roads virtually assured we wouldn't have a lot of competition.

"Buddy, I'll bet we'll have that country all to ourselves," I said.

"Good," he said

I was almost right. There was a pickup hitched to a horse trailer parked at the trailhead and we followed horse tracks for about a quarter mile on the trail going in. At that point the trail, and the canyon, forked. We took the other and neither saw nor heard anyone for the length of the hunt.

We hunted slowly, deliberately, down the canyon. It offered some open grassland in the bottom over the first mile or two but eventually narrowed into a live stream. The flanking hills were steep, rocky, but well vegetated with oaks, piñon, juniper, and ponderosa pine, and the snow that covered about half of the ground was melting ever-so-slowly in the warming sun. This was deer country all right; there were tracks old and new in snow and mud. We periodically stopped to set up a stand well hidden (we hoped) against the flank of a hill where we could look down and bushwhack any deer with legal antlers that might be moving in the flat below.

6

"If you get above them they usually won't see you," I said

"I know, Dad."

But we saw no deer and by early afternoon as we unwrapped some lunch Bud was ready for a new approach.

"There's fresh tracks going off west up this slope," he said.

"It's sort of a mesa up there," I said, "and then you'll come to another canyon with spring water like this one."

"I'm going up."

"I'll wait here; my back is knotting up. Remember, it's dark by five o'clock."

I watched my kid climb until he disappeared into the folds of the mountain. I knew he had a good measure of common sense, for a teenager, a compass and map, and a GPS unit he knew how to use. About an hour later I thought I heard a shot; the muffled report seemingly coming from the mesa above and to the west. Then nothing for a long time. I was starting to worry about how fast darkness comes down in December when he appeared. He took off his coat and held out his arms to show me he had been up to his elbows in a deer.

"Got him, huh?"

"I spotted him from the edge of the mesa, Dad. He was lying down under a tree over across that next canyon. I was above him and he never saw me. According to the GPS it was .26 miles.........about 400 yards. I used the backpack as a rest and held on a point near the top of his antlers. At the shot he got up and took about three steps and collapsed. It took me a while to get over there and find him. I tagged him and then I gutted him and it wore me out. The bullet went in at an angle, through a lung and the liver and stopped at a rib on the far side."

I said something about how Daniel Boone would have carried him out. Bud laughed. He's All-State football, 6'2, 205 lbs. He said, "I actually tried to drag him for a ways." Then he just shook his head.

We made it to the truck just at dark. The next day, in a cold drizzling rain and with some extra help (friends Bill and Gene), Bud went back in and boned out his buck and they packed out the meat in backpacks. The head too; 5 points on a side. The shot was made with a Savage Model #116, bolt action, stainless steel, .270 caliber and a 130 grain bullet. The bullet had mushroomed, performed perfectly, just like you read about in the outdoor magazines. And from stalk to shot to retrieve, I like to think even Jack O'Conner would have approved how it was done.

7

Hunting Dog Tales From Australia

My knowledge of Australia is limited to my having read one book and seen one movie about the land down under.

The book was *Tracks* by Robyn Davidson, a wonderful, non-fiction story about a woman who makes a camel trip across the Australian outback. The movie of course was *Crocodile Dundee* staring Paul Hogan. Dundee's story is pure fiction. But it was an entertaining tale, and while I can't recall much of the plot, some of the Australian vernacular, such as "G'day" and, "No worries," stuck.

Rob Thomson of South Australia is a dog man. Like me, he's not much interested in hunting anything that you can't pursue with some kind of dog, be it sighthound, trail hound, cur, terrier, or mixtures in-between. He'd read my book on coursing hounds and over the years we had corresponded by mail across the Pacific. So last week, while visiting the USA with his family, he rang me up to see if I could show him some of the American outback.

I picked him up at the motel in Silver City and, sure enough, he said, "G'Day," as we shook hands for the first time. And when I apologized for the car, my pickup being once again in the shop, he said, "No worries." On the way to the field I learned something about hunting with dogs in Australia.

"It's unusual to see anyone when you're hunting in Australia," Rob said.

This isn't because there are no hunters, but because this is a nation nearly as large as the USA but with less than 20 million people.

"One station (ranch) where we hunt is 150 kilometers (about 90 miles) wide," he said.

To date, "open space" is not a concern in Australia.

Of the game that dogs pursue in Australia, the only two that were present when European settlement arrived were the dingo and the kangaroo. The dingo is a prick-eared, wild dog roughly between the coyote and wolf in size and highly destructive of livestock. They are scarce in Rob's hunting range but he said that in parts of Australia they are common and there are men with exceptional packs of dogs that can catch one and put it on the ground.

The "roos" are widespread and common, Rob said. As an appealing native species, Kangaroos are technically off limits to hunting. They can be very destructive of crops, however, and can eat the range down to a nub, and thus farmers and ranchers are allowed considerable law in controlling their numbers.

"So hunting roos means getting permission from the landowner," Rob said.

8

Other game are exotics or imports and often exist in plague proportions, Rob said. These includes rabbits (similar to our cottontail only larger), European hares (similar to our jackrabbit), red fox, feral hogs, feral goats, feral camels, and deer.

Rob and his "mates" maintain a pack of at least 6 dogs to hunt a variety of game.

"I have a couple of Jack Russell terriers to rout the rabbits and fox out of holes and brush piles," he said. "Then we use coursing type hounds to run them down. We use the same coursing hounds to hunt the roos and run hares, and then we have some bigger terriers as well, for hunting feral pigs."

Neither kangaroo nor pig hunting is for the faint of heart.

"The biggest species of roo is bigger than a man," Rob said. "They don't run as well as the smaller roos, but when they're caught they'll just set back on their tail and one hind leg, grab a dog up with their front feet, which are almost like hands, and then kick at the dog with their other hind leg. One of mine last year got kicked by a roo and it took 100 stitches to sew him up under his front leg.

"We would rather hunt the smaller roos. They can run like deer and it takes very fast dogs to catch them. But even they can be dangerous. They will run to a billabong (an inland lake or pond) and wait for the dogs in the water. They know how to drown a dog. The roo can stand in there, but the dogs have to swim, and when the dog swims up the roo pushes him under with his front feet. We had one like this a few years ago. The dogs were already 'stuffed' (worn out) when they went in after the roo. We had to wade in to get the roo and save the dogs."

Rob says the kangaroo produces a very lean, dark, flavorful meat. He kills three or four every year to put in the freezer. Kangaroo is also raised commercially and is common restaurant fare in Australia, he says.

A Baptist minister by trade, Rob Thomson does most of his preaching not to adults from the pulpit, but to troubled teens in the great outdoors.

"When I take teens on pig hunts in the outback," Rob says, "I tell them we are going to read the Bible around the campfire in the evening, and kill some meat during the day. I ask them to think about whether they can handle all of that before they go along. It's a challenge, and most of them do quite well."

It takes special dogs to catch and hold a wild pig, and special men to take one while armed only with a knife.

"We use the faster dogs to trail and bay the pig," Rob says, "then we have a couple of bull terrier types to lock onto the head or neck. Once they've got him, I grab the pig's hind legs and get them off the ground, like lifting a big wheelbarrow. Then I can twist and put the boar on his side. One of my mates puts his foot on the neck and sticks the pig with a long knife."

9

With all this excitement in the outback, I feared the jackrabbit hunt I was offering would be a rather plain soup for Rob. But my greyhound Phoebe, and three greyhound/saluki crosses, Cookie, Comet, and Bandit, provided some very exciting coursing as they pursued three different jackrabbits across the Chihuahuan grasslands.

All the hares escaped, but they were good races nonetheless, and Rob commented that our native blacktail jack was definitely faster than the European hares in Australia.

Later, at a cafe, a local picked up on Rob's accent. He started telling Rob about this other Australian who was very much a TV celebrity these days. No, not Paul Hogan. But this fellow also had a strong Australian accent, and pursued crocs, and poisonous snakes, or did, until one of his adventures got the best of him not so long ago.

"What did you say his name was?" Rob said.

"Steve Irwin."

"Yeah, I know who you mean," he said, "but I've got to tell you, I never heard of that bloke till I got to the USA."

Breeding a Better Hunting Dog

Well, what with the heat and wind it appears the pursuit of hare with hound is over till next fall. It was a poor season for my pack, due primarily to the scarcity of jackrabbits on the fields I hunt, but one bright spot was the performance of the pup hound "Phoxy." Born last June, 2010, she came to me this past November from Louisiana, by breeding about 3/4 coldblood greyhound (for speed) X 1/4 saluki (for endurance and heat resistance). Since Christmas, I've been running her with the older hounds; and therein lies a tale.

Even as a pup Phoxy had a tremendous stride, showing all of length, power, and ease of movement. Greyhounds are typically long-coupled (horizontal length, forequarter to hindquarter, is greater than vertical height at the withers) but Phoxy is relatively long-bodied even for a running dog and her tail literally touches the ground. Though a mixed breed dog, she is no accident. Her sire and dam are both good at the same pursuit and she has the chance to be even better.

Dog breeding, and dog breeders, are under constant attack these days from certain "humane" groups who'd just as soon breeding and puppies (and especially pups bred and raised for hunting) went the way of the horse and wagon. But in the right hands breeding is an art and a pup like Phoxy is the proof where perfection of form yields excellence of function. I can't take credit for the creation but a pup like Phoxy necessarily puts me in contemplation of the breeder's art as it pertains to hunting dogs.

I would say that for the serious hunter, whether he fancies sighthound, trail hound, bird dog or terrier, the task is somewhat simplified. The show dog breeder can get all caught up in considerations of coat texture, coat color, head shape, eye color, tail set, and the like. Most of us hunters are concerned with such things only secondarily; we are mostly looking at performance in the field.

Performance in the field can further simplify the breeding process. Many breeds today, including but not limited to hunting breeds, are afflicted with serious defects – congenital eye problems, impotence, hip dysplasia, congenital heart problems, etc. With wild dogs (wolves, foxes etc.) such defects seldom appear because individuals with such flaws don't survive to breeding age. Serious hunters who give their dogs real work in the field will artificially select against the same defects, thus yielding the same long-term benefits to the breed or type. What else is required?

Well, a basic knowledge of genetics and the theory of Mendel is helpful. Plus you should know something of inbreeding vs. linebreeding vs. outcrossing. It's beyond the scope of this column to explain all this here (plus I'm not the best one to explain it), so I'm listing three books at the end of the column that should be helpful. I think my own experience, and mistakes as a dog breeder, can be useful regarding four precepts in the breeder's art.

The first is: "Know what you want." If you're a bird hunter who likes the Brittany spaniel, consider that some lines of this breed work close and some are high powered and work at long range. If you look to breed your Brittany, consider your own needs as a quail hunter and decide ahead of time if you're trying to create a close working or wide ranging bird dog. Hunting coyotes in the snow in Minnesota in the 1970s, I started with big, slow coonhounds that were good at finding the coyotes but couldn't keep up once the race started. I hadn't considered what I really wanted in a trail hound for coyote hunting. I bred in the running abilities of swift Walker and July foxhounds and even faster greyhound and Scotch deerhound, and over time developed trail hounds that "run to catch."

The second precept is: "What ye sow, so shall ye reap." Virtually everything in your hunting dog is inheritable, from obvious physical traits, like size or coat, to less obvious physical traits like nose or speed (these can only be ascertained in the field), to psychological traits like heart and drive or, in the alternative, the laziness of a slacker. The perfect hunting dog has yet to be bred; however if your bird dog lacks a strong retrieving instinct, or your coonhound a strong treeing instinct, he will tend to pass the flaw along to the offspring; i.e., bad traits are passed along as readily as good ones. You might consider not breeding him/her; at the least breed to a dog that is a strong retriever, or tree hound, and thereby provide the opportunity for correction of the flaw in at least some of the puppies.

The third precept is: "Watch out for kennel blindness!" This is not a disease but a flaw of the ego and it afflicts us dog owners rather than the dogs themselves. It's a common affliction, more a sin than a malady, and I confess I've been guilty myself.

The thing is, it's so easy to think that your own "Rover" in your own kennel is the best bird dog or hound in the world, so why not breed him? And if you have a female counterpart in the same kennel, Suzy say, or Swiftie; you probably think she's tops as well, 'cause she's yours. So you do the breeding and when the pups mature you're indignant when an independent assessment asserts that – no surprise – mediocrity begot more mediocrity.

David Hise of Roswell is well known in eastern New Mexico for his fine hounds. He has said: "I don't mind getting outrun by a better dog because then I know where to go to breed my bitch." You don't need glasses to correct kennel blindness, just the ability for a fair and honest critique of your own stock.

The last precept is: "Don't do the breeding if you don't have homes for the puppies." You don't want to be one of those who ends up carting a litter of unwanted pups off to the animal shelter.

Everyone fancies, or at least wishes for, some sort of creative talent. If you can paint, sing, write songs or books, act or otherwise offer some peculiar talent you have the chance to enrich yourself and others and leave your culture a legacy. Most of us flail away and find we just haven't got it; but to produce superior stock offers another field of endeavor. The breeding of animals, whether farm stock, pets, horses or hunting dogs, is an art-form, nowadays enriched by science, that, done creatively, can leave a legacy of rare talent and admirable form within the medium of flesh and blood. Like Phoxy. Not yet a year old, it is already a joy to watch her in the field. By next fall she'll be running down strong hares; and, considering her line of ancestry, breeding and descent, her talents come as no surprise.

For more information on breeding a better hunting dog:

1) *Hunting Dogs* by Rice and Dahl. Out of print but easily found on the used market. Has a short chapter on breeding that is the best introduction I know of.

2) *How to Breed Dogs* by Leon Whitney. A standard work.

3) *The New Art of Breeding Better Dogs* by Kyle and Phillip Onstott. The other standard work.

Wildlife Profile: The Brown Rat – Ugh!

Few can resist a fascination at some point in life with the lowly rat, for the fascination is borne of revulsion. Get up close with a rat for the first time and the experience is there for life. How well I remember!

I arrived home from grade school one afternoon with my dog, Boots. She was a Boxer with four white-stocking feet and she would follow me to school each day, then wait outside for our walk home. As we entered the garage her nose detected something evil lurking behind the trash cans. Her hair came up along the back, she growled; whatever it was she hated it instinctively. Aroused myself, I moved the cans and a huge rat (rats always seem "huge") scurried down the wall. He used my bicycle for cover as he headed for escape at the open door but lost his life as he made his final dash – Boots pounced, grabbed, and killed the rat instantly with a vicious snap of her head. I was exhilarated and displayed the critter by the tail to my horrified mother.

Thereafter, my dog and I hunted rats with passion and a vengeance, at dumps and other feed areas where rats reside. Instinctively, it was so easy to hate them, the chase aroused my nascent predatory instincts, and the kill of a rat is without remorse. Most everybody hates rats. Yet the rat continues to survive, and thrive, and its place in history is secure.

The rat Boots killed was the brown or Norway rat (*Rattus norwegicus*). Whence it came seems a subject of some dispute, but it was certainly in China and eastern Russia before it arrived in Europe around the 17th century, and soon thereafter to the Americas. It was preceded in both locales by its cousin the black rat (*Rattus rattus*), the species that served as a prominent vector during the horrific plague years.

Lore has it that the black rat came to Europe by way of the Crusaders returning from Muslim lands in the 13th century. Then, as now, such war efforts in the Middle East were doomed to failure, and along with a botched attempt at conquest the Crusaders got the black rat for their troubles, an 8 to 12 ounce scurrilous rodent that often carries the bacillus, *Pasteurella pestis*, source of the bubonic plague. The germ lives harmlessly in the blood of the rat but can thereby be passed by fleas to humans where it surfaces in deadly fashion. As detailed by Brian Plummer in his curious book, *Tales of a Rat-Hunting Man*, there is an interesting tale of physiology behind the term, "bubonic" plague.

An early symptom of the disease is the development of swollen lymph glands in the groin and under the arms, swellings known at the time as "buboes." The swollen, inflamed and reddish tissue, circular in shape, was due to the lymph glands trying to filter out the infection. The attempt almost always failed in those days of medical ignorance and the infection spread through the body, often to the lungs, where it produced a deadly hacking cough. Thus the bubonic plague often became a

14

pneumonic plague that further spread the malady throughout the populace. The whole story is still with us today, in a deceptive 800-year-old nursery rhyme we all learned in grade school: "Ring around the rosy; pocket full of posies; ashes, ashes – all fall down."

The "ring around the rosy" was reference to the swollen buboes – the inflamed lymph glands – circular in shape and ringed by a lighter colored skin; "pocket full of posies" referred to the superstition of the time that carrying flowers in the pockets would filter out the evil "vapors" that caused the disease; "ashes, ashes" tells how the dead were taken in horse-drawn carts to the outskirts of town where they were burned, *en masse*; "all fall down" is self-explanatory for the people were dying like flies.

The black rat did not cause the plague years but was merely an evil, if inadvertent, liaison in the deadly process. Centuries later, upon arrival, the brown rat soon dominated the black rat in both Europe and the Americas. It is larger at 12 to 16 ounces and occasionally to a couple of pounds (tales of "a rat the size of a cat" are pure fiction). It, too, can carry and pass along the "plague," along with hepatitis, leptospirosis, and other maladies. The brown rat more easily adapts to field and farm as well as town life. You can tell the so-called house or barn rat – black or brown – from our native cotton rat, wood rat and pack rat because the brown rat has a scaly, hairless tail.

For reasons unknown to me, brown rats seem much less common in the Southwest than back east. I do have two rat tales from the region however, one of which still makes me shudder.

I was living out along the Mimbres River with a pet house cat. This guy was a hunter and one night I was awakened by a terrific ruckus in the kitchen. I went in, turned on the light, and found my tomcat crouched over a monster rat with a scaly, scabrous tail. I was proud; it's not every cat that can finish a rat of that size.

The other story, well, don't read this just before lunch.

At the same house my well water started showing up smelly and discolored at the tap. Single men are famous for not taking care of themselves and I confess I let it go for a while. Finally, even I couldn't stand it. It was a hand dug well, three feet in diameter, and when I shined a light I saw something fuzzy about 20 feet down. I lowered a net and fished out a big barn rat that had been there far too long. I should have been dead already from who knows what that drowned rat might have passed along in the water but I swear I never even got the "scoots."

Of course the Boxer, Boots, is long since gone. But now I have a Jack Russell terrier, Jack. Would I be a rat-hunting man once again? Just show me and Jack a population of brown rats, evil, scurrilous, vicious and diseased. We would hunt them with passion and a vengeance.

Happiness is a Man with Eighteen Puppies

On July 4th my dog Comet, a rough-coated Greyhound, had nine puppies. She was bred to Kyran, a full-blooded Tazi imported from Uzbekistan (more on this later). It was a planned breeding.

On July 24th my dog Mona, a ½ Tazi , ¼ Greyhound, ¼ Lurcher, also had nine puppies. She was bred to Samson, a ¾ Greyhound X ¼ Saluki, but in this case Samson slipped through the fence and the puppies were a shocker. It was my fault, the first unplanned breeding in many years, yet it may turn out the best one in the end. But the sum is, I suddenly have 18 puppies in my life!

Not to panic (though initially I did!), half the pups are already promised to good homes and with the canine benevolence of other like-minded dog lovers who want a "one of a kind" dog, the rest – excepting the one or two I'll keep – will also be homeward bound in the next couple of months. But the experience has been an education in the derivation of our most ancient hunting breeds.

Various authorities surmise that the man/wild dog relationship began to form way back in the Paleolithic period when we were still hunter/gatherers living in caves. A mutual benefit of hunting and defense was a natural derivation of their talents and ours; little by little certain wolves or wild dogs were at least partially domesticated, hunting hip by jowl with our own wild ancestors. But the selective breeding process that produced types or strains of domestic dogs that we would recognize today as breeds didn't begin until well into the Neolithic period when agriculture, stock raising, and "civilization" was upon us.

The first recognized type – generally credited – was what we today call the Saluki, an AKC recognized breed. The Saluki formulation was centuries prior to the advent of firearms (and thus "gundogs") and indeed all the early hunting strains were swift hounds, generally called sighthounds or gazehounds, which could take game like hare, rabbit, fox, deer, antelope etc. without the aid of the human hand or weapon. Numerous ancient examples of art-work from the Middle East of the time clearly indicate that such hunting hounds were at work in the field at least several thousand years before Christ.

But the Saluki had a wide geography, and while all were used for the same general purpose – running down game – they would vary as to topography, tribe, or the game pursued. And in places they became known by another name.

According to Gail Goodman, author of the monumental *Saluqi – Coursing Hound of the East,* as the Saluki evolved from the Arabic countries – Saudi Arabia, Egypt, Morocco, Syria – to the more eastern Asiatic domains like Turkey, Turkistan, Uzbekistan, Kazakhstan, it took the name "Tazi." Again, different terrains, tribes, and exigencies of the

16

hunt produced somewhat different strains, but all were similar enough that the Tazi/Saluki became an identifiable breed or at least "type."

Over many centuries, these seminal sighthounds were selectively bred to become the Afghan of Afghanistan, Borzoi of Russia, and the Greyhound, Whippet and Scotch Deerhound of the United Kingdom. Other selective breeding creativity by hunters produced today's bird dogs and trail hounds. But the middle-eastern sighthounds were the first recognizable breeds.

Did the Tazi or the Saluki come first? I'll let those more expert than I sort that out (I've witnessed some heated arguments) and even then the best of them would be guessing – we're talking about thousands of years of history. But there is no guessing about where most of the hunting Tazi/Salukis are now.

Hunting in the Arabic Middle East has fallen on hard times. The desert terrain meant the game was always sparse. Modern hunting methods, not Salukis but guns and mechanized pursuit, have taken an even greater toll on the wildlife, leaving the ancient pursuit with little to hunt and the hounds that much more rare and esoteric. There are still some good "desert breds" but overall the quality of the hounds has suffered.

In Turkey, Uzbekistan, Kazakhstan, the old ways have survived, both in coursing and falconry. Magdalena author Steve Bodio, like me an enthusiast of the archaic, made several trips to the brutal steppe country of Uzbekistan and Kazakhstan, where it boils in summer and grabs you with iron cold in winter. At considerable expense and effort, the result was the falconry book, *Eagle Dreams,* and the acquisition of three full-blooded Tazi hounds, duly imported to New Mexico. He said all the Tazi of the steppes were hard-boiled hunters, mostly for hare and a large subspecies of the red fox, and fine and valued companions. All eighteen of my puppies are the beneficiaries, to a greater or lesser degree, of this "blood."

The breeding is apparent in the performance. Last winter Mona, barely a year old, and two other hounds did what the Tazi has done for thousands of years, pursue a hare (jackrabbit). The pursuit was sprint, jink, dodge and turn for five minutes – an extreme course – whence the hare, sensing the end, left them all gasping by ducking down a badger hole.

Showing her youth, Mona, one half of a Tazi import, was slightly slower in the early going, just as strong at the end, but the difference came after we had watered and cooled the pack. The other two hounds, a Greyhound and a Greyhound/Saluki cross, were content to follow in my footsteps as we hiked back to the truck. They'd had it; they were "knackered." Within five minutes Mona was back at a strong lope, working out ahead like a bird dog, pure exuberance, using her nose as well as eyes and hoping to jump another jack. I was just as glad we didn't.

You can't teach that, or force it. You can inherit it from a line of hounds that have done nothing but work at their trade, and bond with their hunting masters, for thousands of years. Most of our dogs, like most of us, have gone soft. I "work out," but I could no more keep up with Jim Bridger or Ben Lilly than this year's "best" Saluki at Westminster could keep up with Mona.

Now I have eighteen puppies. I have added some Greyhound blood for that extra dash of speed to the heritage of the Tazi/Saluki. I know from experience that most of the hares will still be too much for us. But win or lose, as the puppies mature, that link to the ancient and archaic will provide all the talent, heart, and satisfaction I could ever want in the field.

To Shoot an Elk, Whistle for *El Cazador*

El Cazador **(the hunter) likes to get after those elk.** And he's good at it. So good, some years ago he was recruited as a hunting guide for a private ranch elk reserve in northern New Mexico.

"I did all right with that elk deal," he says. "People will pay whatever it takes to get an elk. There's lots of elk up there – too many in places – and ………. toss me the map………... and in the summer I guided fly fishermen………….streams in this area here. One thing I learned surprised me: the elk is a bigger animal down in the Gila country; more massive, bigger horns; the North American model will vary from state to state, or by region, and we grow some real trophies down here (Gila National Forest)."

El Cazador has a theory relating to our big elk. The original elk of southwest New Mexico was the Merriam's subspecies. It was reputed to be a large subspecies and photos I've seen of the heads and racks of horns they left behind, and those animals were Boone & Crockett material.

"I'm thinking some of that Merriam's bloodline for size and big racks was incorporated into today's New Mexico elk," says *El Cazador*. Maybeso, though the official line has it that the Merriam's was extirpated by 1906, while the imported Rocky Mountain elk didn't arrive till 1913????

Growing up in rural Dona Ana County, *El Cazador* took to outdoor sport like the proverbial duck to water. Small game was wherever he wandered; big game provided big dreams to a kid who could hardly wait to get old enough. By the time *El Cazador* became acquainted with my son Bud (17 years old), and myself (never mind), he had experienced successful pursuit of virtually all of New Mexico's big game. Yet such was his enthusiasm for the chase, he would offer his skills as an extension of friendship, *por favor*.

"I was unable to draw an elk tag this time around," he said, "but helping Bud get a cow in this youth hunt will be almost as good."

We met near Reserve, last days of December, 2012. We piled into *El Cazador's* pick-up and headed up into the Ponderosa pine. Every half mile or so we'd stop. Bud and *El Cazador* could grasp the landscape with these stops, using binocular to scan the far ridgelines.

"Is that a cow?" Bud said.

El Cazador said, "I see it too; it's not a cattle cow."

"I think it's a cow elk."

"It *is* a cow elk………let's go."

We looked at the map and they marked a route to the sunning elk and even I could see her now, with the naked eye. It was a good stalk and

19

they were getting almost to rifle range when the crunching of their feet on the snow alerted the cow; when next I looked she was gone.

We saw two more elk at distance and Bud and *El Cazador* would try to sneak up on them, too. Bud had done so in the past but these were wary animals and always heard them or smelled the men coming and moved on. And so the day ended and we all knew now it wasn't going to be easy. We dropped *El Cazador* off at his travel trailer near Cruzville and went into Reserve. We got the last motel room in town and the two cafes were staying open till 8 o'clock to accommodate the youth hunts in the area; we picked one out, ordered a couple of big, ol' chicken fried steak dinners, and ate like harvest hands.

The next day was more of the same: cold, crisp air, lots of sunshine, and a cover of snow that let us know there were some elk in the area. But for the longest time it seemed we couldn't find them.

Late afternoon we went deeper into the woods. A cat hunter, following his hounds on a lion trail, advised that there were lots of elk and tracks "over that-a-way." We followed the general direction of his arm, drove a ways then got out and walked. We walked until the "road" narrowed into a two-track trail. And then a small pickup, carrying two hunters, came bouncing down the two-track route. They went by, waved, then disappeared down the trail as they crossed over a narrow ridge. Then we heard a shot.

"Get ready!" It was *El Cazador*. "Those guys may drive them right to us."

Bud was ready, it seemed, but when the elk came over the ridge there must have been forty of them, all cows, and they were moving, fast. I had warned Bud about downing big game on the run.........it's oh so easy to lose your bullet to a gut shot, the animal just keeps going, or a hip shot, in which case you may bring the animal down but your bullet placement leaves a big chunk of elk blood-shot, the meat spoiled. So Bud held back, seemingly helpless as the herd ran past, maybe 120 yards on a line. That's when *El Cazador* whistled.

If you've been around them much you know a whistle is one of many sounds elk use to communicate. Of course an elk's whistle is distinctive; if your whistle sounds like a hockey referee stopping an off-sides at the blue line it's not going to fool an elk. But when *El Cazador* whistled the last cow running past came to a halt, confused, then wandered off into the trees, Bud quickly got a new position, lined her up, and shooting off-hand scored a good hit in the lung area with a single shot, .270 caliber, 150 grains. The big cow bucked, walked a short way, and lay down for good not a quarter mile from the "road." With three of us including the expertise of *El Cazador* and Bud's rangy, muscled frame, it didn't take long to get the meat boned out, tucked away in plastic sacks and hauled to the truck.

Nearing 18, Bud will soon have to leave it to chance to draw an elk tag; no more can't miss youth hunts for him. But he'll always remember his last one, when *El Cazador* showed us how to bring an elk to a stand-still with just a whistle.

Drawing by Fred Barraza

21

Elk Tracks in a Hard, Cold Country

It's a hard, cold country up there in Catron County at the north end of the Gila National Forest. An ocean of mountains, pine forests and grassland parks grab the visitor; only later do you realize that none of it is leavened with any running water. The sparse human population is a plus. To the hunter it is Game Unit 15 and if it had a flowing stream, it would freeze at summer's end.

No place in America gets so cold that far south – Reserve, NM and Atlanta, GA are very close in latitude, worlds apart in climate. Take that triangle from Reserve northeast to Datil then back west to Quemado and the Arizona state line and you'll have a fair picture of the geography and the map. Santa Fe at 7,000 feet is known for cold with an all-time record of -22 below zero. Reserve is only about 5,800 feet and 300 miles south yet it is colder with a record of -23 below zero. Taos is even higher than Santa Fe, further north, and one night dipped to -27 below zero. Not even close to Quemado at 6,900 feet and a record low of -33 below. Name a colder town in New Mexico! No, not even Chama at 7,600 feet and a record -30 below right on the Colorado border.

Game abounds in this hard cold country though, particularly Abert's squirrels and elk. Two weeks earlier we'd had a good squirrel hunt. Our terrier, Jack, put them up a tree and Bud sharpened his shooting eye, bringing them down with a bolt action .22 magnum. We had a fine squirrel stew but even then Bud was already contemplating his youth elk tag for any antler-less animal in that unit. Of course we had to power up from that .22 magnum. I had the only centerfire arm in the house and we took it to the range to sight it in. Bud handled the gun well and we did a competent job, as it turned out; tuning up the inherent accuracy of the gun.

I said, "Bud, you group them in the field like you do on paper and you've got a dead elk."

I had a tip from a local hunter for an area to camp and hunt, and we came prepared to pitch a tent, hunt meat rather than horns, and try to stay warm, especially at night.

That first afternoon, before season, we set up camp on a cool,, sunny day and set out on foot to scout. We found tracks and elk droppings most everywhere, but no place in particular. More than one informant had warned: "That Unit is no good anymore…wolves got most of them." It appeared not. There was plenty of elk sign, fresh enough that we knew they hadn't all been taken down by wolves in the last week, but it appeared the herds were broken up and scattered (wolves will do that) and we would need to cover some ground to find elk. Fair enough; we were hunting after all.

The next morning we were up before dark and set up before first light in a small stringer of pine close to a feeding area. The thought was the elk would be out in the open park under cover of darkness and we would bushwhack one coming back into the Ponderosa about legal shooting time. It was a good plan but did not produce sight or sound of an elk. As the sun rose we did enjoy the sight of an antelope herd at play on a dry lake bed. They never saw us so we were doing something right. Then we retreated to camp for breakfast and a nap. We hiked out a good section in the afternoon, then, toward evening, attempted to dry-gulch one, as before. No luck. We also made it to an over-look of a nice meadow below.

"You think they might be down there early some morning, Dad?"

"Maybe so, Buddy"

It sure got cold that night – I found out later it went below zero at Quemado – and getting up to answer a call of nature at 3 a.m. was a real test of manhood. Or so it seemed, standing in the snow on bare feet away from the tent in your long johns, shivering, while you did what had to be done. I surmised that no place in New Mexico was colder that night.

In the morning friend Jeremy arrived to show us how to hunt elk. Though a young man, he's killed some 15 elk lifetime which was 15 more than we'd killed and he wanted to help. We hunted a day of futility, ranging further afield on foot, and it was easy to see where they'd been. But where they were now was still a mystery. We climbed a big bluffy mountain and looked all around. Amazing how herds of animals that weigh 500 lbs. and more apiece can melt away when the hunt is on.

It began to snow in the afternoon and the water jugs were still frozen from the night before. We took to heating up cans of stew or hash on the grill over the fire and then eating it right out of the can…like I said, a hard, cold country,

In the morning the white stuff lay on the ground and we were all thinking, "a tracking snow!" And sure enough we spotted some elk – maybe 25 – from that same high bluff Bud and I visited two days before. We slid and climbed down the bluff as the elk meandered off the meadow into the trees, into mountain country, headed east. But they did not seem to have seen us and in time we entered the big woods ourselves, saved by a tracking snow.

With three inches of white stuff on the ground it wasn't hard to follow a group of cloven-hoofed wildlife that weighed upwards of 500 lbs. apiece. In about an hour, in our most surreptitious way, we stumbled into five bedded down together. Still, they saw us before we saw them and, once spooked, Jeremy said it was "not likely" that they would bed down again.

Elk tracks merged, divided, merged again; as each big print took on its share of the falling snow it was easy to tell which was the freshest track. But these elk were not following the ridges, they were crossing them. Everything was uphill or down and they were making better time. Still, Jeremy urged us on, and we stopped at the crest of each ridge to peer across the next canyon, on the off chance that a sub-herd would stop to feed.

At first, looking through the weather, I didn't believe my eyes. None of us did. Were those elk, or the ghosts of elk, or just a snowy mirage of 500 lb. animals reaching and eating high into the branches, far across the canyon?

"Incredible, they've stopped to feed!" Jeremy whispered.

Logical, Bud got in a prone position at the ridge crest, rested the gun on Jeremy's backpack, and shot her at 160 yards with my Browning lever-action .308. The 150 grain bullet angled into the front quarters, then the biggest cow on the hillside staggered three steps back and went down like a house of cards. The one-shot kid.

So we had a 500 lb. ungulate near the bottom of a canyon and two miles from camp. Jeremy boned out the meat and we carried it all out in backpacks. It took two trips by each of us and from the first cut till the last bag we made it to camp just before dark. It was a workout but there were three of us packing meat fairly earned and nobody complained.

Now fourteen, Buddy will always remember the elk tracks in the snow, the stalk, getting into position, surreptitiously, and the 160 yard shot across the canyon. Me?

I'll remember how pleased I was for my son, that at the core I'm a houndman, not a rifleman, and that I wouldn't have been bragging on the kid without the help of the one guy there who knew what he was doing.

And I'll always be grateful for that hard, cold land. From 3 lb. squirrels to 500 lb. elk, it is game country.

24

Primitive Pursuit Sustains Man of the Cloth

The bird, a year-old, male, red-tail hawk, looks right at home, perched on a high snag overlooking a brushy arroyo in the Burro Mountains of Grant County, New Mexico. I am close underneath and could hit him with a rock, but he is not spooked by my presence. Nor is he curious. He has his eye on the man who took him from the wild not 3 months ago, seen beating the bushes for rabbits up ahead.

In a book on coursing – my favored primitive pursuit – I wrote that the sport pre-dates firearms by thousands of years and commented that the coursing hound is "a companion of the hunt rather than an instrument, who may respond to and reciprocate emotion both in and beyond the field." I also inform the reader that this singular class of hunting dog can be a fine pet as well a catcher of game.

Falconry, too, is thousands of years old, but one look at the fierce eye and singular intensity of this bird tells you that hunting hawks are not pets. Tractable though he is (remarkably so after just three months), this bird is bonded to his master only by the most tenuous of threads; he is "tame" only in so far as he is plied with rabbit meat and the opportunity to hunt. Mishandle his diet or his hunt regimen – for example, falconers try to avoid flying their birds in a high wind – and this bird could abandon all his training and disappear forever with a few flaps of his broad wings.

"His hunt weight is about 965 grams (a few ounces over 2 lbs.)," Paul Moore, falconer and Rector at Church of the Good Shepherd, Silver City, told me on the way out to the hunt grounds. "That's when he's keen to catch. At 1000 grams or more he's increasingly lethargic. Fly him when he's too light and he's weak; a jackrabbit might turn and kick him off. Fly him when he's too heavy and he might not hunt at all. He might, however, fly away."

Growing up in Ecuador, the son of missionary parents, and in Dallas, Moore was am amateur bird watcher by high school age. That's when he acquired two kestrels (sparrow hawks) and largely taught himself the rudiments of taming and handling wild birds. Raptors held a particular appeal; all are predators but Moore said they demonstrate different styles of pursuit.

He described the red-tail, like the golden eagle, as a buteo, a soaring hawk, but they can also hunt like an accipiter, like the Cooper's Hawk or the Goshawk; which fly off the fist, pursuit by sprint; and he admired the true falcons, like the prairie falcon and the peregrine; they may "stoop" from on high, attaining speeds pressing 200 mph, striking and killing far larger birds with transcendent force.

And the Harris hawk, at home from our southwestern border states to Argentina, is popular with falconers.

"The Harris hawk is a blend (buteo and accipiter), a para-buteo" Moore said. "A good one is almost too good. I had a female for six years, three years in Weslaco (Texas), three in Killeen (Texas). She would take 50 cottontails in a season, and nearly that many jackrabbits. But she was increasingly broody each spring season. I couldn't help her with that so one spring I took her back to Weslaco, where there are lots of Harris hawks, and gave her up to a male bird……..returning a gift to the wild."

Back at the dry wash in the Burro Mountains, Moore's red-tail is free to roam but keeps his eye on the falconer. As the human hunter moves off through the brush, the bird largely follows of his own accord, landing above on a new snag. When he occasionally gets too far off, Moore raise a long stick with a "T" perch at the tip and whistles. The bird comes to the perch like he heard a summons, gets a tidbit of meat, then flies to the next tree. I express surprise that the bird is quick enough to catch a cottontail (he got his first last week), fast and strong enough to take a 7-pound jack.

"A cottontail flight is typically over within 50 yards," Moore said. "The rabbit is caught or gets away down a hole or in the brush. A jackrabbit can run 40 mph and the flight might go 500 yards. A red-tail can fly 50 mph and probably hit 80 mph when he dives or stoops. They learn to bind onto the head of the jack; kill quickly with their talons, otherwise the jack may turn over with the bird and kick him off. This bird needs to catch three or four more cottontails before I start him on jacks."

Neither rabbit nor hare is plentiful this year in southwest New Mexico. Flights are few this day. Gliding toward a new snag, I see the bird suddenly drop like a stone on to………..we don't know.

"Probably a mouse," Moore says, retrieving his bird. "A quick snack for a red-tail."

Then Moore's rabbit dog, the long-haired dachshund, Aldo, gives cry. A rabbit is on the run and the bird is in flight. His acceleration off the snag is impressive but he accelerates yet again as he folds his wings to dive into a swooping pass at the cottontail. For an instant the talons seem to have, then do not have, a rabbit; the bird sails up onto a new snag and the bunny is safely lost in the brush. Two questions remain.

Can we go again, maybe try jackrabbits some time? And, what's an ordained Episcopal priest, a man of the cloth committed to peace and pastoral duties, doing out here in wild nature with blood on his hands, sharing an ancient atavism with a not so tame bird? And the answer is:

Yes. And: "The predator-prey relationship creates a kind of dialogue, a dynamic tension that, through the bird, I am able to share. It's a communion of sorts, the bird and I each nourished by the flesh of the rabbit, and the attempt to catch and the attempt to evade ultimately makes each species better. So out of the death of the rabbit there is a resurrection of life."

Communion? Resurrection? Sounds like the Church of wood and nails and stained-glass windows reaches all the way to the Church of the Open Field. Here the pursuit is as much spiritual as it is physical; a service any sentient hunter might want to attend.

Leave Your Shirt, Find Your Dog

I wonder what it would be like to smell like a dog? Of course dogs, like people, vary as to smell, with some certainly smelling better than others. But I mean, what would it be like to have the nose a dog does, to be able to detect and distinguish smells as a dog can? It would be a revelation.

Having had hunting dogs since I was a kid, I have long been intuitively aware that a dog, as the saying goes, "has a good nose." But I got a better appreciation of the facts upon getting to know Gail Burnham, author of *Play-training Your Dog*, some years ago. Gail breeds Greyhounds and trains them for, among other things, tracking and scent discrimination. I had witnessed dog tracking work many times in the field but the scent discrimination test was something else.

In the typical event, three dumbbells are placed at the far end of a field. The owner of the dog being tested places one of the three dumbbells on the ground; only the briefest handling is required. The other two dumbbells are placed adjacent by others. Greyhounds are not noted for "nose," but they are still in a realm of their own as compared to humans. I've seen greyhounds race to the end of the field, pick out the right dumbbell – the one handled by the mistress – with the merest whiff, and retrieve it to hand. They just never missed.

How much scent resides on a wooden dumbbell handled briefly by a human, and what is the difference in that scent from the scent found on the other two dumbbells handled by someone else? And why does the dog prefer the scent of his (her) master? It is a form of knowledge dogs have that we humans can only imagine.

Appreciating what a dog knows with his nose can be a real help in the field. It has helped me to recover a number of fine hounds I might have otherwise lost.

In this column I told a while back of the foxhound, Grits, who got in on a timber wolf chase in northern Minnesota. This isn't something one does on purpose, but the old fox track faded out, the fresh wolf track appeared and the race was on. The sounds of the chase disappeared into the boreal forest, I lost the dogs for some eight hours, but at dusk Grits' two companions came back to the forest road near where the chase began – this is the homing instinct you want in a hound. But Grits didn't show. I knew it was possible she had been taken down by the wolf, but I left my coat in the bar ditch along the road and went home to do the chores and get some supper. It was near midnight when I returned.

Grits eventually homed in just like the others, but not finding me there she could have become disoriented and wandered off to places unknown. But of course with that nose of hers she found the coat, knew immediately it was MY coat, and was sleeping on it when I arrived.

It was more serious when the coonhound, Charley, got lost. He failed to come in from a long coyote chase on deep snow. That night a cold front settled in and it dipped to near forty below zero. Again I left my coat near the source of the chase, and this time made sure it was in a spot out of the wind, for at that temperature, plus wind chill, a slick-haired blue-tik hound might not survive the night.

Charlie was there in the morning, sleeping on the coat; we were awfully glad to see one another. I would have to believe that as soon as Charlie smelled that coat he knew it was just a matter of time and we would be together again.

Something similar happened just last week in Dona Ana County. This time it was a young sighthound that was lost and rather than the cold I worried about the heat.

The hounds had gone off on jackrabbit chase. It was a very long run, they went out of sight; even in this wide open country I couldn't find them and I can only surmise what happened. I believe they caught the hare (one hound showed blood on the muzzle) but jumped another jack on the way back. This hare easily outran the tired hounds and scattered the pack – the three older hounds came in to the source of the chase an hour later but Mona, a 10-month old pup, failed to show.

I waited for another hour. At two hours I began to drive the ranch roads, standing periodically on the roof of the truck and scanning with the binoculars. I even had a friendly rancher helping me look, which I much appreciated. But before I went searching by vehicle, I left my sweaty t-shirt by a bush and near where the chase had begun. It took four hours in all, but when I came back to the spot, there was Mona curled up by that bush. When she saw me get out of the truck, she stood up, grabbed that smelly t-shirt in her mouth, and ran over to greet me.

Dogs get panicky when they lose their human companion in the field, just like we worry over them. But if you'll leave your shirt you can offer up an assurance that's almost as strong as your being there yourself. Your friend will go no further and will be waiting by your scent when you arrive.

Brush Wolf Hound

The creation of a hound that can trail a coyote effectively and with open voice on a hot track in wooded or hilly terrain, while retaining the sprint speed to sight chase and catch the little wolf when he comes into view, is a new concept in dog breeding to most houndmen. Yet I've seen it done and further I think we may be on the cusp of the formation of a new breed of hunting dog – the Brush Wolf Hound.

Coyote hunting with hounds in North America began not in the East, which had few to none of the predators prior to 1900, but on the western plains where such as General George Armstrong Custer, Earnest Thompson Seton, and Theodore Roosevelt used leggy coursing hounds – smooth-coated greyhounds and rough-coated staghounds – to take coyotes in sight chases of 1 to 3 miles. Then, ironically, as settlement and coyote hunting moved west, the coyote began to migrate into the wooded eastern states, filling a biological niche as the timber wolf was extirpated there. In the wooded East the sighthounds could not function well, but coon and fox hounds could, finding and trailing coyotes and, on a good day, driving one or more to the gun. Though both are rightly called "hounds," the coursing hounds and trail hounds are so unalike they have been separated by more than the geography of east and west. The trail hounds show a relatively broad head and muzzle that is part and parcel of their highly developed olfactory system. In conformation they are built to run all day, rather than sprint, and thus more closely resemble bird dogs than they do their sighthound cousins. In contrast, the lean, lithe sighthounds resemble nothing in the dog world but themselves. Separated by geography, conformation, function, and "look," I never thought of cross-breeding trail hound with sighthound, or saw evidence of it, until a hunting trip to Nebraska circa 1972.

It was the Sand Hills in mid-winter, there was snow upon the rolling grasslands, and rancher and houndman Paul Krajeski had a pack of coyote hounds. One of them was a rangy male, a dark, slick-haired brindle with a big head that Paul called "Cooner." He said, "He's one-quarter coonhound," it being understood that the rest of him was some mixture of leggy coursing hound, like the remainder of Paul's pack. Cooner was far from the handsomest dog in Paul's hunt truck. But time and again I watched him take the scent trail of a coyote that had crested a couple of hills and come unsighted from the pack, lead the pack over another hill or two to where the coyote had foolishly slowed, thinking he was safe, then start the race in earnest when he went from loping trail hound to galloping coursing hound upon sighting the little wolf once again. Cooner didn't always get there first but he had speed comparable to a field sighthound. He was silent on trail, which Paul wanted for coyote hunting in open country, and when despite Cooner's best efforts the coyote gave all the slip, we sometimes had a long wait for Cooner who would trail beyond the pack. But Paul knew Cooner was worth waiting for. I went back home with my own coursing hounds, impressed with Paul Krajeski's Sand Hills pack, and one hound in particular. Yet I missed the implications of trail hound crossed with sighthound for my own coyote hunting in northern Minnesota.

Living in Lake of the Woods County, I hunted coyotes (called "brush wolves" locally) in an admixture of woods and farm fields – trail hound terrain. To the west was the open prairie where my sighthounds could stretch out coursing jack rabbits and red fox. But for the brush wolves closer to home I started with a stout, grade blue-tik hound named Charlie. That first winter it was just the two of us, plus a pair of snowshoes and a Savage Model 24, .22 magnum over 20 gauge. Far from a speedster, Charlie could and would trail a coyote all day; usually the coyote would eventually circle and we got a few late in the day, far back in the woods, when the hound pushed the tiring coyote within range of the gun.

Things got more interesting the next winter when I added a Treeing Walker (Skeeziks) and a Running Walker (Grits) to the pack. Skeeziks was faster than Charlie and Grits was faster than Skeeziks; at times, hunting in deep snow, these two gyps could actually run a coyote down, bay him up, though it would take them several hours to all day to do so. Meanwhile, between brush wolf hunts, my sighthound pack was active mostly on jackrabbits near the North Dakota border. And despite having the living materials at hand, I was yet to connect the dots that might lead me to breed a dog like Cooner – a trail hound/sighthound combination hunter. A 45 lb. speedster named Cricket would show me the way.

Cricket was a throw-in as part of a dog trade with coyote hunter Pete Mathwig of Dunnell, Minnesota, the main acquisition being a high-powered Running Walker named Harvey. She was a slightly built, red-coated staghound, the runt of the litter. "I figure she's a little small for the coyote hunting I do," Pete said, "but she's smart as a whip and can run and I think she might give you something for jackrabbits and fox." He proved right about that and we named her Cricket because she was so quick in her movements and athleticism. And she turned out to have talents no one suspected.

Although all sighthound, Cricket had a wonderful nose. Out jackrabbit hunting she alone among the sighthound pack could wind a jackrabbit camouflaged in its form and go straight to it and jump it up. Or she would pick up the trail a jackrabbit had recently made and trail it to the hare in its form. Up jumps the hare and the race is on. She provided the same talents on red fox. She had a fine combination of speed and endurance and was very quick and agile at the catch. Back home in the wooded country, she was so smart and such a good companion, I took to letting her ride in the front seat of the pickup while we drove around the section line and forest roads as we tried to keep track of Charley, Skeeziks, Harvey and Grits on their coyote runs. At times I would turn Cricket loose as a catch dog on coyote and she would run the wolf down and hold it up till the trail hounds arrived. And then one day her hunting entered another dimension.

Off a fresh jump, my trail dogs pushed a coyote across a section road headed south into a large boreal patch of the Beltrami State Forest. I stopped and stood at the crossing and listened with satisfaction to the sounds of the chase. Cricket wanted out so I let her out. She went over to the coyote's crossing in the deep snow of the bar ditch, nosed the trail, and without a sound disappeared into the woods. Forty-five minutes later I heard the singular sounds of dogs who have a coyote bayed up. I snowshoed in to the catch and of course Cricket was there. Skeeziks and Grits had never bayed up a coyote in less than 3 to 4 hours. Cricket, the sighthound, had pursued the coyote in deep woods and deep snow by scent. But in catching the coyote in less than an hour she had trailed with sprint speed. It was a revelation.

But there were problems. I caught more coyotes running Cricket with my trail dogs but I eventually gave it up. Because she ran silent I never knew where Cricket was. On a chase of many hours she would drop out and one time I spent days getting her back. On other chases she'd get way ahead of the pack. Only I wouldn't know where she and the coyote were; one time she had a big brush wolf alone for I figure an hour or more and got chewed up pretty bad. She was too valuable to lose so I went back to using her on jackrabbit, red fox, and as a sight-chase catch dog on coyotes. But the revelation was forming into a plan and one evening at the local café after a hunt I wrote three names on a napkin: Cooner, Charlie, and Cricket, and let my imagination go its way.

"It won't work," an old houndman in Roseau County told me. "It's been tried," he said (though he had not tried it himself), "and they're just too different. You'll get a trail hound that can't smell or a sighthound that can't run." Veteran of the chase Pete Mathwig said he'd never heard of such a thing, but added, "With that Cricket anything is possible; go ahead and try it."

I bred Cricket to Charlie. I picked the cold-nosed Charlie rather than the faster dog, Harvey, as I was hoping to get a voice on the one I kept. The pups were of all colors and different types of coat and some looked more trail hound and others more like sighthounds. Few hunters were interested and most of the pups ended up in pet homes. But one leggy male with Cricket's red, rough coat seemed the perfect blend of hound traits. I began to favor him early on and called him Redman.

Cricket taught him a lot. At night she would jump the kennel fence, catch a snowshoe hare, then bring it back to her pup. As he matured I took them on walks. Cricket would pursue the smaller hares, bigger jackrabbits, and fox. Redman of course would chase anything she did and I noticed he would use his nose to trail these critters too, at least for a short distance. I wasn't worried about him trailing hares once he got the evil smell of coyote into his experience.

This came in November with the first snows of winter and Redman about 14 months old. The first few hunts my "experiment" reached no conclusions. Hunting now with Charlie and the other trail hounds, Redman was baffled by cold tracks. Once the coyote was jumped he would follow the pack for perhaps a quarter-mile then come running back, looking for me, or Cricket. I put this down to puppy insecurity and counseled myself towards patience. After all, Redman came from hunting stock and I knew he could run.

One December morning a foot of new snow blanketed the ground. It was a little above zero. The sun was so bright on the new snow, dark glasses were a must. A northwest breeze of 15-20 mph was disconcerting but not so severe as to spoil the chase, and once you got back in the woods it was pretty quiet. A houndman needed to be out there looking for tracks. Ten miles away, near the frozen shores of Lake of the Woods, Charley took a cold track into a patch of woods. When he jumped the coyote I fed Grits, Harvey and Redman into the race. They disappeared into the woods and Harvey and Grits were soon sounding off on the hot track. Of Redman I heard nothing but at least he was still in the woods and not back at the truck. And then I heard an odd squall amongst the baying hounds. It had to be Redman and it certainly was not the voice of Bugle Ann. Indeed you might have thought the hound had just been jabbed with a cattle prod every time he sounded off. But he had joined the race and was open on track. The way they were headed, it appeared they would soon cross an open field.

I drove the section and was able to flank this open field on the north side. I could see the coyote's running track as it crossed the field on new snow; the little wolf was already gone into the woods to the west. But hot on his trail was Redman, squalling, running with his head up and due to the wind taking the scent out of the air ten yards downwind of the track. He was already 100 yards ahead of two fast Walkers, Harvey and Grits. He was running the track on his own, he was open on track, and he was trailing with more pure speed than any straight trail hound was ever built to achieve.

I finally saw the coyote about an hour later. He emerged from the woods onto another agricultural field, recently cleared, as there were a number of large standing rock piles and burnt brush piles scattered along the perimeters. The game made for one of these rocks piles and ducked into a crevasse. The reason? Redman wasn't 50 yards behind. He bayed him up in the rocks and the others soon arrived as I snow-shoed out to the catch to take the pelt. I had a sighthound that could run a track. And he was open on track. I had a trail hound with sprint speed. All in the same dog. The experiment was completed, though far from over. Nobody could tell me now that "it won't work."

That winter, led usually by Redman, the pack took about 25 coyotes, including the largest Minnesota coyote in my experience, 51 lbs. Many other coyotes of course eluded us one way or another; the species will never be an easy mark. In chases of two hours or less my "combination hound" invariably led the pursuit. In longer runs the advantage gradually shifted to the Running Walkers. Redman's rough staghound coat served him well in hunting coyotes on snow. For the record he stood 26 ½ inches at the withers and weighed 70 lbs. And Redman and Harvey learned to kill every coyote they caught.

The following summer I had reason to move to my present location in southwest New Mexico. Here a dog like Cooner could be an effective coyote hunter while Redman was somewhat "out of his element" in the open country. He would end up going to legendary houndman Ben Hardaway and his famed Midland Foxhounds of Columbus, Georgia, where he made his contribution as hunter and stud dog within the Midland pack. Before sale however, Redman was bred to a cold-blood greyhound named Gracie, out of which breeding I kept a pup named Goofy. At ¾ sighthound X ¼ trail hound, Goofy was a dead ringer for Cooner, with the same ability to silently trail up a coyote then run him down in open country. Only Goofy was faster and also very good on jackrabbits; the best all-around coursing hound I've ever owned. For the record he stood almost 28 inches at the withers and weighed 75 lbs.

Redman was also bred to Skeeziks to produce a ¾ trail hound X ¼ sighthound. litter. From this breeding I kept Rojo, a smooth, tireless, effortless runner who missed his natural calling as a north woods coyote hound but who nonetheless was an aide to the pack in the desert southwest. He did not lose his nose by being ¼ sighthound and was in fact an effective trail hound with extra speed. And a descendent of Rojo I bred, named Chance, is about 1/3 trail hound, 1/3 staghound, and 1/3 saluki/greyhound. He has proven a good find for a New Mexico falconer, teaming with a goshawk in the hunting of jackrabbits.

The basic tenants of breeding a combination hound? Know ahead of time if you want essentially a trail hound with speed or a coursing hound with a nose. If the former, the off-spring should be at least ½ to ¾ trail hound and should be open on a hot track. If the latter, the end product should trail silent and be at least 2/3rds coursing hound by blood.

Yes, trailhounds and sighthounds are "different" from one another. But good specimens of each type of hound have a common drive to "run to catch" on appropriate game. Used in a judicious program of cross-breeding, with the off-spring employed properly in appropriate terrain and climate, these hunting dogs with combination traits and talents could indeed in time breed true to type and yield a new hound for coyotes, particularly in the north woods – the Brush Wolf Hound.

An Introduction to Lamping

"I'll take the light," Matthew said. "You handle the dogs...there's one now!"

Matthew had come over from Scotland. Now we were along a dirt road in a remote expanse of public land in Dona Ana County, New Mexico and he had an American hare, a jackrabbit, in the beam of the lamp. I stopped the truck and my son Bud and I got out. It was already past his bedtime, it was a school night, but he would not be denied his first look at lamping.

"Keep your eye on the rabbit," I told him; "I'll turn the hounds loose."

Directly, Beech-Nut, Phoebe, and Rhoda leaped out of the back of the truck. Trained lamping dogs know to follow the beam to the game but Phoebe and Rhoda were bewildered, sniffing about in the dark and squatting over bushes while Beech-Nut paused to lift his leg. In time I got Beech-Nut, a lanky, rough-coated greyhound (staghound), to look to the hare, hopping about unconcerned in the light. The hound made a dash. Matthew skillfully kept the beam on the race but the dodging, shifting jack soon raced beyond the reach of the lamp, leaving Beech-Nut in the dust.

"Aye, there's a trick to the lamp," Matthew said. "These dogs don' know what they are about."

They would learn, however. Soon the hounds had the method: when they were let out of the truck it meant a jackrabbit was sitting in the grass at the end of the light. Follow the beam and you get a chase. Chase fast enough and you may catch a hare.

We saw some wonderful races. Matthew had the trick of keeping the light on the action (you have to beam the hare, not the hounds), even when the chase was pushing 40 mph. Beech-Nut, a dark brindle, was practically invisible unless directly in the beam, but the fawn Rhoda (5/8 greyhound/3/8 saluki), and the parti-color Phoebe (coldblood greyhound) fairly shown with speed as they raced with the beam in pursuit.

Of course most of the hares escaped. We must have seen at least 30 jacks and the majority did not stay around to be hunted. Those that did usually eluded the dogs till sprinting beyond the reach of the beam. Once beyond the light the dogs lost sight and the chase was over. These hares are constantly chased by coyotes and a variety of raptors, by day and night, and are masters at eluding pursuit.

I was relieved that each hound was good about quickly returning to the truck or the leash for it's easy to lose a dog in the dark. In the end we had perhaps a dozen chases and one was a classic.

The hare was well off the road, barely visible in the light. Beech-Nut got the break, sprinted and turned the hare who made a 180 degree maneuver and began a long circular sprint around the truck. Bud said later he had never seen our hounds running with such intensity, and so low to the ground. Thirty seconds later the jack bolted off on a tangent and was nearly out of the light beam when Phoebe reached at high speed and picked the hare up. Like my other hounds, she kills a hare instantly, and then she retrieved as good as any Labrador. Another race went even longer, with clouds of dust rising in the light, but in the end the jack escaped. We went home at midnight with 4 jackrabbits, enough meat for hounds and hunters.

On a more recent trip, Matthew, Bud and I were joined by photographer Dan Gauss, determined to add action shots of lamping to his already fine coursing portfolio. For hounds we had Mona (1/2 Tazi X 1/2 English lurcher), her daughter Ashley (a mix of Tazi, lurcher, and coldblood greyhound) and Jack, an oversize Jack Russell terrier we brought along for comic relief. The hares were particularly spooky this night, and quick on the dodge, and foiled us time and again. But as Ashley caught on she became a real help to the experienced Mona and after about a dozen maneuvers one of the three dogs (it might even have been Jack who was so frantic in pursuit he was squeaking in excitement with every bound) caught a hare just beyond the reach of the light. And our only other catch was also a thriller.

This jackrabbit used every jink and dodge available as it circled the truck, eluding the hounds at the last instant time and again. But Matthew followed expertly with the beam and just as I was thinking the dogs would run out of wind, Mona put on a burst and rolled the hare in a tumbling catch not a stone's throw from me, Bud, and Dan's camera...lamping at its best.

In retrospect, I'd say two hounds is ideal for any single chase. A hare at night is just as fast as in the daytime, but they do tend to jink, dodge and circle more when lamped and that can lead to high-speed collisions. On one chase I had the hare run right between my legs; the following hound spun me for a loop!

I checked with the New Mexico Game & Fish enforcement people and lamping with a hound is legal for rabbits, hares, coyote and other furbearers and so-called "non-game" animals.. However, you must not have a gun or other weapon in possession, in your truck, or anywhere around or you could be in serious violation of game laws. Each state has its own rules on hunting at night with a light. Also, off-road vehicle use is against the rules on public land; you must stay on identifiable roads daytime or night. For off-road lamping I have acquired a strong light with a portable battery so I can hunt on foot, like the coonhunters. In that case, I have a hound or two on a slip lead, to be released only at the right time. Whatever the lamp, you need a minimum of 250,000 candlepower, and a half million or more is better.

Expect everybody but the driver to sleep on the way home. Bud slept on my lap while Matthew rolled the seat back and said good night till we arrived in Silver City. I didn't have anyone to talk to but had plenty to think about in the way of swift hounds in hard pursuit of hares that fairly flew in a moving light.

Matthew Bowes

New Mexico's Last Grizzly

He was the "Monarch of the Gila," over seven feet from tip to tip, no matter which way you measured the hide, and double the weight of the trophy black bears that are still relatively plentiful in the mountains of southwest New Mexico.

But this King was a grizzly, still technically a bear but enough different from his lesser cousin that, for nearly a decade, he spawned an odd admixture of fear, hatred, and respect from those who tried to raise cattle on his range. One family ranch account names this bruin for the killing of 26 head of stock from the summer of 1930 to the spring of '31. His demise shall now enter the lexicon of the Western Myth, told in unadorned detail herein for the first time; and leave a legacy, for the last of his kind, albeit a beast in the Wilderness, is just as timeless and singular as the first to top Everest, and Hillary was some kind of man.

The bear had a range generally covering the drainages of Mogollon, Sacaton, and Rain Creeks – the south side of the Mogollon Mountains, Gila National Forest. The Rice and Shelley clans were the principal ranch families thereby; they raised cattle there, but by necessity in a tough, homestead, live-off-the-land fashion. A rogue grizzly that could swat a grown steer senseless could not know he was creating a feud with wilderness pioneers as tough and attuned to the rigors of outdoor survival as himself. The story of the inevitable clash, and climax, is best told by participants, starting with Blue Rice, as recorded years ago in blue ink by his wife, Minnie.

"In the spring of 1924," Rice would recall, "I came to the PIT ranch to work. At that time it was known that there was a grizzly bear killing cattle on the ranch. It had been around for several years.

"In the spring of 1925 we found where this bear had killed three cows in Rain Creek...Jim Henry set a bear trap and caught this bear by two toes. In the struggle to get away, the bear pulled the two toes off and did get away...over time we would find where (this bear) would kill a cow or calf and move on.

"About 1928, a man was prospecting on Sacaton Creek. As he came upon this big bush, he heard a noise and looked over the bush...there was this big bear standing up on his hind legs. The man (had a rifle) and shot, but the bear ran away into the brush and was lost from sight. This man and his partner came to the ranch and asked me to take my dogs and help them trail up the bear. I didn't have any hounds, only a bulldog. I went with them and we were able to trail him quite a long way until the bleeding stopped.

"Up until April, 1931 we didn't know much more about this big bear, except we would find where he had killed some stock, ate, and moved on.

38

"In the first days of April 1931, we found where this grizzly bear, and we could tell by the tracks it was a grizzly bear (grizzlies have long, heavy, non-retractable claws – ed.), had killed a cow in Rain Creek. He had partly ate the cow.

"On April 8, 1931 my brother Carl and I took four hounds...and when we found his tracks he was going towards Rain Creek. This bear had gone down through this steep, rough country. The dogs were able to trail him and we found the trail he had been using, which since then we call the Grizzly Bear Trail. The bear went off and up the creek to where the dead cow was, ate another fill, then went up on to the side of the hill into some thick oak brush and bedded down for the day. All this time the dogs were trailing on his tracks.

"When Carl and I got up to where we heard the dogs bayed...we climbed the hill a little north of the thicket into an open place and out on to a big rock...(then) this bear walked out of the brush, not more than fifteen feet from us. We both shot at the same time. The bear went down, then raised right up on his hind legs and let out an awful roar. We both shot again, he went down again. The bear kept trying to get up and we kept shooting until he was dead."

Carl Rice would recall they had to dismount during the pursuit in rough country and, climbing afoot, remembered the final confrontation this way: "The bear was fighting the dogs on the ground but, when the bear saw us, he quit the dogs and he came right at us. I had a little .351 Winchester (semi) Automatic and Blue had his Model 94 Winchester .30-.30. We 'lit' him up as he climbed to us. When we finally killed him I was out of shells and Blue had one cartridge left in the chamber. Directly, I tried to roll a cigarette but I couldn't keep the tobacco on the paper."

Blue Rice's account reports that, upon skinning the bear, they found the prospector's lead bullet just under the hide. The bear also was missing two toes from a front foot. This indeed was the rogue grizzly that had taken livestock at will off several adjacent ranches over nearly a decade in time. The animal would also make the pages of the local Silver City *Enterprise*, and history.

From the definitive "The Grizzly in the Southwest" by David Earl Brown (1985), the author writes: "So far as I know this is the last written account of the taking of a grizzly in New Mexico."

Who gets the credit here, and/or the blame?

The *Enterprise* reported that the permit to take this depredating bear out of season came through "Supervisor James A. Scott of the State Game Department." In this quintessential Old West Saga, that lacks any taint of fiction, each participant played their part; the bear by killing all that livestock; the hounds by trailing him down bringing him to bay; the men by killing the bear in a retribution driven not by revenge but their own economic survival.

Myself, I take no more pleasure in the demise of the last grizzly than I would the demise of the last working rancher, sold out to a developer; both are part of the legacy of the West I love and the two have a lot in common. It just wouldn't be the West without ranch culture, or big predators.

Is there a place for the grizzly in today's Southwest? At this juncture I wouldn't touch the issue with a long-handled hoe. I only know that in the early days of the Great Depression, April 8, 1931, four hounds, two men, and a really big bear played out a drama that was at once perfectly true, and the stuff of legend.

The author is indebted to Steve Wilmeth for providing the primary materials for this document.

Montague Stevens: The Philosophical Bear Hunter

Of all the stalwarts, notables, and reprobates who roamed the mountains of the Gila – and this includes such legendary characters as scalp hunter James Kirker, indefatigable Ben Lilly, raconteur Nat Straw and incorrigible Bear Moore – none left a legacy to match that of Montague Stevens. For Stevens told his own story and, albeit it tells a tale from the late 19th century, within it is wisdom for today's dog lover, horse lover, hunter, conservationist, and anyone inclined to take the road less traveled.

Iconoclasm was Stevens' most notable trait. Born in England, and educated at Trinity College, Cambridge, he came to the western frontier in the 1880s a "remittance man." Having butted heads in youth with traditional parents, the family simply paid him off – a remittance – so that he would seek his livelihood elsewhere; what Stevens wanted all along.

Out West, Stevens promptly lost an arm in a hunting accident. This would have ended the frontier adventures of a lesser man, leaving him a school teacher, salesman, or clerk in a store. Determined, Stevens bought a cattle ranch in what is now Catron County, devoted himself to cattle, horses, hounds, and pursuit of the grizzly bear, as if to say, "I have but one arm, but no handicap."

Few hunters, then or now, ever attempted the grizzly bear with hounds. Unlike the black bear, grizzlies won't tree, yet they can run forever. Hounds can be found to trail them, and terriers to fight them, yet even with good horsemanship, the race soon goes out of hearing. Even if the hounds eventually bay the bear, how do you find him in the vast mountains of southwest New Mexico? Stevens pondered, and in time found the answer. He crossed trail hound with English sheepdog; the hound blood to trail the bear, the sheepdog blood that the dog would relate to the hunter rather than the pack. These hybrid "slow trail" dogs stayed with Stevens and his horse on a long chase, but with their nose eventually led him to the bayed-up bear. The innovation turned Stevens' bear hunting from a problematical "hit or miss" pursuit, to one where a dead bear became a "reasonable certainty."

Stevens after all was a cattleman, grizzlies were not endangered in the 1880s and they regularly killed his stock. Stevens went after these stock killers and reveled in the pursuit. Yet within a dozen years or so, Stevens viewed the grizzly becoming increasingly scarce in the Gila country. In his book, *Meet Mr. Grizzly*, Stevens wrote: "...and feeling that I had already had my full share of them, from that time on, I became a zealous convert to their preservation, to prevent so noble an animal becoming extinct."

41

Others were not so prescient, however, and the grizzly is now gone from the Southwest. But Stevens' numerous training innovations, based on kindness rather than the force of discipline, are detailed in *Meet Mr. Grizzly* and remain invaluable to any dog owner today. Here's one of his insightful observations on hounds and scent:

"While there is no yardstick by which to measure the keenness of a hound's scent, there is, however, a way in which to get an approximate idea. When a hound approaches the scent trail of a man or animal at a right angle and scents the trail in the air, how does he know if the man or game went to the right or the left? Usually, he takes the right end of the trail; that is, the way the man or game went, the other way being called the backtrail. But sometimes, due probably to the wind or some other atmospherics tradition, the hound is not sure which way to go and he will run some twenty yards in each direction alternately several times, until he has fully made up his mind which is the right end of the trail to take. In my experience he is invariably right. The question therefore arises: How much difference is there in the strength of the scent twenty yards one side or the other of a given point? That difference is the measure of the keenness of a hound's scent."

Stevens training techniques also applied to horses. The usual technique of horse breaking at the time was to tie the horse stem to stern, force on a saddle, then let the "buster" ride the horse, over and over again, till he quit bucking. No slave to tradition, Stevens found the practice abusive, dangerous, and, he said, it took the spirit out of a good horse. Again, he pondered.

He found the solution in a milling machine, powered by a team of horses that walked in a circle, grinding the grain. Stevens harnessed an unbroken colt to the machine, saddled it, then turned the harnessed work horses lose to begin their circle. Overpowered, the colt had no choice but to walk in a circle with the others. Once he got used to that, a rider mounted the colt. He couldn't buck, harnessed as he was, and the colt was soon at a steady walk, getting used to a rider on his back.

Stevens found he could "break" multiple horses at a time, easily and safely; a large improvement over the tradition of bronco busting. Yet, he reports, the majority of the cowboys were so macho and imbued with the Western tradition, they refused to ride a young horse broke by a machine!

A working philosopher, Stevens saw problems as opportunities for resolution – fun puzzles in effect – rather than obstacles that couldn't be met or transformed.

Living in remote country, northeast of Reserve and far from law enforcement, Stevens was temporarily stumped one time when word came that a band of thieves were working the country, stealing large bands of horses. He knew he lacked the means or the men and arms to stop them. Stevens pondered.

42

The next day he ordered his men to round up the remuda and shave off the tails of all the horses. The men thought he was daft but did as they were told. Stevens writes:

"I heard, sometime later, that the thieves had rounded up my horses in the pasture, and when they realized that it was impossible to steal them, owing to their easy identification, they were very indignant!

"My readers may wonder what this theory has to do with my secret ambition of catching grizzlies with reasonable certainty. My answer is, that this example, and many similar ones that followed, which seemed very difficult to solve, but had equally simple solutions, encouraged me to stay with the grizzly bear problem."

Shortly thereafter, Stevens began to fashion his breeding program for adding "slow trail" dogs to his pack, the simple solution that achieved his goals as a bear hunter.

Stevens did not write his memoir until well into his eighties; he lived well past ninety. His observations on the natural history of bears, dogs, horses, and hunters remain remarkably new and fresh today. His approach to hunting, that relied on skill, innovation, and endurance, offers a lesson to today's high-tech, road-bound nimrods. He was one of New Mexico's noblemen and he left us a classic.

A New Computer, An Ancient Sport

I suppose it was bound to happen. My kid has a birthday coming up and he's asked for a new computer. Not that he has an old one, but he's played around with mine. Now he wants his own. I guess it was inevitable.

Birthdays past, he wanted a fishing rod, or a BB gun, or a fishing vest, or a backpack – the same sort of stuff I got for my birthday when I was a kid. Back then, we didn't need no stinking computers! Today a computer, and the word processing skills to go with it, is a necessity. With the world of the Internet and video games just a finger-punch away, I have to wonder if the lure of the outdoors will soon seem hopelessly antiquated to a kid. With that in mind, and the new computer looming on the horizon, I asked Bud last week if he'd like to go hunting. "Sure," he said.

He knew I meant hunting with the hounds, and the way we do it, it would be hard to imagine any pastime further removed from the world of the Internet. Hounds just like ours decorate the walls of ancient caves and tombs, depicting a time and a sport that precedes by several millennia centerfire arms, black powder arms, gun dogs, trail hounds, and even bows and arrows. In those days, the hounds were an aid to survival. Yet the art work reveals that even in that faraway time the ancients reveled in the chase.

We are up at five and away before six with three hounds in the truck. Today we will run Samson, Angie and Patch, leaving Hazel, Mona, and Comet at home. Just past seven we find our field somewhere in Luna County, New Mexico and turn out the pack. It is springtime and already warm; we will need to find some game and get in our runs by ten o'clock or lose the day and the sport to the heat.

It sure is pretty when the sun balls up over the desert. I love those early hours, and a hike over the grasslands of southwest New Mexico is an exercise in solitude for almost everyone else goes to the mountains. Our pine-clad mountains draw summer hikers and our desert mountains draw those bent on a winter ascent. We can see the mountains, but they are far away, spaced by miles of grama grass, tabosa, snake weed, and so much else of the Chihuahuan grasslands I cannot name, most of it wonderfully green now from rare spring rains. With the right perspective, the hike, and view, is as good crossing the desert as ascending the peaks.

"Dad?"

"Yeah."

"You think Samson is a fast as Angie?"

"Angie's only nine months old; I think Samson is faster than Angie."

"But when Angie grows up?

"I think it will be quite a race."

44

Samson is our new acquisition from a kennel in Georgia, a very tall, leggy hound (¾ coldblood greyhound X ¼ saluki), and my kid is showing interest in the subtleties of the chase. I am pleased, though we say nothing more as we hike a flat, open, grassy expanse so broad we need the mountains in the distance to stay oriented. It takes more than an hour but we finally get one going.

It's a hare, named "liebre" south of the nearby border, or blacktail jackrabbit (*Lepus Californicus*) in the guidebooks – the same animal, the hare, so commonly pursued by the ancients and depicted on the walls of caves and tombs so long ago. It is an animal that was born to run. I let out a whoop and the race is on.

That Samson can really go! He alone sees the hare at the start and his sprint is impressive. He overhauls the jack in an awesome gallop, and when the hare turns sharply to avoid the take, Angie and Patch cut across the field to vie for the lead.

That Angie can run! Though still a pup she briefly holds the lead and presses hard on the dodging hare. There follows a series of straightaway sprints and artful maneuverings by hare and hounds. Each hound has the lead at times but Samson is the dominant runner until Patch, way out there but still in sight, surges to the front and rolls the jackrabbit.

"I like Samson," says Bud

Of course he likes Angie too (also ¾ greyhound X ¼ saluki), and Patch (5/8 greyhound/staghound X 3/8 saluki), both of whom he helped raise. The hounds are with us again and I give them water while Bud finds and retrieves the hare. We rest and enjoy a shared moment with the hounds following success in the field. All this comes naturally to both canines and *homo sapiens*; as Ortega y Gasset, author of *Meditations on Hunting*, wrote: "The only logical response to an animal that lives its life obsessed with avoiding capture, is to chase it."

It is definitely warming up and we head for the truck, now some two miles away. And then, there goes another one!

This hare gets up from under my feet and all the dogs see it straightaway. It is a stronger hare and stretches the run out over two minutes. Again Samson is dominant much of the way with Angie close and Patch coming on at the end. Through the binoculars I see they have the hare run down – turning it at will – when it ducks into a badger hole. There is a momentary disappointment, then relief; it was a great race and it is good to leave some for seed.

It takes Samson a long time to return and he arrives thoroughly "knackered" and contending with the heat. I give him water to drink, wet him down, and here's a secret for working dogs in warm weather. About 10 ccs of 50% dextrose solution, squirted into the mouth, will revive a dog who might otherwise go down from over-exertion or heat stroke. The information comes from a friend, a DVM specializing in canine sports medicine whose clients include several greyhound kennels in the

Deep South. This solution can save your dog; and, absent sometimes hard-to-find dextrose, more recent experience indicates Gatorade can yield similar benefits

It revived Samson and we leash them up and make it to the truck, load the dogs, and then drive to a Deming café. My son will soon be home, that much closer to his birthday, and a new computer. With Bud just a finger-punch from the Internet, I wonder if the traditional country sports will still hold a place in his life.

"Dad?"

"Yeah."

"I think Samson and Angie are a good team. You think they could win the Pack Hunt next year?"

"Well, they'll have to outrun Patch and Mona and Comet and Hazel, not to mention the hare. And our competitors have got some good hounds themselves. It should be quite a race."

The Gun Show: Old Debates and a New Rifle

We had a table at the Silver City gun show last week, selling books about guns, hunting, and Western history, especially the sub-genre of outlaws and lawmen where guns and shooting are invariably part of the story. We did all right in sales, but I hadn't figured into the weekend budget that either Bud or I might come away with a new gun.

Silly me. Any veteran attendee of gun shows should know that even leaving your checkbook at home won't necessarily protect you from a hefty purchase, not with all those firearms on display, priced to sell, and you can pick them up and handle them, too! Once you succumb to handling a good one, turning the gun back to the dealer can make you feel like you just rejected a puppy in need of a good home.

I was tending to book sales Saturday morning when Bud and Cherie showed up. He passed by the table just to let me know he was there, then moved on. "I'm going to look at some guns," he said as he disappeared into the crowd.

Returning some time later, he was stimulated, as one might expect. "Dad, I think I need my own gun," he said.

I reminded him he already had a .22 rifle, a.22 magnum rifle, and a Remington 20 gauge pump shotgun.

"Yeah, but a real gun, like yours."

Well the guns named are real enough but I knew what he was getting at. Last fall he borrowed my Browning lever action .308 and got his first elk. At 14, he was already in the grips of big game hunting and he wanted a gun – his own gun – that could do it all on large game in North America and maybe hunt the larger varmints to boot!

"There's this one guy," he said, "has some real nice ones…a real nice table."

I felt like I knew who he was talking about already. He was a neighbor, always had a table at the Grant County shows; and, unlike so many of the gun vendors at any show, he not only had an attractive array of both long-guns and hand-guns, he had complete descriptions of each gun – model, make, caliber, price, etc, – neatly printed on reference cards attached to each item. Handy for the potential buyer, you knew all the essentials about each arm, and could handle it, without the awkward phase of having to ask the basics – and give away your interest – to the vendor.

Bud led me over to the table and I was right. Gradually we narrowed down our criteria – price, caliber, action, etc, – to one that seemed close to right: a Savage Model 116FSS "Weather Warrior," a bolt action gun with both barrel and action in stainless steel, a tough synthetic stock, a Simmons/Deerfield 3 x 9 variable scope already mounted; the caliber was .270, the condition "new/never fired," and the price $695.00. We both handled it, liked it, except Bud thought the caliber "too light."

"I think I need a .308 like you, Dad, or a .30-06, or one of those 7 mm magnums."

"No hurry," I said. "We'll look at everything here at the show and we can study up on anything of interest tonight. Then tomorrow we'll know which one we want…or maybe we'll just wait."

In fact I did most of the research that night on the Internet. Therein the old gun debates roared on, much as I remembered reading them in the old *Hook & Bullet* magazines that lay about, battered and worn, in the barber shop, circa 1959.

The lever action vs. bolt action debate was alive and well, the bolt boys claiming greater accuracy, the lever fans claiming a speed advantage in the action and comparable accuracy in Savage Model 99 and Browning BLR. But the Model 99, I was surprised to learn, went out of production about a dozen years ago.

Jack O'Connor and Elmer Keith are gone but their old argument lives on. O'Connor descendants still believe the .270 "is adequate for any big game in North America, including moose and grizzly," while the followers of Keith advise a self-imposed limit for use of the .270 to "medium-sized, thin-skinned game."

As for the .270 vs. .30-06 vs. 7 mm Remington magnum, everyone it seems had a story to tell. And for every doubter who claimed the .270 wounded big game, another claimed the same caliber a marvel of accuracy, proven since 1925 as the all-around hunting cartridge. And they still use O'Connor quotes to solidify the claim!

Shooting left-handed, I'm partial to lever action myself. But Bud said, "No, I want a bolt." With the help of O'Connor however, I did convince him of the speed, flat trajectory, accuracy and all-around effectiveness of the .270. And the testimony and experience of numerous hunters/shooters in favor of the practical Savage "Weather Warrior" went a long way. Plus without the scope, in .270 caliber and 22" barrel, this useful, all-weather arm only weighs 6.5 lbs.

The next day when the vendor offered to knock off fifty bucks from the listed price he had a deal. And so did me and Buddy.

"This was your idea," I said. "But if you'll put up $325 from your savings (that is mostly garnered from the care of chickens and sale of eggs from our homestead farm) I'll cover the other half and you'll walk out of here with a hunting gun good for a lifetime."

We shook on that and, since he got the gun and at half price at that, it might seem that Bud came away the most pleased of all. Well, maybe. But in these times any of us from the old school must get an indescribable lift whenever a lad looks beyond the boob tube and video games for a connection to country sports and the natural world. Such inclinations should face no impediment and indeed may be deserving of a boost.

An unexpected purchase meant we about broke even on book sales at the gun show. But the knowledge gained from old debates and a new rifle put the whole family in the black.

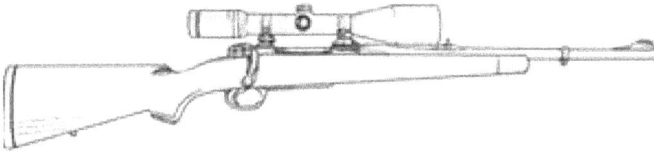

Wildlife Profile: Coyotes I Have Known

I've done a handful of these wildlife profiles over the years – ravens, gray fox, and brown trout come to mind from recent efforts – and it occurs to me from the list that I am drawn to the critters that we humans view as "clever" or "smart."

Ravens of course are famous for a variety of clever antics. Gray fox must be smart – they are heavily trapped for fur here in New Mexico yet remain widespread and plentiful. And any experienced flycaster will tell you the brown is the "smartest" and most wary of the trout. Yet none gets pressured so much, yet survives so well, as the coyote. This animal impresses in so many ways, even as you feel sometimes you want to kill him.

Adaptability is one measure of the coyote's arsenal of talents. In less than a century he has transformed himself from a resident solely of our Western states to an inhabitant of every state but Hawaii. I got a first hand look at this when I used to live in northern states.

An old trapper in Minnesota told me he first start seeing, and catching, coyotes in the north woods about 1920; before that the coyote kept to the Dakota plains. They spread across northern Minnesota, Wisconsin, Michigan, and by the 1940s were established in northern New York where I grew up. Today they are common in New England and have made a similar invasion of the wooded southeastern states where they have essentially inbred the red wolf out of existence and driven the once-common red fox into the most furtive haunts.

Whatever sort of animal you are, life on the Great Plains or desert Southwest is much different from that in the north woods yet the coyote, or brush wolf as he's called up north, does equally well in either locale and is inclined to dominate any competing predators wherever he lives. Are coyotes really smart? Or is it just instinct? Anthropomorphism is a slippery slope, but consider this: One time in Minnesota the hounds and I had a coyote on the run. He was circling in the woods on deep snow and I was so sure they were going to catch him I didn't take my gun with me when I went into woods to hear and see the race.

It was a frantic pursuit and the bawl and chop of all three hounds told me they were close. In time I saw the coyote, he maintained his lead, and I noted he was running the same circular path, round and round. This redundancy in time left his scent as all powerful all along the route and the hounds became confused, no longer sure which way he was going in the circle. As soon as that confusion came into their voices, and they began to run the backtrack, the coyote left the circle and headed out cross-country, never to be seen again.

Was this escape by "intelligent design" or just instinctual good luck? Can't say, but I was impressed.

Speed is another coyote trait. One time near Roswell, famed houndman Dave Hise and I turned out three running dogs on a coyote, not twenty yards off his stride. His two were veteran coyote hounds of coldblood greyhound breeding and my dog, Chief, was registered. All three had the speed of their breed but twenty yards was as close as they ever got to that coyote.

The race was even for a quarter mile or so, with Chief having a slight advantage over the other two hounds, but in time the coyote began to lengthen his lead and by the time the race topped the rise in the far distance he was home free. Now this was not your average coyote – this one had undoubtedly been run before – but the best coyotes have a sprint speed to rival the fastest canines, selectively bred.

Endurance? I put three trail hounds down on a coyote track one February morning not a quarter mile from my Minnesota home. They soon jumped the little wolf and the race was on. It went all day, here and there, never more than a mile from home. About five that evening the falling temperatures robbed the pursuit of its scent and I pulled the hounds off the track. They had run hard for nine hours and never pulled hair on that coyote.

Of course coyotes sometimes impress us in not such a good way. Raise watermelons and they will eat them. Raise sheep or chickens and they will eat them. Let your cats run loose and they will eat them.

In the north woods coyotes are larger – 30 to 40 lbs. on average and 50 to 60 lbs. on occasion – and coyotes that size can have a real effect on a deer herd. Here in New Mexico they are smaller but just as voracious. I have had a constant battle with the critters getting my chickens. Much of this raiding took place at night, so I narrowed the entrance to the coop so a chicken can get in but a 25 lb. coyote usually cannot.

Still, they will sometimes risk a daylight raid and just this summer I ran for my gun as one took a barred rock hen and scrambled over the six foot fence. I was too late.

And just last week they got one of my turkeys. I didn't see the actual raid but the trail of feathers the next day told the story. And, somehow, that coyote had taken that gobbler over that six foot fence. So I guess we can add strength to the weaponry of the coyote.

My friend Big Jon Finn says New Mexico coyotes are hardly worth skinning this season; their pelt price has fallen out with the surfeit of hides still available from last year. But you can bet I will put a hide on the wall if I catch a certain coyote climbing fence with one of my turkeys in his mouth – another coyote I have known.................

For Real Hunting, Use a Spear!

I first heard of Alexander "Sasha" Siemel many years ago for even as a kid I would read about any hunter who follows the hounds. Siemel used hounds to hunt jaguar. Unlike other houndmen, however, he would sometimes get face to face with his quarry, just like his dogs. Siemel wrote his own book of his adventures, called *Tigrero.* I read it early on and found it something of a disappointment. The book does have several remarkable photographs of Siemel killing a jaguar with a spear but most of the text is taken up with other conflicts that have nothing to do with hunting. Books by others who knew Siemel fill out the story: *Green Hell* and *Tiger Man* by Julian Duguid*; Sashino* by Sasha Siemel Jr., and *Jungle Wife* by Edith Siemel.

Born in Latvia in 1890, Sasha Siemel drifted into South America while still in his teens. At 6 feet and 180 lbs., and with a lust for adventure, he had both the physique and the temperament to come to terms with the jungles of Brazil, Peru and Bolivia, as wild then as our own Wild West decades earlier. Like our own West, cattle raising came with early settlement and where our stockmen pioneers struggled with cougars, wolves and grizzlies, the scourge of the industry as jungles were cleared in South America was the jaguar.

By tradition, the *Motto Grosso* (or Big Woods) of Brazil holds the world's largest jaguars, some of them exceeding 300 lbs. Hunters who have tried them, all say that the jaguar is more unpredictable than the cougar when pursued by dogs, more likely to bay up on the ground rather than tree, and subject to attack the man or dog that approaches too close.

Siemel found that the European settlers, not surprisingly, used guns to kill a jaguar brought to bay. The natives traditionally would approach one in groups, armed with spears. But a few, a very few, of the native hunters were known as "Tigreros" for their ability to meet a bayed jaguar one on one, armed only with a spear. Much like Montague Stevens, who became obsessed with becoming the best grizzly bear hunter in our own Southwest, Siemel sought to be the only white man who could qualify as a true "Tigrero."

In time he found a mentor. Drunk in his hut, the wizened, leathery old man hardly impressed Siemel as one who could kill a jaguar single handed with a spear. But he was widely reputed to be one of the last of the true Tigreros and he offered to show Siemel how it was done.

In subsequent hunts, the old man proved true to his word. When not on the bottle he was amazingly strong and active for his age and knew the tricks of meeting a jaguar head on. When the beast would charge and leap, the old man would place the butt of his spear to the ground, along his instep, and stand his ground as the jaguar would impale himself on the blade.

When the cat would charge low, he showed Siemel how to hold the spear low, between the arm and the rib cage, with a long, forward thrust that kept the cats claws from the man when he met the blade. Footwork had to be perfect or the force of the charge would bowl the hunter over where the cat would certainly gain the upper hand. In time, age would prove too much and the old man lost his last battle with a jaguar. But by then, Siemel was a Tigrero in his own right.

He fashioned a hardwood shaft 7 feet long with a foot-long, iron spearhead at the tip, sharpened on both sides. There was a crosspiece at the base of the blade to keep the cat from sliding down the blade to reach the hunter. It appears that Siemel did not really like killing jaguars, but merely the challenge and adventure of meeting them, and he limited his hunts to confirmed stock killers. Still, over a long career in the jungle he is credited with killing some 130 jaguars, approximately one fourth of which he took with a spear. Anyone who doubts it can see the photos in the book, *Tigrero*.

Hunters and fishers are sometimes criticized for not giving game "a chance." It's true we don't kill rabbits or quail or trout with our bare hands, and if we hunt a potentially dangerous animal, like a cougar, the "chance" the animal has is to get away, and most of them do. The hunter who contrives to meet dangerous game head on is unusual. Beyond Sasha Siemel and his spear, the only comparable hunting I can think of is the pursuit of wild hogs, where a few hunters still approach the bayed hog with a spear or long knife. I participated in just such a hog hunt myself. Still, a hog is not a jaguar. Sasha Siemel was as fearless, quick and strong as the cats he hunted, who refused to tree and turned to meet the pack and the man with the spear on the ground.

Jaguars still roam Central and South America, including the Sierra Madre of Mexico from whence they occasionally cross into southeast Arizona and the "Bootheel" of New Mexico. They receive a measure of protection from hunting in most countries, even as population growth and settlement continues to deplete their habitat. The future of the jaguar is clouded.

Meanwhile, Sasha Siemel had a long, adventurous life in South America, was a good citizen and raised a family, and sometimes came to the States in the 50s' and 60s' to relate his adventures to hunters. He died in 1970. His goal never was extermination and over time he became increasingly an advocate for jaguar conservation. Yes we have wild hog hunters who can kill a bayed-up boar with a knife. But a jaguar? We are not likely to see the likes of Sasha Siemel again.

Tales of Squirrels and Squirrel Dogs

After the fall hunting season last year I ran into the game warden. He included in his range of responsibility Unit 15 south of Quemado, had given us a tip or two on where to camp and look for elk, and now with the season over was curious how we'd done.

I told him his advice was good, that on the last day son Buddy had shot a cow elk in a remote canyon and that with help we managed to bone it out and pack it two miles to camp. I also added that on a scouting trip a few weeks earlier we'd had a good hunt in the same area for tassel-eared squirrels.

"You went squirrel hunting?" He remarked. "I think I've only checked one set of squirrel hunters in my six years in that section."

"There seemed to be quite a few squirrels in that unit," I said. "We only got four but there were others we passed up and some got away."

"Oh, I always see squirrels," he said, "but nobody hunts them."

Well, almost nobody. Our southwestern tree squirrels are, in that overworked term of the outdoor writer, "under-utilized." Take this past weekend when Buddy and I again went squirrel hunting in the mountains south of Quemado.

The woods were crawling with elk hunters. Actually it was more the forest roads; once we got back into the woods we didn't see anybody. Of course an elk hunt is a bigger deal than a squirrel hunt but to go for elk you have to get drawn and your odds are under 50%. Then if you do draw a permit your odds of getting an elk are less than 50%. Your season is less than a week long, the elk tag is expensive, and many locales will be crowded with fellow elk hunters.

As squirrel hunters our license is cheap, is bought over the counter, and the season is two months long (October and November in southwest New Mexico). The limit is eight squirrels per day and we seldom get skunked. Competition from other squirrel hunters is minimal and, perhaps best of all, you can hunt them with a dog.

Of course, you can hunt them without a dog, too. That's the way I started hunting them – without a dog – when I moved to Catron County in 1979. I'd spot a squirrel out on the ground feeding early in the morning; he'd invariably be on the run before I could get a shot with my .22 magnum. So I'd run after him, hoping to force the squirrel to tree before he got out of sight.

Sometimes this worked but it's foolhardy to run with a gun through the woods. And I had a companion at the time with a trim, smart, prick-eared mongrel. One day a light came on and I thought, "What about Taccoa?"

My friend liked to hunt and was eager to try her dog, who was "just a pet," on squirrels. Toccoa took after that first squirrel and put him up a tree in half the distance I could have managed it, if in fact I didn't fall on the run and shoot myself. Once he was up in a big ponderosa, Toccoa marked the tree and learned to keep her eye on the squirrel. She never really learned to use her nose in squirrel hunting but with her legs and good eye she was very useful and made the hunt more interesting.

Alas, for reasons outside this story, both the companion and the companion's dog were there for only two seasons of squirrel hunting. Since, my son Bud has been the perfect squirrel hunting companion as he has grown up. But that still leaves us missing the dog. I've tried greyhound, coonhound and a couple of Jack Russell terriers. All had their talents and liked hunting squirrels but none was as effective as Toccoa. And now we have "Jack."

Jack is a mostly Jack Russell terrier but a little too big to be a purebred specimen of the breed. We got him to be a companion to Buddy growing up – "just a pet" you might say. That's a noble calling by itself and Jack and Buddy have shared many adventures. But a few years ago when ground squirrels invaded the barn Jack showed he had some hunting instincts as well. It's an on-going battle with those incessant diggers and grain feeders but Jack has caught and killed a half-dozen that I know of. I said to Buddy, "Jack may be our squirrel dog!"

This past weekend was Jack's second season on tree squirrels. Last year he got the hang of it right away to push those on the ground up a tree. And he would "locate" on the tree. He was a bit gun-shy, however.

Last weekend I took to holding him while Buddy did the shooting; the extra security seemed to work as he barely flinched at the shot and was on those squirrels as they hit the ground. And he proved he could locate a squirrel by scent; i.e. one that already treed – a "lay-up" squirrel.

One squirrel treed ahead of us but we never saw him. Jack trailed him a hundred yards or so, sniffed the trunk of a certain Ponderosa, circled the pine a time or two, jumped up and sniffed the bark, and as much as told us in plain English, "He went up this one, guys." We circled the pine and looked up and Jack was right.

No, we didn't come home with a lot of squirrels, But we got that one and a few others and it would have been maybe half that without Jack and, as always, it was a better hunt with a good dog.

Stags, Shags, and Scotch Deerhounds

The great majority of the coursing hounds used for fox, coyote and jackrabbit hunting on the western plains today are unregistered, mixed breed hounds commonly lumped under the generic term, "longdogs." Among them there are as many sizes, forms, coats and colors as there are dogs, but they may be divided into two phenotypes – those with relatively short, smooth coats, and those with long, rough coats. The smooth-coated hounds are generally not described by their coat but rather by what they hunt; e.g., "he's a coyote hound," or, "he's a rabbit dog." The ones with the long, rough coats are commonly termed "staghounds" (or "stags" for short), as in, "he's a staghound," or, "he's a stag." More recently, the term "shag(s)" is sometimes used to describe the same dogs, an obvious reference to the type of coat.

The smooth-coated longdogs I will leave to another time, but in reference to stags and shags I'd like here to consider: where do they come from?; what is their relationship to the rough-coated coursing breeds, the borzoi (Russian wolfhound), Irish wolfhound, and Scottish deerhound?; what should a good one look like and how should he perform in the field?; and, since few of them hunt deer, why do they call them staghounds?

The best source of information about the early coursing hounds on the plains is to be found in writings by and about General George Armstrong Custer. He wasn't the only one who used rough-coated coursing hounds back then, but he has left us the most information. In 1868, just three years after the end of the Civil War, Custer received orders to proceed to Ft. Hays, Kansas, to join a campaign against hostile Indians. In *Life on the Plains* he wrote:

"At Ft. Leavenworth I halted in my journey long enough to cause my horses to be shipped by rail to Ft. Hays. Nor must I omit two other faithful companions of my subsequent marches and campaigns named Blucher and Maida, two splendid specimens of the Scotch staghound, who were destined to share the dangers of an Indian campaign…"

A handful of photos of Custer with his various hounds have survived, covering the years 1868 to 1876, when the General went down at the Little Bighorn. Although the individual hounds are not named, all the rough-coated ones strongly resemble what was known then (and now) as a Scottish deerhound. The breed is described in the official AKC standard as, "a rough-coated greyhound of larger size and bone," and was originally bred in the highlands of Scotland to take the large Scottish stag without the aid of firearms.

In the days before game laws, Custer hunted most everything with his "stags," including jackrabbits, coyotes, fox, antelope, deer, elk, and buffalo! Custer writes of the kill of a yearling bull on the Kansas plains.

56

After a long running fight, the buffalo was brought to bay by the hounds. Bringing him down was another matter:

"Finding escape by running impossible, he boldly came to bay and faced his pursuers; in a moment both dogs had grappled with him as if he had been a deer. Blucher seized him by the throat, Maida endeavored to secure a firm hold on the shoulders. The result was that Blucher found himself well trampled in snow, and but for the latter (Maida) would have been crushed to death. Fearing for the safety of my dogs, I leaped from my horse and ran to the assistance of the stag-hounds. Drawing my hunting knife, I succeeded in cutting the hamstrings of the buffalo, which had the effect to tumble him over in the snow, when I was enabled to dispatch him with my pistol."

Clearly, these early staghounds had the right stuff.

Blucher and Maida would not last long sharing the dangers of an Indian campaign. The dog was killed at the Battle of the Washita, the bitch in a firearms accident. But Custer would soon import others from the United Kingdom (UK), by some sources from a Lord Berkeley Paget in 1870, and perhaps also from the kennels of Queen Victoria. Among his favorites was the bitch, Tuck. In a letter to his wife, Elizabeth, Custer wrote:

"Did I tell you of her (Tuck) catching a full-grown antelope-buck, and pulling him down after a run of over a mile, in which she left the other dogs far behind? She comes to me every evening when I am sitting in my large camp chair... First she lays her head on my knee, as if to ask if I am too much engaged to notice her. A pat of encouragement and forefeet are thrown lightly across my lap; a few moments of this posture and she lifts her hind feet from the ground, and great overgrown dog that she is, quietly and gently disposes of herself on my lap... She makes up with no other person."

If you've ever owned one, you know the "lap dog" description, and the aspect of singular loyalty, fits the Scottish deerhound to the letter.

In *Boots and Saddles*, Elizabeth Custer wrote:

"With the staghound, hunting was so bred in the bone that they sometimes went off by themselves, and even the half-grown puppies followed. I have seen them returning from such a hunt, the one who led the pack holding proudly in his mouth a jack rabbit... Once when the staghounds were let out of the kennel for exercise, they flew like the winds over the hills after a coyote. The soldier who took care of them could only follow on foot, as the crust on the snow would not bear the weigh of a horse. After a long, cold walk he found the dogs standing over the wolf they killed. When he had dragged it back to our wood shed he sent in to ask if the general would come and see what the dogs had done unaided and alone, for he was very proud of them..."

Little is known of Custer's staghounds after the Little Bighorn. One hound, Cardigan, went to a clergyman in Minneapolis, who later had the dog mounted on display in a public building. One can assume that the others were dispersed with new owners. It is evident that Custer had already begun breeding these hounds and their new owners doubtless did, too, but if further of their hunting exploits survive in print I'm not aware of it.

The use of borzoi and Irish wolfhounds on the plains before 1900 is less clear. In response to my query on the Internet, I learned from several borzoi breeders that the first of the breed was not brought to the USA until about 1890. The first Irish wolfhound was registered with the AKC in 1897. There may have been a few Irish wolfhounds in the states before then, but the breed was still in its formative stages prior to 1890. The original Irish wolfhound died off with the wolf of the United Kingdom before 1800. The breed was recreated by Captain Graham in the UK between 1860 and 1900. None of these hounds hunted wolves, and with rare exceptions the re-creation to this day is, in my opinion, too tall and heavy to be of much use as a coursing hound, even for its original quarry.

Certainly borzoi and some Irish wolfhounds were used on the western plains after 1890, and they no doubt were crossed with the various greyhounds, longdogs, staghounds and deerhounds that were already there. It seems clear however, that it was the Scotch deerhound, imported from the UK by General Custer and others as early as 1868, that formed the basis for the unregistered rough-coated longdogs we know today as "staghounds." In the early days, the deerhound/greyhound cross was likely the original source of staghound puppies; since then, staghounds have been crossed, and produced, by a myriad of combinations. The deerhound connection also answers the question as to why the term staghound came into common use on the western plains, where most of the hunting was for coyote, fox, and jackrabbit. Staghound is a derivative of deerhound, and Custer was calling them "Scotch staghounds" as early as 1868.

What, then, is a staghound? To me it's any mixed breed coursing hound with something of the rough, wiry coat that is characteristic of the Scotch deerhound. I've heard the term "smooth staghound" used, for smooth-coated dogs in an otherwise rough-coated litter, but for me if it doesn't have something of a rough, wiry coat it's not a staghound. Stags come in all colors and color combinations, and in size may range from 25 to 27 inches at the withers (jackrabbit and fox) to 28 to 30 inches (coyote, deer, and other large game).

It may seem surprising that no breed standard or registry has emerged for the American staghound, though they have been around for well over 100 years. Well, we Americans have proved to be great dog hunters, but not great dog breeders. Yes, we produce some great individual dogs for the field. And we have developed a few new breeds – the various coonhound breeds (or are they strains?) come to mind, as well as the Chesapeake Bay retriever. But within the coursing hound set, all our breeds come from overseas. The aesthetics required to standardize a breed as to type as well as function so far do not appeal to the American coursing hound enthusiast.

And what of the original Scotch deerhound that Custer brought over from the UK? This is an AKC registered breed; however, there are less than 200 new registrations (mostly puppies) in the USA each year. Logically, the breed probably totals more than 1000 individuals in North America but relatively few of these are ever used for hunting. I've owned three; I hunted with them, and I've seen others in the field. Though breeding for show has had its bad effect on the breed, there is still some ability there. The most common faults in the field are too much size to allow for good action, and a lack of desire for a long race. The breed does seem to have retained much of its courage, however. Bob Schulz of Minnesota tells of his deerhounds Mo (a Donna Brookman breeding) and Tonto (from the Fernhill Kennel in Ontario). I owned Mo for a time and he was the better runner. But Bob said that Tonto was the most awesome coyote killer he's seen. Tonto would usually arrive late at the catch, Bob said, but would grab the little wolf by the neck and shake it with such force that he would literally throw the other hounds off the kill. Tonto needed no help to kill a coyote. With but one exception, however, none of the deerhounds in my experience have had the running ability of the many good staghounds I've owned or seen on the Great Plains.

If I were once again a deerhound owner and breeder, I would immediately outcross to a good-running staghound to start a new foundation that would recreate the kind of Scotch deerhounds that accompanied General Custer in his hunts on the plains. Part of the strategy should be to change the AKC deerhound standard back to the original as to size. For dogs: 28 to 30 inches and 85 to 110 lbs.; for bitches: 26 inches or more and 65 to 80 lbs. The standard should state that deerhounds over 32 inches at the withers "are not to be considered representative of the breed." Size wins in the ring but not in the field. A strict size limit is the only way I know to get away from the current tendency towards the over-tall, stilted dogs that win in the shows.

A literary descendent of Custer as a houndman was Leon Almirall who hunted with what he called Scottish deerhounds on the plains of Colorado between World War I and World War II. Some of the hounds pictured in his book *Canines and Coyotes* are clearly mixed breed staghounds. But one of his favorites was Jeff, photographed in several outdoor scenes. Whether Jeff was an AKC registered Scottish deerhound cannot be known. My guess is he wasn't. But he looks very close to being a purebred Scottish deerhound with a sandy coat; certainly the deerhound influence is strong. The fawn-colored deerhounds were more common in the early days, and the color acceptable and even well liked, though most today are dark blue-gray. Another deerhound impressed Almirall greatly:

"A Scottish deerhound, Sandy, came to join this pack of mine in the high-up country. Owned by a rancher and ill-treated, he foraged for himself largely. One day on a high mesa he ran into two coyotes. These varmints, apparently believing there was safety in numbers, planned a little fun for the deerhound. In this they got the jolt of their lives. They had reckoned so wrongly that one was jolted right out of his life. Sandy had the fun and I saw the battle. The deerhound tied into both coyotes with such fury that he put one to flight and killed the other --no mean feat if you know coyotes..."

Due to a warm climate and a focus on jackrabbits, I am mostly working saluki crosses these days and have just one staghound in my kennel. He's a lovely young pup named Beech-Nut, out of a track greyhound mother and a black staghound father who is proven on coyotes and jacks. Beech-Nut got his sire's staghound coat, colored dark blue-gray; at first glance you might just call him a Scotch deerhound. With his bloodlines, he'll run to catch.

The staghound of today has, with few exceptions, been a mixed breed hound for many generations. Go back far enough, however, and you'll find he got his rough, wiry coat, size, strength, endurance and tenacity from an old breed, the Scottish deerhound. As the deerhound contributed to the abilities, character and traits of the staghound, it will be interesting to see if today's staghound, used judiciously as a cross, can restore the original Scottish hound to the greatness he knew when such as General Custer and Leon Almirall rode with him on the plains.

Wolves and Hounds North and South

Shades of the Old West, last week a wolf incident made the front page of the Las Cruces *Sun-News.* The hounds of a Mimbres hunter got "balled up" with a pack of wolves (2 adults and 5 pups) near Brushy Mountain in the Gila National Forest.

Two of the hounds were seriously injured in the fight but at last report would recover. The wolves, spooked by the hunter on horseback, fled the scene. And the hunter commented to the paper that he would join with the New Mexico Cattle Growers Association in a suit to force a removal of these and other Mexican wolves from the wild if the agency wouldn't do it on its own.

I have some personal experience with hounds and wolves in the wild; I can empathize with any hunter re: the perils of hunting dogs that confront large predatory animals. Ultimately, however, my response to wolf/dog incidents has been quite different from that of the Mimbres hunter.

I arrived in Lake of the Woods County, Minnesota in 1970 and within several years had built a pack of trail hounds for hunting coyotes (known as "brush wolves" locally), red fox, bobcat, and raccoon. The timber wolf was also common in that section but by 1973 the species was totally protected under the Endangered Species Act. Fines for killing a timber wolf were severe but I had other reasons for giving the critters plenty of room.

The local game warden from across the Rainey River in northwest Ontario told me a story one day over coffee. The year before a man from Missouri had come north to Canada with a large pack of hounds.

"We have no lack of wolves," the warden told me. "That Missouri man turned his whole pack out on a bunch of fresh tracks in the snow. The hounds got a race going but those wolves only ran so far. Then they stopped and waited for those dogs. Three of the hounds never came out of the woods. The ones that did were cut to ribbons. That was a wiser man who went back home to Missouri."

I was tempted to add: "Guess those wolves 'showed' him," but thought better of it.

In those days I sometimes hunted brush wolves with Percy Erickson of Roseau, Minnesota. I related the warden's story to Percy. He said, "That's not how you do it."

Percy said he killed a number of timber wolves in the 50s and 60s hunting with hounds. "The trick," he said, "is to find the tracks of one traveling alone. If the hounds can catch him, then they need to badger him like a bear or a boar hog. If they try to jump him you're likely to lose some dogs. But when they would bay one up then I'd come in on snowshoes from downwind and sometimes I could get close enough for a shot."

If you hunt with hounds in wolf country incidents may occur; we north woods hunters learned to live with this. My pack had several encounters with wolves in northern Minnesota. It wasn't on purpose in any case, but one incident gave both the hounds and I a real scare, and a memorable look at a big predator in the wild.

Early one morning I found the track of a red fox going into a large section of woods. I put three hounds – Charley, Skeeziks, and Grits – down on deep snow and they took the cold track into the bush. They jumped the fox and we had a race. A red fox will generally stay within a square mile of territory and this fox did that for a half hour or so. I was thinking of putting on my snowshoes and going into the woods to try to intercept the fox with a shotgun when the race changed; the hounds began to sound more frantic in their pursuit, almost fearful, and the run lined out going south.

I drove south and came back west on another remote forest road. I got out of the truck and could hear the race coming my way. The hounds were really burning up the track and whatever they were chasing he was leaving the country. I supposed my pack had lost the fox track and were now on a brush wolf who was in full flight and would cross the road momentarily not far from where I stood.

He did, but it was no brush wolf. It was a timber wolf and in that country a mature specimen can weigh 90 lbs. or better. He cleared the bar ditch in one running stride, the road in two, then landed in a powder of snow as he disappeared into the woods on the other side.

The hounds crossed in frantic, yelping pursuit and I strapped on snowshoes and followed the race into the woods; I spent the better part of the day there. But the race went due south into an endless track of the Beltrami State Forest and was soon out of hearing. I had plenty of reason to worry. All three hounds were veteran coyote hunters. But I knew if they piled into that timber wolf it could be curtains.

Mid-afternoon, Charley and Skeeziks came out to the road, worn down but unmarked. Grits didn't show. By 8 P.M. it was long past dark and well below zero. I left my coat on the edge of the road where the race had crossed that morning and drove to town for supper at a café. I considered that I had probably lost a great hound to a big predator that I never wanted to chase in the first place. But I don't recall that I ever blamed the wolf. Really, there was no one to blame; hound and hunter know that the pursuit involves risks and, as the saying goes: "If you hunt long enough, it'll all happen."

By 10 P.M. I was back at the crossing and found Grits sleeping on my coat, near frozen but otherwise sound. I'm not sure which of us was more glad to see the other. I only wished she could have told me what happened once the race was out of sight and hearing.

I recall that winter as a great season of hunting. Grits, Charley, Skeeziks and I caught a number of brush wolves and a half-dozen fox. The hides sold for good money in the late 70s. But I believe I'd trade every dollar for the sight of one timber wolf that cleared a road in full stride, landed in deep snow, and (thankfully) got away. North or South, hunter or naturalist, any country is richer for having them around.

Drawing by Fred Barraza.

"White-out": A Close Call in Winter

Coming home from a jackrabbit hunt the other day, and passing through Deming, I tuned into Garrison Keillor and his "News from Lake Woebegone" segment of *A Prairie Home Companion*. Garrison Keillor said something like this: "On this day in November," he intoned, "1975, three partridge hunters from the Twin Cities were caught in a blizzard up north in Lake of the Woods County and never made it out of the woods......" I was taken back some 30 years, for I lived in Lake of the Woods County at the time, and I too went hunting that day. I don't recall any storm warnings on the radio re: weather. A congenital sleepy-eyed boy, maybe I just missed it. Or wasn't paying attention. I should have been.........

......It was abnormally warm that November morning; indeed I recall the entire fall as one long Indian summer. I'm sure I felt no need of gloves, ear-muffs, long johns and woolens, Sorel felt-insert boots, and other accoutrements of Minnesota winter garb. A pair of bib overalls and a light game jacket to carry the rabbits and ammunition seemed reasonable, considering the weather. This was going to be a lark; a morning afield with my two Bassett Hounds, Suzie and Phoebe, hunting for snowshoe hare. No snow on the ground and the hares were already turning an almost perfect white. After the first week of November, you don't often find bare ground in Lake of the Woods County, Minnesota, hard on the Canadian border. What could possibly go wrong?

I was well armed, too: a Savage Model 24 with .22 magnum in the top barrel and twenty gauge full choke shooting #6 shot in the bottom. I drove to a remote section of the Beltrami State Forest – vast, flat, boreal woodlands – and turned loose the hounds.

We had a good hunt. Suzie, black, brown and white, a leggy Bassett, was of hunting stock and the leader; Phoebe, lemon and white, was more compact, but tireless and all heart and she had the better voice. Even with big, obvious white hares I proved I could miss my share of running rabbits driven hard by hound music. But I rolled three over in spite of myself – that was enough meat for all of us – and late morning I came out of the woods and sat on the tailgate, drinking coffee and waiting on the hounds. They were capable of running hares by the hour just for the fun of it but once she realized I was no longer in the woods backing her up, Suzie came to the same dirt road. She saw me and ran to the truck. I thought, "We could have some good running on the south side of the road here, too." But Suzie sat there on the forest road and looked up at me like she was done. Odd! But I took her hint, opened the door, and she jumped in the cab of the truck.

Missing her hunting partner, Phoebe shortly came to the road as well. She, too, was oddly ready to quit. So I loaded her up; by this time a light snow had begun to fall and the wind had picked up. I poured more coffee and started a leisurely drive – about 15 miles – for home. With the dogs warming up the cab, steaming up the windows, and all of us happy from the hunt, it should have been a pleasant drive. But we almost didn't make it.

By the time we were halfway there I was having trouble seeing the road. It was a mixture of falling snow and blowing snow, there was no definition between the road and the bar ditch, everything was white – a "white-out." If I wasn't already familiar with the road and the few turns required I would surely have driven into the ditch. As it was I crawled along in third gear and nearly missed my own driveway. Indeed, I passed it but saw the mailbox and backed up. Even then I had to get out and get a fix on the turn down the lane; there was a bar ditch there, too.

I got to the barn, got out, and noted that the temperature must have dropped 40 degrees from earlier in the day. Working without gloves, my hands started to sting and ache as I secured everything from the coming storm. The two bassetts thought this was all great sport; they played in the snow but stuck around till I was done and followed me into the house. I built a fire in the stove, made coffee and some lunch, cleaned three hares and knew I wouldn't be going anywhere for the next few days.

In time the county snowplow opened up the county road and my driveway. I went to town and little by little caught on to how lucky I'd been. Garrison Keillor, some 30 years later, was right – two (or it may have been three), partridge hunters from southern Minnesota, hunting just a couple of miles from Suzie, Phoebe, and me, got caught in the same "white-out" while still in the woods. Without a compass, and totally disoriented by the storm, they never made it to the road. I doubt I would have fared much better if the hounds and I had not the luck to quit early that day and head for the barn. Indeed, if it wasn't for Suzie, the clairvoyant bassett, I'd likely still be there, hunting the Elysian Fields on the south side of the road.

Photo by Jacelle Ramon-Sauberan.

MISCELLANEOUS
SPORT, ISSUES, REVIEWS, HISTORIES

Mountain Men and a Family Feud

He was a mountain man all right, known as "Hunter" Thomas Jefferson Wood. Folks relied on him for skins, hides, wild meat. For a price of course. But he was a homesteader as well, with a place in the upper headwaters of the Gila River, near Iron Creek, about as far from a road as you could get, then or now. He had a bear story from his youth.

According to an article in the Silver City *Enterprise*: "Wood narrowly escaped death in the jaws of a silver tip (grizzly bear). The bear struck Wood on the side of the head, gouging out an eye and inflicting scars which he bore for the remainder of his life. As the bear stood over Wood, (George) Parker shot the bear and it fell dead across Wood's body."

Parker, a black man, would prove a good partner to Wood. In 1877 a particularly vicious outlaw gang, the Nelson bunch, had a headquarters nearby, also back in the Gila near the headwaters of Sycamore Creek. Notorious horse and cattle thieves, they were also implicated in more than a dozen murders. Perhaps because they knew the country so well, and had a reputation for fearlessness, Wood and Parker were unofficially deputized by Grant County Sheriff Harvey Whitehill to eviscerate what they could of this outlaw gang.

The rest of this vigilante work comes straight from the *Enterprise*: "He (Bob Nelson) arrived at the cabin with a companion known as Portuguese Joe a little ahead of the five other men. Wood and Parker fired from close range, Parker killing the Portuguese, while Wood missed Nelson. Nelson fired a second shot, which also went wild and as he tried to escape was shot from his horse and killed by Wood. The remainder of the gang didn't put up much of a fight and three of them were killed, two escaping."

Tom Wood was known from then on as a mankiller; he was already a vigilante, hunter, and near victim of a grizzly bear; in many ways a man of a reputation both feared and respected on the frontier. But life in the wilderness was really all he always wanted, and mostly to be left alone with his family, for this mountaineer had a domestic side.

He brought in a young wife to his camp, Tomasita Cisneros, who left a traveling circus to join him there. They built a cabin along Iron Creek, just across Turkeyfeather Pass from the upper West Fork of the Gila, had a garden, hunted, fished and trapped, raised some stock, and three children; the middle one, a son named Charlie, who had his father's flair for dangerousness. By all accounts this was a family that preferred the wilderness life and were comfortable with and had largely solved its hardships.

Into the midst of this wilderness tranquility, in 1885, came the Grudgings brothers, Henry, Willie, and Charley, who built a cabin and established a homestead of their own along the West Fork, not far upstream from what is now the Gila Cliff Dwellings National Monument, but at the time as nearly remote a locale as Tom Wood's "property" further up in the mountains. The West Fork is more than 30 miles long; you would think there was room for more than one homestead, one cattle range, and at least several mountain man personalities, however independent, in this vast section. Apparently not.

The Grudgings brothers were cattle rustlers, according to more than one report, including the say-so of Tom Wood who threatened to expose them. Meanwhile the Grudgings had it on record, they claimed, that Charley Wood, now fifteen, would butcher a Grudgings' steer, jerk the meat in the arid mountains, and sell it as deer jerky at substantial profit on the streets of Silver City. However vast the wilderness, and long the river, a family feud developed, and they knew how to find each other.

On October 10, 1892, Charley Wood, returning with supplies on a pack train from Silver City, made camp with a companion along the West Fork, well above the Grudgings' cabin. His body was found there in camp the next day by a passerby. Head lacerations indicated he had been pistol whipped before being shot through the head. The companion too was dead but everyone knew that Charley Wood was the target. Nothing was stolen; the pack stock, burros, and supplies were still in camp. There were no suspects, but one could easily intuit a motive of hate.

Physical evidence was lacking but in time Tom Wood focused on the Grudgings, and Willie Grudgings in particular became the marked man. The family feud was already there. Rumors fly, even in the wilderness, and a dying cowboy, bucked off a horse and breathing his last, claimed he was there when it happened; it was Willie, he said, who killed 15-year-old Charley Wood. Or so some said he said.

Tom Wood would deliver his own justice. Whoever did it was foolish, for he had killed the son of a man with a reputation.. On October 8, 1893 Tom Wood shot and killed Willie Grudgings, outside by the corrals, at the Grudgings' homestead along the West Fork of the Gila River. Within days he had turned himself into the law, said he did it because Willie Grudgings had "killed my son." Held at Cooney, a tiny mining town with a crackerbox jail, he promptly escaped, slipped back into the wilderness and hung about the homestead for the better part of three years. As historian Jan Devereaux noted in a recent western journal, it's likely that, with Tom Wood's reputation, nobody wanted to try and arrest him, especially on his home ground.

But, on the lam, Tom Wood was not a free man and that, rather than guilt, may have weighed on the mental wellness of a lover of the wild. In 1896 he surrendered again, got a good lawyer in Silver City, or at least a better one than the prosecutor, and was acquitted. He'd said he did it. Did the jury find him innocent, or simply justified? The record is silent. He returned to his mountain home and lived most of the remainder of his life there, seemingly content with the history he had created, and died of natural causes at 78 years.

Willie Grudgings was buried by his brothers near the family homestead. The cabin remained long after the U.S. Forest Service took over the property, but burned in a forest fire in 1991. A headstone remains along the West Fork for those who can find it: "William Grudgings, Waylaid and Murdered By Tom Wood, October 8, 1893, Age 37 Years 8 Months."

Charley Wood, too, is buried deep in the Gila Wilderness. It all seems quite odd today. I was fishing along there just the other day and it would be hard to find a more idyllic locale than the wilderness waters of the West Fork of the Gila River. The Willie Grudgings headstone rests quiet and cryptic in a bucolic park. Yet long ago, that pristine flow was witness to a pistol whipping, a double murder, and revenge that might have equaled it in crime.

Note: The author is indebted to Jan Devereaux for research included in this column.

"Oh, On That Day We Play Baseball"

The Gila and San Francisco Rivers went above boards last week; I mean over-the-top! Here in New Mexico, both streams spiked close to 30,000 cubic feet per second (cfs) for a time, a near record for either one. And – most unusual – the Mimbres River has been running all the way to Deming for weeks. That has all the locals talking.

Not surprisingly, some hikers and river runners got caught by the flood waters and the rescue on the Gila of a family of hikers by helicopter made the papers. One group of kayakers made it through, while two other river runners I know of got walled up in a canyon and had to temporarily cache their boats and gear and hike out. It all put me in mind of a canoe trip of mine on big water many years ago, in northern Quebec.

Still in our teens, my cousin Hank Soule and I wanted an outdoor adventure before packing off to college. We weren't deliberately courting danger mind you – neither of us was inclined to want to get on the edge of what whitewater can do to you – just looking for a doable adventure in remote country where we could catch some fish.

I think it was Hank's uncle suggested the Megiscane River, though he had never been there, and he loaned us a canoe for the trip. It stretched 18 ft., was all wood – looked like mahogany – and was immaculate; the sort of classic model they use in picture books to sell lake frontage. Of course this was before the popularity of Royalex and Ram-X and other synthetic models that can take a pounding. I liked the looks of our canoe, but looking at that hand-crafted wooden elegance understood that it would just take one mistake to smash it on the rocks a long way from home.

The rain started as we crossed into a foreign country, a steady drizzle up through Ottawa and on into the vast, relentless boreal forests of French Canada. Nobody, it seemed, spoke English, though most seemed to understand it well enough, and it was still rainy as we took a two-hour, dead end gravel road to the only dwelling on big Lac Faillon, a nascent fishing lodge owned and managed by one Jean Abel. He did speak English, albeit with an engaging French accent, and he apologized for the weather.

"This is a three-day blow, and this is the fourth day, so this is the last day for sure of this rain," he said.

And the sun did shine for awhile in the morning. Marcel, a guide at the lodge, took us to the river, 40 to 50 miles upstream on the Megiscane, and dropped us off. Jean Abel had warned us of the river running high in all the rain, and "big rapids," but "the map will show you the portage, or else on some you'll line down.......but you boys are canoe-men......"

71

We boys waved goodbye to Marcel who gave us a cheer that meant something hopeful, I think, in French. We were only vaguely aware that we were on much bigger water than either of us had ever canoed before. And then it started to rain.

And it drizzled, most of the time, for the next week. Jean Abel's well meant "for sure" did not end the soggy weather; August is a wet month in Quebec, and since we were several hundred miles north of Ottawa, it was cold too; more like October than the last days of summer.

The map Jean Abel gave us, saved us. Northern Quebec is *voyageur* country where people have traveled by water since the days of birch-bark canoes. Every time the Megiscane funneled up into big rapids the map would show the rapids with cross-hash marks and a portage trail that would get you around it. If no portage trail accompanied the warning of rapids, they figured we could run that one. Or at least line down.

We used all three approaches at different times – we learned a lot. Some of the portage routes were a mile long, lining down in cold wet weather is always work, and running a rapid was fast and exciting but as remote as we were, we could not afford a wreck. We were working hard and making it.

The fishing was spotty. But we caught some every day. We threw daredevils at them, and flat fish, various spoons and plugs, and hooked walleyes at 2 to 3 lbs. and the occasional northern pike. I got the biggest pike at 7 lbs. or so but we only kept the walleyes to eat.

Little by little most everything got wet – clothes, tent, bedrolls, some of the food. Campfires were difficult but we'd get one going come evening and fry fish and talk about how we would dry everything out the first sunny day we got. But no sunny day arrived and that last morning we boiled coffee, ate Fig Newtons for breakfast and I said to Soule: "Looks like we got about 10 miles of river and 12 miles of lake; I say let's pack up and paddle and make a big push for the lodge."

Soule had had enough as well. We had one portage and ran the only other rapids. We dodged the boulders and rode over the haystacks and shot out the lower end working both paddles and by noon reached Lac Faillon. The wind had the lake in whitecaps but we had to cross it sometime.

I'd had the steering paddle in the stern all morning but crossing Lac Faillon Soule took over the rear seat. More than once I thought we were swamped but Soule was adept at keeping the bow head-on to the waves and we baled water on the go. We threw it out as fast as it came in and hopped out and jumped and cheered for ourselves when we finally reached the far shore.

Of course we had to deal with a fierce head-wind, following the shore-line, but we pulled onto the beach at the lodge in time to rent a cabin, change to dry clothes, start a fire in the woodstove, and eat a supper of roast pork and potatoes, and in that remote lodge nobody asked our age when we ordered a thick Canadian beer. We ate like harvest hands and I got a laugh out of some French-Canadian girls at the next table when I summed up the trip with a notation that "even the Fig Newtons had gotten wet."

The next morning as we made ready to pull out Jean Abel was extolling our skills to the other guests – "these boys are sure good canoe-men" – and swearing to anyone who would listen that this was the last day "for sure" of the rain and cold.

"Well," I said, "what do you do in the summer here in Quebec?"

"Oh," he said with a smile, "on that day we play baseball."

Changes Apparent in a High, Green Land

A friend and I hiked up to Bead Spring a few weeks ago. We traveled just ahead of the current spate of monsoon rains that have blessed us here lately in southwest New Mexico. At first glance, everything looked much the same as the last time I visited the spring, 23 years ago. But looks can be deceiving and, upon reflection, change is coming to our local lands and waters as seen from a high, green land.

High and green because Bead Spring is one of the source waters of the Gila River. The hike begins at Sandy Point at some 9,000 feet and you are over 10,000 feet by the time you get to the spring – elevation and a unique topography elicit a quick transformation from scrub piñon and juniper to a boreal jungle. This is where the rain and snow falls that makes the Gila River a reality instead of a dry wash in an otherwise desert land. Even before the monsoon rains the trail to Bead Spring is startling green in summer.

Well above the Transition Zone of Ponderosa pine and oak, we hike through aspen trees, blue spruce, Engelmann spruce, ferns and mushrooms – plants that require a cool climate and 30 to 40 inches of precipitation a year.

A Deming resident, where one hopes for an average of 8 inches of precipitation a year, marvels at the 16 inches a year granted to Silver City just 50 miles away. But what does one say about the 10 feet of snow that topped the snowtel in March of 2005 at Hummingbird Saddle, just up the trail from Bead Spring! I remark that Hummingbird Saddle holds Hummingbird Spring, a source water of Whitewater Creek, a seminal flow for the San Francisco River. My friend, who is a photographer, is intrigued.

I've been too long away. Once on the trail I marvel at how much I had forgotten about the Canadian aura and Hudsonian biome of the source waters of the Gila/San Francisco drainage. Here it looks more like Alberta than the state where the coatimundi and javelina live not 20 miles away.

At the spring the flow emerging from the ground is a bit less than I recall from 1983. It is still enough to form the beginnings of a perennial stream, Willow Creek; if we follow it a ways, I tell her, we will find trout. But my friend is a photographer and she is already hard at work.

She has a book in process, not her first, for she already has another under her belt; it too is full of pictures. Anybody can take a picture but the good ones – the real photographers – create pictures and leave images that make you think certain things should not be sullied by the machinations of man. What she did for New Mexico's Great Plains, over east, she now wants to do for a river in peril from – you guessed it – the machinations of man. To record the river's source waters on film is both a challenge and an opportunity.

She is long and willowy in form and often bent at impossible angles, which must be uncomfortable, and gets improbably close to the plants and waters of Bead Spring, but her camera can make minutiae big. She goes "click, click, click." My only contribution is to find a wonderful purple flower of a surreal tint, it's only failing its small size. Well, maybe not. She finds the flower, and the focus. "Click!" And then, this being a digital age that has passed me by, she shows me the image of a tiny purple flower, nourished by Bead Spring, that looks as big as an orchid.

"Wait till you see Gilita Creek," I say on the hike back to the truck. "Wait till you see those trout!" But no. Before we get there, or even to Willow Creek campground, the road is blocked by the Forest Service. The Bear Fire of early summer charred more than 50,000 acres and rendered Gilita Creek to black ash. Only by a miracle could a trout survive and we can't even get through to find out. I can't recall the last time I went fly fishing and never even strung up the rod.

In the weeks ahead I would learn more. The Bear Fire was a wildfire, unplanned, and it burned hot. It closed popular campgrounds, and fishing streams, and will keep them closed for a year at least. And when the monsoons finally came this summer, they sent black ash from the fire down the tributaries into the Middle Fork of the Gila suffocating none knows how many fish. It will be long past your time and mine – if ever – before that 50,000 acres looks like it did before the fire. It was just luck, and hard work by the firefighters, that the Bear Fire didn't get Bead Spring and Hummingbird Saddle, too.

But the headwaters of the Gila/San Francisco drainage have seen wildfires before; they were the historic norm, the process that kept the forest properly open and spared of overgrowth. Ashes to ashes, dust to dust, but the monsoons, as in eons before, will spur an early revival of new green growth.

The fish will make it too; not many, but enough to start a new generation of wild trout and other species to please angler and naturalist alike. And in some waters this fire may be a spur to rejuvenate lifeless flows with introductions of the recently down-listed native Gila trout.

The photographer and I obey the Forest Service and turn around at the closure and head back towards Sandy Point. With the giant spruce, fir and aspen all growing close along the narrow road, it is rather like driving through a tunnel. But there is one place where a rock slide has created an opening where one can see far to the north. A photographer can't pass that up.

Before she is done we are getting rained on; the sunlight that blessed us, and her camera, at Bead Spring has left us and the dark clouds of the first monsoons are closing overhead. It is time to get off the mountain.

"Next time," she says, "I'd like to hike all the way up to Hummingbird Saddle. I'll bet there's some good shots up there."

"There are," I say. "Some big vistas. But they may not all be pretty. There's been some changes in this high, green land."

Photo by Jan Haley.

Bear Attacks are All the Rage!

Having email access means being on the email circuit and that means all manner of stuff arrives unannounced and often unwanted. Most of this stuff is just junk, some of it is reprehensible, but there is the occasional nugget of real interest. Such was the case this week when someone forwarded an item making the rounds re: an attack by what may have been the largest grizzly bear on record.

A forest service employee in Alaska was out hunting when he was charged by a grizzly. Armed with a 7mm Remington Magnum, he got several shots into the bear which went down just a few feet shy of the hunter's boots. A few more shots finished him off.

Now I'm innately skeptical of claims arriving via gratuitous email but this missive came with photos of both the bear and the hunter and this was a monster animal. He dwarfs the hunter such that it is entirely believable that he weighed, as claimed, just over 1,600 pounds. The weight, according to the document, was certified by Alaska Game & Fish and the bear is to be mounted and displayed at the Anchorage airport. Further advancing his place in history, the bear carried within him the remains of two humans, including a missing hiker!

How big is a 1,600 lb. bear? Well, he's eight times as large as a 200 lb. man. The download I printed out says this particular bear, standing up, was 12 feet tall at the shoulder and 14 feet to the top of his head.

"To give additional perspective," the download goes on, "consider that this particular bear, standing on its hind legs, could walk up to an average single story house and look over the roof, or walk up to a two story house and look in the bedroom window."

Bear attacks are all the rage! A quick scan of my used book shelf shows four recently published volumes on bear encounters. The most recent (2005), *Death in the Grizzly Maze – The Timothy Treadwell Story*, by Mike Lapinski, is worth reading.

Lapinski's prose is strident but I think nonetheless accurate in debunking Treadwell as the "bear whisperer." A Malibu, California ne're do well, and possibly bi-polar, Treadwell earned fame, and appearances on nation-wide TV shows, by getting himself filmed standing, sitting, and conversing with grizzly bears that roamed just a few feet away. Over a span of a dozen years he dallied with bears like a child wandering amongst so many big, fuzzy dogs. He claimed he was protecting them from poachers and bringing the plight of bear conservation to a wider audience.

Lapinski thinks Treadwell was a charlatan, a thrill-seeker who took the adulation offered by certain animal rights groups, and activists like the infamous Captain Paul Watson, and ran with it. In October, 2003 in Alaska, Treadwell and his girlfriend, Amie Huguenard, were killed and eaten by one or perhaps two grizzly bears in Katmai National Park. The next day the two suspected bears were killed by park officials investigating the scene of the maulings.

I got wind of this incident through, you guessed it, unsolicited email! And it was not only news release that came through. Somehow the photos of Treadwell's partly eaten body, which should have remained in official hands, got out there on The Web. Next thing I know I had full view of the "grizzly" corpse; what was left of Treadwell was distributed and viewed nationwide with electronic speed.

Even more gruesome, apparently, is the audio of the final minutes of Treadwell and Huguenard. Their video camera was set up that morning to record bear encounters. Unaccountably, the lens cap was on when the killer bear approached, but the audio of the camera was functioning and, Lapinski reports, it recorded a six-minute ordeal during which the two humans battled for their lives with a killer bear. Of course the bear won.

The audio, so far, has remained in official hands, but photos of one of the dead bears that had eaten Treadwell also made it to my email address. This bear weighed "only" 1000 lbs., by estimate, but it still had a paw that would lop over a dinner plate.

Bear attacks are all the rage and it is human nature to find attacks on our species by wild animals as endlessly fascinating. The drooling bear was standard fare on the covers of "hook and bullet" magazines for years. Stalking cougars and vicious wolf packs will never go out of style. But midst the rage it is good to put it all in perspective.

Lapinski reports that Alaska has a total of about 40,000 bears and they average a mere six bear attacks per year. The great majority of these attacks are not fatal.

There have been but fifty deaths by cougars in North America, going back to the 1700s and handful at most by wolves. By comparison, bees, wasps and hornets are much more dangerous than large carnivores, and a recent study I saw recorded an average of 24 humans per year in North America gored by cattle.

The last time I got close to a bear was a few years ago while fishing the Gila River. A medium-sized bear of a reddish-brown pelage crossed the river just below, climbed the bank and took his time crossing a ridge behind me before disappearing into the hills. Certainly, he was bigger, stronger, faster than I. Yet there was nothing to fear and much to admire in this Gila forest bear. I didn't bother him and he didn't bother me.

A drive through the Big-I in Albuquerque at rush hour is more dangerous than a walk in the woods where bears reside. Still, bear attacks are all the rage. Don't be surprised if you encounter one some morning while checking your email!

Beavers: Sometimes Dam Building is OK

I was up along one of the Gila streams the other day. I didn't catch any fish, and hardly tried, but it was a good hike along the waters and the main thing I noticed is that the beavers had been hard at work. It seems they are coming back.

They were once along our local waters in great numbers. In 1824, James Ohio Pattie descended the Rio Grande from Taos with fellow trappers. They took beaver all along the great river on down to what is now the area of Truth or Consequences. The party then crossed the Continental Divide, apparently near what is now Emory Pass (Pattie was an imprecise geographer in the *Personal Narrative* he left behind) and trapped the Gila drainage up to the area of the Gila Cliff dwellings.

Pattie marveled at the beaver populations along the Gila. Later the group descended the Gila, then ascended the San Francisco River from its confluence with the Gila near present-day Clifton, Arizona. They got good numbers of beaver there as well and with luck could have returned to Taos with a small fortune. Alas, luck is fickle, is very difficult to trap, and Pattie lost his fur cache to an Indian raid. But we know from early mountain men like Pattie and James Kirker that both the Rio Grande and the Gila drainage in southern New Mexico held prosperous native beaver colonies historically and in spite of human activities they are still with us today.

Known by the Latin name *Castor canadensis*, the beaver is native to a wide span of North America, from northern Canada to northern Mexico. In an interesting essay, "Nature's Hydrologists," Alice Outwater quotes an estimate of some 200 million beaver in North America before European settlement. At home virtually anywhere there exists a perennial flow, these 200 million rodent engineers built dams everywhere they lived and thus created millions of acres of wetlands that multiplied biodiversity in ways a beaver could never know and we humans were slow to understand.

Some beaver lore is well known: their teeth are constantly growing so chewing and feeding on trees, brush and bark is a necessity; they are incessant workers; and they are known for their strong family values, taking up to three years to raise a family of kits. But unless you've seen one up close you may be unaware as to how big they are.

Years ago, at my 240-acre place in Minnesota, I had beavers on the back forty. It was quite a swamp after the spring snowmelt and a friend came by to trap a few. He set out several Connibear traps and got a half dozen beaver; one monster he stopped to show me weighed 65 lbs.! That's well above the average of course but a grown beaver is a massive rodent and can provide big dividends in meat and hide.

79

Beavers are strict vegetarians and the meat is said to be excellent by those few who have tried it. They are more commonly killed for their pelts. Of course the beaver trade helped settle the West but here is what my latest issue of *Fur-Fish-Game* has to say about the current beaver market.

"Beaver prices just can't seem to turn that long-awaited corner where the big, good shearing types will be worth a premium over what is being paid for commercial types and smaller sizes. Again, expect tops of $25-$30 for the better straight-haired goods, with a few heavy types netting $35. Smaller skins will average in the low to mid-teens, and lower grades will continue to move at $5 or less."

Ms. Outwater estimates that the historical beaver population of 200 million is now down to about 10 million. Although the dams beavers build are sometimes a nuisance around settlements, the overall effect of large-scale beaver removal has been negative. Here's how Ms. Outwater describes the loss, to both biodiversity and aquifer recharge:

"When the beavers were removed, their old dams slowly collapsed, and the streams were released from the series of ponds that had been built throughout the watershed. The watersheds lost wetlands, and the water that had seeped quietly down to the aquifer now flowed rapidly to the sea…in the undammed land, the water table soon dropped. Wetlands disappeared by the acre as the frontier rolled West."

Beavers can overpopulate at times and at times there is a place for beaver trapping, even today. They are a renewable resource like many other furbearers. But we can hope that the days of every beaver and his dam being seen as a problem are over. Indeed, they have a great potential in watershed and ecosystem restoration, augmenting other wildlife that birders, anglers and hunters all appreciate and value, if for different reasons.

They will only thrive where there is a perennial flow, but imagine the aquifer recharge possible if we humans became beavers and all the arroyos and ephemeral streams in southern New Mexico had check dams that held water back, promoting aquifer recharge and reversing the down-cutting of gullies that mars so much of our precipitous terrain. There is much concern these days that Texas and Arizona are getting "our" water. We could learn from a rodent and employ ourselves as so many beavers and hold some of that water back. Better yet we could foster and help spread our local beaver populations and they could do most of the work for us.

Some years ago I canoed through the Bosque del Apache Wildlife Refuge. I saw several beavers and lots of beaver sign; the critters added to the trip. Later I canoed from Caballo Dam down to Leasburg dam and was similarly rewarded. On the San Francisco River one evening I camped by a dam and watched the beavers build it higher, pushing all the trees and sapling stem first into the flow. On the East Fork of the Gila I have caught smallmouth bass up to 20 inches on wooly buggers out of a deep pond created by beavers.

Then, just last week, I came upon a similar pond on another stream in the Gila Forest. Though it was mid-winter, some of the cuttings were fresh. The beavers were hard at work at what they do. And I'll be back in the spring to see how the game fish like their new impoundment.

Alternative Energy Not Always "Green"

It is said that traditional energy development (here in New Mexico that largely means oil and natural gas) has its problems, most of them environmental. And it's true. Oil and gas rigs fragment wildlife habitats, have a strong potential to pollute or contaminate our scarce and valuable water supplies, and at the burning stage produce greenhouse gases – the so-called carbon footprint – that contributes to global warming. Plus oil and gas are finite resources that must over time decline and leave us increasingly dependent on foreign providers.

All this bad news about oil and gas (not to mention coal) has given a big boost to so-called alternative or renewable energy, particularly wind and solar power, as a new direction in energy development – no pollutants, no carbon footprint, and you don't "use up" wind and sun like you do oil, gas, and coal. But a cost/benefit juxtaposition of traditional energy with the new "green" energy options reveals there's no pasture entirely free and green on which to feed our huge appetite for energy.

I caught on to this at a public meeting in Lordsburg a while back. SunZia Transmission, LLC (a consortium of power companies) proposes "up to two 500kV transmission lines" to run "approximately 460 miles" from substations in Pinal County, AZ to those in Socorro or Lincoln Counties, NM, requiring "rights of way of up to 1000 feet in width." These lines purport to carry new wind and solar generated power (along with some traditional energy) and concurrent new wind and solar generating fields in New Mexico are seen on the maps provided.

At first I thought, "Great; these new alternative energy lines will replace older lines – no new impacts and cleaner energy!" How naïve. The BLM and representatives of the energy companies hosted the meeting, everyone was polite and tried to be helpful, and I was informed that energy is a "growth industry." So we were looking at a whole new array of transmission lines and energy generation fields; all the old power lines and oil and gas development would still be there while the new alternative energy development would add its own impact to our lands and waters. That impact varies according to where it occurs and whether it comes from the transmission lines per se, or the wind or solar energy fields.

The transmission lines themselves appear to be no better or worse than the ones we have now. They are unsightly but apparently necessary, fragment open space and may impact wildlife to some degree depending on where they're placed. One possible route for these new alternative lines crossed the bird flyway between the Sevilleta and Bosque del Apache Wildlife Refuges near San Antonio. Secondary routes as indicated on the map avoided this conflict and appeared friendlier to birds. In general, all I could think to recommend in my comments and letter to the BLM was to avoid special areas like wildlife refuges and our remnant Chihuahuan desert grasslands, and parallel new lines with existing major roadways or extant power lines whenever possible. I was told by both agency and industry personnel that those were "good suggestions" and that "nothing on the map is cast in stone." We shall see.

For wind farms in southwest New Mexico, there was one on the map, projected for the Goodsight Mountains. For these "windmills" they of course look for wind corridors and usually these are along ridges and low mountains, I was told. Wind generator blades can chew up a lot of birds so, again, one hopes they avoid bird migration routes. Also, wildlife professionals have developed guidelines to make transmission lines and wind generators easier on our birds.

Of more concern to me were the solar panel fields of which there were half a dozen proposals for southwest New Mexico. In this form of renewable energy development, fields are leveled, solar panel units are installed in close proximity, and wildlife habitat, grazing land, and recreation land is not merely fragmented or altered, it is essentially eliminated over the reach of the units.

I noted on the map a 23,000 acre project proposal, most of it BLM land, called Mason Draw Solar Study Area. I am familiar with this largely grassland expanse about 25 miles west of Las Cruces, favored by rabbit and quail hunters and predator callers. It is also good grazing for at least a couple of ranches and invariably I see golden eagles and pronghorn antelope when hunting there.

Is this the best place for a solar panel field? Not, I'd say, when there are huge expanses of creosote, mesquite and catclaw flats nearby that are much less productive of wildlife, recreation, and grazing forage.

Renewable energy does hold benefits over drilling for oil and gas or mining and burning coal. But none of this energy development is wildlife friendly or without negative impacts. We can mitigate those impacts but we're still going to get new energy development because we're growing. Further, why are we developing all this renewable energy a thousand miles from where it's to be used? Individual solar or wind units should be developed on the spot for every home, building, business, or town that wants or needs one.

A letter in a recent issue of *High Country News* notes that global greenhouse gases are up 70% since 1970. No coincidence; so is population growth worldwide (3.8 billion to 6.2 billion) and in the USA (roughly 200 million to 300 million) over the same span.

Canada is larger than the USA and is a net exporter of energy while we import much of ours. Is this because Canada produces more energy than the USA? No, it's because Canada has about 33 million people; we have nearly ten times that number. Some day we will have to face up to the crux of the problem; until we stop growing, new energy development is upon us, the best of which is still just a pale shade of green.

Author Writes of Eagles, Sporting Books

Writing "coaches," faculty at writing conferences, and would-be authors with literary pretensions are forever counseling the less skilled among wordsmiths to "use your imagination" and to "write what you know." This is generally good advice as imagination and what you know can easily combine to put a certain enthusiasm onto the printed page. And enthusiasm – if the author "translates" well to the reader—will if nothing else save a weak book from boredom. And it might render a good book into a classic.

Steve Bodio of Magdalena, Socorro County has a myriad of enthusiasms among his belongings. His voice carries, his eyes penetrate, and whether the subject is the survival of the planet or how to feed his pigeons, Bodio in person or on the printed page will capture your interest or even hijack your spirit if you don't watch out. In the past year he has seen the publication of two more books, both vintage Bodio.

An Eternity of Eagles: The Human History of the Most Fascinating Bird in the World (Lyons Press, Guilford, CT, 2012, 212 pgs., $26.95 hardcover), is a volume the author was surely busting to write; eagles stir our imaginations and Bodio is intrigued by the quest.

"We need new ways of imagining the minds of the 'other bloods' with whom we share our world," he writes. "Eagles contain power and intelligence in a body that weighs only twelve pounds. They appear and disappear like magic in seconds and can fall out of the sky to kill a one-hundred-pound antelope or a five-pound flying goose with no tools but the muscles of a hollow-boned body smaller than a child's. Those talons exert a ton of pressure at their tips."

Without so stating, Bodio seeks – and is close to realizing – the essence of the eagle. He's on a roll…….

"Too many writers," he says, "who write about animals either pretend to a scientist's assumed 'objectivity,' using the passive voice and a deliberate flattening of affect to distance themselves from the subject on the page, or they anthropomorphize their protagonists……."

"……I am human, and wish I could fly with eagles and, liberated to the air, hunt with them like a human mate – blowing down the wind like a thought, a shadow on furled wings, falling from the sky like a sentient thunderbolt to kill with my own suddenly powerful hands. This wish to know, to understand, and even for a moment to be something different, something other than human, is an entirely human desire; an eagle would neither comprehend nor care. Our dreaming species lives within a larger context that predates us; it is one that needs us less than we need it."

Bodio is not all dreams and speculations of course. There are long chapters on natural history of eagles (there are related sub-groups of sea eagles, snake eagles, hawk eagles and the Aquila group which includes the golden eagle, fairly common here in New Mexico and a superior hunter, even among eagles). And there is eagle hunting.

No, you can't hunt eagles in the USA (certain Native American tribes have wrangled a controversial exemption) but people have been hunting with eagles for thousands of years, world wide. I was astounded to learn that eagles up to 20 lbs. have been used in big game hunting including the take of fox, coyote, wolf, deer and antelope. Bodio recounts hunts he attended in Central Asia. Most USA eagle falconry is for jackrabbit.

Profusely illustrated, mostly in color, *An Eternity of Eagles* is at once scholarly, informative, and inspired by the enthusiasm of its author.

Bodio has been busy; his second book of the year is out: *A Sportsman's Library: 100 Essential, Engaging, Off – Beat Fishing and Hunting Books for the Adventurous Reader* (Lyons Press, Guilford, CT. 2013, 255 pgs, softcover, $18.95). A long-time book reviewer for *Gray's Sporting Journal* and *Fly Rod & Reel,* Bodio is a bibliophile. He reports that when first presented with the idea of introducing readers to the 100 "best" sporting books of all time he had no trouble listing on a note pad some 130 titles drawn from the top of his head. And you can bet your last six-pack he's read most of them.

Bodio is as effusive about good sporting books as he is about eagles. Each title, named and delivered, gets 2 to 3 pages of review coupled with a color photo of the cover. The selection process is necessarily arbitrary, but Bodio is nothing if not eclectic with his literary tastes and so there is something for everyone – venerable classics (*The Art of Fishing with an Angle*/Dame Juliana Berners, 1486); modern classics (*Green Hills of Africa*/Earnest Hemingway, 1935); books you've heard of and have probably read (*Maneaters of Kumaon*, 1946); books you've never heard of (*Tales of a Rat Hunting Man*/D. Brian Plummer, 1978).

As with the Eagle book, Bodio's enthusiasm comes through on each page; he must have chuckled over the assignment; they would pay him to delve into his principle academic interest – books! He tells you what he likes and doesn't like:

He likes *Trout Bum* by John Gierach. He quotes another well known fly fisher, Seth Norman, who commented on Gierach: "More often than not, the greatest appeal is the faith Gierach conveys to the reader that lets us think: I could do this."

He likes *Big Woods* by William Faulkner – "America's iconic hunting saga" – about a down in the dirt southern bear hunt, but doesn't like the animal rights movement – "Where will the hounds go when all is forbidden?"

All said this is an astounding collection that only Steve Bodio could have produced; nobody else in my view could be as lively and cogent in his critique while digging up such a captivating list, from the venerable titles to the esoteric, otherwise lost to time. Of course there will always be quibbles with a list of the "best" since you can't list them all; I would have included Harold Blaisdell's *Philosophical Fisherman* among the angling books.

For that matter, I would have included one of Bodio's own sporting books – *Eagle Dreams: Searching for Legends in Wild Mongolia* – in the review. Quibbles aside, *A Sportsman's Library* is more than just a "good read;" it's a service to literature.

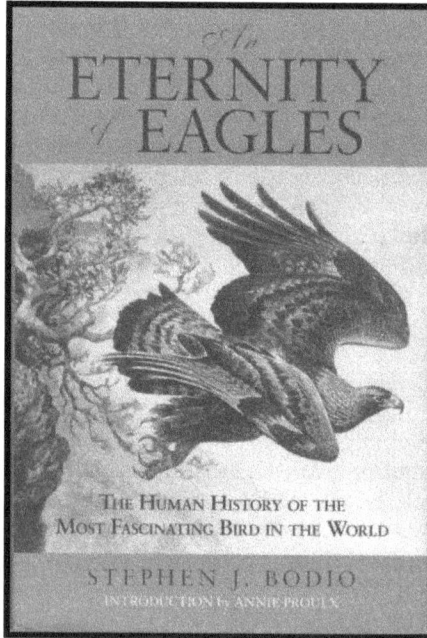

Campfires to College: Trailing the Kid

My father hunted, fished, was in all ways an outdoor man and, with a face "beat back by the weather," he even looked the part. Many years ago he offered up that outdoor life to me. Had he pushed me into outdoor sport and fascination with the natural world, I might have resisted. But out there he was more teacher than parent, yet offered knowledge by way of opportunity and a positive example rather than directives, and he knew how to make each day fun for a kid. I was hooked an early age.

My own son was born 18 years ago and this column began some 2 years later. "Bud" has appeared in numerous stories within this newspaper. Like my father, I have tried, not always successfully, to be positive rather than preachy. But in the end I had to trust in the Red Gods to steer my kid into a love for, rather than an aversion to, the outdoor life. From the book *The Catfish as Metaphor*, here's how I saw the prospects in 1997 when Bud was 2 years old:

> It's possible of course that John Pomeroy "Bud" Salmon II won't even care to fish. He may not care to hunt, either; in a disapproving world awash in TV selections, computer games and urban blight, the eternal verities of nature and pursuit may leave him cold. But I doubt it. Recently, he saw his first fish, a bullhead his father caught out of Elephant Butte Lake, and though just old enough to walk and too young to talk, he stomped his feet and pointed, and shouted questions we couldn't understand.
>
> In the evenings when his father goes to the barn to feed the hounds and chickens, and feed and milk the goats, he carries the egg basket and won't be left behind. He has seen the squirrels in the walnut trees, the raven on the fence post, and he has fallen into the creek; his wandering and wondering in the natural world have already begun. In time he will know a brown trout from a rainbow, a channel cat from a blue, a jackrabbit from a snowshoe hare. He will understand that the natural world is worth fighting for, and to leave some for seed. He will feel the singular thrall of the chase.
>
> He is learning things I feel he will never want to be without. This knowledge will be his benefit no matter what direction he takes in time, and with luck he will one day be able to say of his own father – though flawed he did not fail.

A good start for the two of us but would it hold? From the *Sun-News*, here's Bud – now seven – on a bullfrog hunt with a BB gun:

"You hit that one, Bud!"

"Can we eat him?" he asked as I retrieved the trophy. I'd made a big deal earlier about how good frog legs are. But I had to tell him that his frog was too small to eat.

"What are you going to do with him," he asked?

I had also made a big deal about how you don't just kill things and then just leave them lay. So my own brand of ethics was now on the spot.

"We'll feed him to the chickens when we get home," I said. That seemed to satisfy him.

At home, sure enough, we took the boy's trophy out to the chicken yard. They made short work of that frog.

"Look at that, Dad!" the boy said, pointing, as the birds scrapped at the meat like a flock of politicians over a pile of cash. Then we gathered up the eggs and headed for the house.

We had some memorable fishing days – fly fishing, spin casting – but memorable too was bait fishing on Father's Day 2007. We had hiked half the day to get to try the "big pool" where a "big fish" was anticipated, only to find we were stopped short by high water. From the *Sun-News:*

He was disappointed, but I explained to Bud there are always other pools and hidden haunts along the Gila and we stopped at one on the way back. I suggested a certain backwash pool; he ignored me and cast his hellgrammite nicely to a deep quiet spot well downstream against a cliff face.

"Not a bad idea," I thought, and soon he was into a fish, a good one that ran his line and I splashed ashore to help. The fish proved tenacious but Bud made him work against the rod, and the drag on the reel, and he eventually beached a flathead catfish over two feet long.

"Don't let go of him, Dad!"

No chance; the fish had gripped most of my hand in a way I would remember for days.

"He looks freaky; is that a flathead catfish.......I've never caught one of them before."

Indeed it was a flathead, and we kept this one, for this is as fine an eating fish as swims fresh water.

On the way home I asked Bud if he had gotten me a gift for Father's Day.

"I think Mom did."

'That's fine," I said. "You don't need to buy me a present, Buddy......we'll just leave it like it is."

The memories come unbidden. The mule deer hunt; a fine buck stalked in the wilderness, shot at long range, boned out and packed out the old way..

And the extended camp-outs. Like the time we took the pack goats and went in for 4 days along the Gila. Nights we stared silently into the fire. Days we caught every kind of fish in the river, including a brown trout and flathead catfish caught out of the same pool.

Of course we got skunked too, often enough – hard work, bad weather, and an empty creel or game bag. He took that in stride too.

Alas, this could not last! One day he grew up and the next day he went off to college. Actually, it was just last week. Campfire to campus! We'll still get out there of course, when we can. Between times, the reader of this column will perhaps indulge the author if from time to time he brings Bud along as we revisit and recount the old haunts and primitive pursuits.

Bud cooling off at East Fork campsite.

Carrying Capacity in Phoenix

I have fished the Gila drainage perhaps a half dozen times this spring with predictable results. One stream produced but one fish but that was perhaps predictable too as it suffered an ash flow last year. Otherwise fish populations have shown themselves to be fair to good in various streams but nowhere over-loaded to where specimens appeared stunted by too many fish. I've fished with both flies and bait, have caught stream smallmouth to 16 inches; channel cats to 22 inches; a flathead catfish and carp exceeding two feet; numbers of rainbows and one brown over a foot long; and a 19-inch Gila trout. Nature, when not overly influenced by man, tends toward something biologists call "carrying capacity" and over time populations tend to work out a rough balance somewhere between too many and not enough for the available range. Not so for human populations in the Phoenix Valley.

I bring up the Phoenix area after reading a fascinating article in the April 16, 2007 issue of *High Country News*. Titled "Phoenix Falling?" by Craig Childs, the piece informs us that the current boom in "greater" Phoenix, which now totals nearly 4 million people, is not the first. A thousand years ago a people called the Hohokam (a Pima word meaning "all used up") achieved an even greater sprawl, if not quite as many people crammed within similar boundaries. This is now known because legislation in force requires all new building and renovation in the area to be surveyed first by archaeologists to uncover, study, and remove for protection elsewhere, all signs of previous native American life. And everywhere the developers go in the Phoenix area they find the Hohokam were there before them.

The Hohokam in fact first settled the Salt River Basin as much as 3,000 years ago. They entered a "boom" phase, Childs reports, about 2000 years ago. By the 14th century (600 years ago) they had peaked; by the 15th century they had reached "overshoot," where carrying capacity is exceeded. After that the decline of this civilization was rapid, the valley essentially abandoned long before the first Anglo 19th century settlers saw the converging waters of the Salt, Gila and Verde Rivers and began to have big plans of their own.

What happened? We can guess. Surely the waters proved insufficient to a population that didn't know when to stop. Life-giving irrigation dried up. Surely the soils were depleted, and racked with salinity, by overuse, abuse, and agricultural ignorance. Surely as times got tough health was broken, *en masse*, and societal norms, which kept everyone working more or less in harmony, went awry. Starve people; break their health, and some of them will get mean.

Whatever, the Hohokam society collapsed. Since today's Phoenix is built upon a revealed civilization that ended in disaster the obvious question arises: could the same overwhelming decline overcome this huge, burgeoning, modern city that is now covering up an ancient one? Almost to a man (or woman) the archaeologists Childs interviewed said, "It's not *if,* but *when*"

They speak of course in archaeological time. The Hohokam boom lasted nearly 1500 years; on balance they may have done well to last so long. The boom in Phoenix didn't come till after World War II – about 50 years ago – with the advent of air conditioning. Childs reports: "Some of the archaeologists say Phoenix has another 300 years to go; some guess it is more like 50. Either way, they agree the end of this luminous city is inevitable."

One who disagreed, a Republican real estate developer, noted the water infrastructure provided by Lake Roosevelt and the imports of water from the Colorado River. He saw no end to growth.

And indeed a recent report from a major Arizona water conference anticipates (and promotes) an additional growth of some 5 to 7 million people in the adjacent counties of Maricopa (Phoenix), Pinal (Casa Grande), and Pima (Tucson), over the next 50 years. The lessons provided by the Hohokam are nowhere mentioned in this document.

But Childs, and the archaeologists, say it is precisely this reliance on imported water that makes these communities so vulnerable to a second monumental collapse. The Gila and Salt Rivers are already dry in Maricopa County and even flowing waters, while renewable to a degree, are not infinite, especially in the face of unbridled growth. Plus we now have global warming throwing an unpredictable and dangerous wrench into the works.

I'd say, enjoy Phoenix while you can (if you can; it's too bloody hot!). I'll submit the archaeologists will, sooner or later, be proven right about overshoot and carrying capacity in the Salt River Basin.

Meanwhile, for an example closer to home, the Las Cruces City Council recently voted to annex some 6,000 acres of what has been open space, mostly State Land, paving the way to double the population of another city in the desert and proving once again that the growth syndrome trumps common sense almost every time.

And I could write a whole column on the "wisdom" of the current U.S. Congress in their rush – both parties are guilty – to boost our nation's population through various means of increased immigration, putting us on course to have to provide resources for some 450 million U.S. consumers by 2050.

Over on New Mexico's Gila River, Mother Nature knows better. Fish populations rise and fall but are stable over time. Carrying capacity is never exceeded for long. Overall resource health is maintained.

And recall my complaint in this column the past two summers about the over-abundant non-native crawfish and their negative effect on gamefish, non-game fish, and the prey base. I should have had more faith.

There are still crawfish in the Gila but the surfeit is gone. Did the bass and catfish eat up the surplus? Did disease get them? Something brought them down to normal populations.

All is mostly well along the Gila, in a rough harmony, where critters with pea-sized brains have learned to populate in balance with their range and resources. Meanwhile, out Phoenix way, the lessons offered by the history of a creature far more advanced are tossed to the winds by modern day growth mongers. Growth trumps carrying capacity until nature, in her slow but ineluctable way, responds. And unless we change our ways, she will.

Lee, Fountain, Garrett, and Little Henry

The disappearance of Col. Albert Fountain and his 8-year-old son, Henry, on remote lands near White Sands, February 1, 1896, is likely New Mexico's most enduring and perplexing "who done it." Only a court can convict. But authors and readers can have a fine time trying to figure out the culprits, for despite 100+ years this murder mystery is still very much alive.

The first book written entirely on the murder itself is the recent *Murder on the White Sands* by Corey Recko, University of North Texas Press, $24.95 cloth). Recko is not the story-teller to match the previous Fountain murder scribes, C.L. Sonnichsen (*Tularosa: Last of the Frontier West*) or Arrell Gibson (*The Life and Death of Colonel Albert Jennings Fountain*), but he is astute. He notes that Fountain was a fundamentally honest prosecutor who acted fearlessly to get more than 20 indictments against various cattle rustling syndicates, including the prominent Oliver Lee and his principal henchmen, Billy McNew and James Gililland, during court proceedings in January, 1896. How he got Lee & Co. indicted is a fascinating story of Old West police work.

Lee, *et al,* would double-brand someone else's steer to make it look like it was his. It worked on the surface but the ruse showed up inside the hide. Fountain told his livestock inspector, Les Dow, to gather the evidence. At the appropriate time Dow took hold of McNew and hand-cuffed him to the cook's wagon. He then took one of the suspicious steers, shot it between the eyes, and got the cook to help him skin it. Sure enough, sign of the new Lee brand showed up overlain over that of the rightful owner on the inside of the hide. That hide made Lee & Co. cow thieves and Fountain a marked man.

The indictments were achieved at court in Lincoln, leaving Fountain and Henry a 3-day wagon ride back home to Las Cruces. They never made it.

Recko lays out evidence that it was two other Lee men, Jack Tucker and William Carr, who trailed the Fountains horseback from Lincoln to La Luz. They then rode south to Lee's Dog Canyon Ranch (near present-day Alamogordo), alerted Lee, who picked up the trail with McNew and Gililland on February 1st. The three riders were seen by the Fountains and two mail carriers during the day, never close enough for personal identification. But one man rode a large, almost-white, horse.

Late in the day, at Chalk Hill not 10 miles east of San Agustin Pass, the Fountains were ambushed. Evidence found by the posse indicated three horses and three men, one of whom kneeled behind a bush and expended two shells.. The wagon horses bolted 40 yards off the road, then were stopped by riders. Albert Fountain, according to all three authors, at that point was almost certainly dead; he fell out of the wagon and left a pool of blood in the sand. The boy's handkerchief was found blood-soaked and powder-burned in the wagon. The posse, two days behind, followed the trail of three mounted men, wagon and team, southeast, in the general direction of Lee's Dog Canyon Ranch.

After five miles the buckboard was abandoned by the killers; a few miles beyond they stopped for bacon roasted on sticks. But, whatever the effort, they kept the bodies, using one, then the other, of the wagon horses to carry the essential evidence tied across the backs of the weary stock, destined for a burial still unknown.

The posse held several experienced trackers. They noted that one of the fugitives, due to a hitch in his stride, left a distinctive down-at-the-heel boot mark whenever he was off his horse. This trait would later be traced to Bill McNew.

Another fugitive rode a horse shod extra large; his hoofprint could be trailed through a horse herd by a good tracker. Such a man was Carl Clausen, veteran of the Indian Wars. When the fugitives split up, Clausen readily tracked this big-footed horse to a Lee line camp, Wildy Well. The horse was there, almost white, and the man who came out of the camp to ride him away was Oliver Lee, leaving the same distinctive big, shod print he rode in on.

The other two men were trailed to within several miles of Dog Canyon Ranch, the author says. A herd of cattle wiped out the trail but the posse could have gone on to Lee headquarters to see what, or who, they could find. Rain, sleet, and perhaps a certain loss of nerve effectively ended the pursuit. Nor was a search warrant ever issued for the Lee Ranch.

Pat Garrett, 6'5" and a proven (and provocative) lawman in 1896, has taken much of the heat for the fact this crime was never solved; nobody paid the price for these particularly heinous murders. But as Recko notes, Garrett was brought in as sheriff after the killings, he did get McNew in jail and gave him every possible reason to squeal – not bad police work – and he did eventually bring Lee and Gililland to trial. The prosecutors were no match for Albert Fall of the defense, and how do you get a guilty verdict in the 1890s with no body to prove anyone got killed?

Lee, McNew, and Gililland still have their defenders; others, they say, could have done it. Maybeso. But Recko, and Gibson, convinced me. Lee was tracked to his guilt by Carl Clausen who followed a big, shod, almost-white horse right from the crime scene to the man himself; McNew was Lee's right arm in those days and his boot track was telling;

Gililland? He talked about the killings late in life and named himself, Lee, and McNew. All three men had motive due to Fountain's prosecution. And Recko provides an interesting anecdote.

"At a later date," the author writes, "when Gililland lived at Hot Springs, he handed Burris a Masonic pin. He said he took it off the

Colonel's body and asked Burris to give it to Albert Fountain (the younger) when he was gone. Following Gililland's death, the pin was given to the Fountain family, who pronounced it authentic."

Conclusive evidence? There is none in this case. It is certain however, that this is one of the legendary mystery stories from the Old West and Recko's book has made a competent stab at the truth behind it.

Pat Garrett.

Some Horse Races I Have Known

Well, American Pharaoh did it; won going away at the Belmont Stakes, taking the extra quarter mile in stride over the Derby and Preakness distances to win the 1 1//2 mile race just 2 ½ seconds off the track record set by the indomitable Secretariat in 1973. Put another way, to win the Triple Crown of horse racing you need to be an equine who can average nearly 40 mph for three consecutive races from 11/4 to 11/2 miles in length. No wonder no horse had done it in 34 years! Secretariat, American Pharaoh, War Admiral and Seabiscuit; these are legends of American sport; as great and laudable as Jesse Owens, Michael Jordan, or Larry Bird. For there is something about a horse race. .

And I've often thought, to be the jockey, the rider, of one of those major league horses has got to be one of the most physically exhilarating experiences in sport; indeed in all of life! I say that as I've been in a few horse races myself.

Mind you, these races were not around a track, nor were they scheduled events and they didn't involve Thoroughbred or any other high-toned breeding of stock. But even a cow pony can run, fast, and if you're aboard any thousand pound quadruped at 40 mph you won't forget it any time soon. I found this out when I was seated on a horse named Red Wing when she took a run at a wild cow called Old Yeller.

I wrote this up in this column a while back but in short, I arrived at a ranch job in south Texas in 1963 (17 years old) not knowing a curb bit from a snaffle but granted the privilege of riding, at different times, every horse in the remuda, from Fino Blanco who was untrustworthy and had a hard trot that would loosen your fillings by the end of the day, to Red Wing, who was *muy mancito* (very gentle), a smooth traveler who knew cows and could run like the wind.

And so when we emerged from the brush onto an open flat there was the wild cow Old Yeller already in full flight. Red Wing "built right to her" with no urging or direction from me and I simply turned her loose and concentrated on not falling off. And that's when I learned something about riding a horse at speed – although scary, it's probably a horse's smoothest gait.

As Red Wing came up to full gallop, her neck came slowly down and she was reaching out with head and muzzle like she could smell a fresh apple just ahead and with that, at full pace my seat in the saddle smoothed out with the length and ease of her stride. It was a race all right but not a fair one as she soon over-hauled and flanked that maverick cow, allowing the foreman, Mr. Ott, to come up on the other flank and throw a loop. Old Yeller was caught, Mr. Ott earned and got the credit and even I didn't look too bad, thanks to the horse.

96

Later, in Minnesota, there was Jesse, my first horse under my ownership. Jesse was a mixed breed paint horse, otherwise nondescript and certainly nothing to match the elegance of my girlfriend's Arabian gelding with his arched neck, finely chiseled head and muzzle, and short-coupled, muscular frame. One day when the Arab was prancing along on a dirt road in a cold wind, she said, "Let's turn them loose to the section line road up there," and the race was on.

Well Jesse might have been of ordinary conformation but she could sure run and she had the Arab by three lengths when we crossed the section road after about a quarter mile run…she split the breeze!.

The third equine in my horse race memoir, well, I can't recall his name. But he was a gelding owned by a fine old gentleman, Mr. Albert Hebbert (1905-1999) of Ashby, Nebraska. This was a Sand Hills pony, and Mr. Hebbert said, "He's a top-notch cow horse and he loves to hunt coyotes." Well hunting coyotes is what we were to do that day and I knew as I stepped on I was well mounted; he was tremendously alert, eager, and responsive. And Mr. Hebbert was right about his being a hunter; indeed, I'll just call him "Hunter" for this story.

As we rode out over those remote, wild Sand Hills grasslands with the hounds, Hunter was constantly on the lookout for a coyote. He could see better than the hounds due to his height and he spotted two of the little wolves at very long range before I saw them myself. But they were well out of range. The third coyote that day was close enough for all to see and the race was on!

Now among those who had preceded us in hunting coyotes and jackrabbits on the plains with coursing hounds was General George Armstrong Custer, Theodore Roosevelt, and in New Mexico, naturalist Earnest Thompson Seton, and the cowboy-novelist Max Evans. All I'm sure would agree that the idea is not to race the hounds to the catch (too dangerous) but to use the horse's mobility to keep sight of the hounds and get a good view the race. But apparently Hunter didn't think so.

Hunter wanted to go right with the hounds, and when I tried to pull him up he took hold of the bit and went on…………when I tried harder he took to pitching about such as I thought he would throw me. I suppose a better rider would have kept him under better control but rather than getting pitched off I turned him loose……….

My gosh what a race that was, uphill and down, dodging yuccas and jumping soap weeds; and a thousand yards later when the hounds rolled that coyote, I mean I was there! When Mr. Hebbert rode up at a sensible pace I said, "Mr. Hebbert, this is quite a horse you gave me to ride." And he said, "Oh, he's a little fiery."

No, it wasn't the Belmont Stakes, but it was still quite a ride!

Gamefowl: On the Edge of the Wild

With cockfighting much in the news these days, I recall the time I viewed these "chicken-fights" first hand. It was years ago, deep in the desert of Coahuila, near Muzquiz, Mexico. In that country cockfighting is hardly debated, it is simply practiced, and during my visit in 1970 it was practiced openly near Muzquiz at what we would call a county fair.

It wasn't just the roosters that were colorful. The crowd was animated, exuberant, and intensely involved. The avid spectators ranged from patrician *hidalgos* of the *rico* class to the most common *vaqueros* in spurs and down-at-the-heel boots. None of us could take our eyes off the birds.

The roosters surged with color, myriad and variegated. Their strut caught your eye; their blind courage was scary. The athleticism was too quick for the eye, flashed the colors, and usually led to the death of one of the birds. The handlers left with blood on their hands but nobody seemed to mind.

I didn't mind either. Neither approving nor disapproving, I was simply enthralled by another culture, another world. But upon reflection it is easy to see how such a practice could enrage an urban citizenry unused to a blood sport steeped in such archaic revelry. It is also easy to see how its fans and practitioners would go to the mat to save it.

For a young Anglo from across the line, the "county fair" near Muzquiz was a cultural delight – the Mexican brand of rodeo, the impromptu horse races, the smell of spicy meats cooked over open fires, and especially the cockfights. Yet I have not attended a chicken fight in 35 years and have no desire to see another.

The issues. First, is cockfighting a cultural tradition in New Mexico?

Of course it is. If you doubt that then simply attend a cockfight in Luna County (mostly Hispanic) or a cockfight in Lea County (mostly Anglo) and open your eyes. For some people – maybe not you or me – it is a way of life and goes back untold generations. It is not only a cultural tradition, it is a multi-cultural tradition.

Is it cruel? Arguably, yes –eventually it is a bloody end for most of its avian participants. On the other hand, gamecocks live well beyond a year on average, while cockerels on modern egg farms are euthanized by the millions shortly after birth (chicken infanticide). In this debate, it is easier to kill a lifeway and ignore an industry.

Of course "humaneness" has always been selectively applied. Feral horses are revered and adopted and protected by Federal law; feral hogs have been here as long but are nowhere protected by any law but are despised and hunted as pests.

Does cockfighting deprave its human participants? There is no evidence that cockers are more prone to violence or crime than the rest of us. At the fair near Muzquiz, I mistakenly left my wallet on the table with an empty Tecate; it was an hour later before I realized my loss. Resigned to my fate, I went back to the table without much hope. My empty Tecate had long since been picked up and discarded; my wallet was still there! With all the money!

Was Abe Lincoln a cocker? Not exactly. But there is evidence that as a young man in frontier America Lincoln used to referee cockfights, his inherent honesty and fairness already apparent and much in demand. He is said to have said: "As long as God permits intelligent man created in his own image to fight in public and try to kill each other while the world looks on, it's not for me to deprive the chickens of the same freedom." Who knows? But the syntax is certainly Lincolnesque.

I like to keep a gamecock on the place, and half a dozen game-hens. As a homesteader, this is how I came to truly appreciate these birds. Game-fowl are the closest thing we have to the jungle fowl of Indonesia that are the ancestors of all our domestic chickens. Most domestic breeds, like leghorns, barred rocks, and Rhode Island reds, are thoroughly domesticated and have been made stupidly dependent. On modern factory farms they need not even reproduce themselves naturally, let alone raise a brood of chicks. Game fowl are still on the edge of the wild.

The game hen will fiercely guard her clutch of eggs, pecking fiercely at your hand if you try to grab a couple for breakfast. Once they're born, she keeps the chicks safely under wing till they are ready to walk about. At that point you want to give her plenty of room. I've had game-hens flair at my face when I got too close to her brood. And she will fight to the death to protect them in the face of a predator or another, cannibalistic, chicken.

Game fowl can fly, can scratch around and feed themselves, and are predators on beetles, ants, worms, grasshoppers, and even mice. And I once introduced a young gamecock to my chicken yard where another, larger, mixed breed rooster had control of all the hens. I thought, "I better wait and see how this plays out."

Nobody got killed, but that gamecock quickly whipped that big rooster into second place on the pecking order; when he was done winning he crowed loudly for a victory you couldn't help admire – the little guy had won.

Like most gamecocks, that little rooster had colors to match his spirit. It is no wonder that fly tiers value that hackle as part of the lure, and lore, of another sport.

As a legal pastime in New Mexico, cockfighting is almost certainly doomed. Like dog fighting, it will be forced underground. I won't miss the fights, but I hope the gamecock, and gamehen, can survive on the farm or back yard in something close to ancient form. Thoreau said: "In wildness is the preservation of the world." In an era of factory chickens, homogenizing cultures, and urban angst over blood sports, there is something inspiring in a bird that will fight to the death out of pure atavism, spit in your eye if you get too close to her babies, and live on the edge of the wild.

Note: In February 2007 cockfighting was legally banned in New Mexico. Rumor has it the pursuit maintains a furtive life regardless.

Of Grasshoppers, Catfish, and a Deadly Meal

According to one Internet article, there are over 200 species of grasshoppers in the Southwest. Just one of them is the main subject of our amateur entomology investigation in this story; finding, gathering, identifying, fishing with and eating the big, six-legged creature known as the Giant Horse Lubber Grasshopper of the desert grasslands of southeast Arizona, southwest New Mexico, and west Texas. They have a considerable range across the border in old Mexico too of course; I couldn't describe that range by State but I'd guess the Horse Lubber over there favors the same habitat as our big hoppers here – desert grassland at less than 5,000 feet elevation.

That's where I first found them years ago in early fall at about 4,200 feet and moving across the road in droves, near Lordsburg, on my way to fish for catfish on the Gila River. I had never seen a grasshopper that size, or as colorful: the biggest near 3-inches in length, built like linebackers, with black backs and bright yellow stripes around the head/eye area and a look that, face to face and up close, could stop traffic or put a banshee into cardiac arrest . I gathered a half-dozen in my hat and slipped them into a clear baggie with some beef liver I had and sped on to finally descend on foot to a deep canyon called "Catfish Hole" in a warm afternoon.

The wonderful slow swirl of this big deep hole made you think "a very large catfish must live in here!" Well, maybeso. Or maybe somebody had already caught him and took him home. Regardless, these hungry meat-eating hoppers had already eaten half the beef liver in the baggy. I put one on a hook and tossed him out on a spinning rod into the center of the pool. I didn't know then that the Horse Lubber hopper is considered by some as poor bait and virtually inedible (one Internet site says they can be "deadly") by man or beast due to severe "biotoxins" in their system!

Well, you don't want to believe everything you read on the Internet because the fishing while not fabulous was still pretty good. I caught three channel cats on those hoppers, from 15 to 22 inches each, and took them home and had a good fish fry.

It was fun but I confess I hardly thought about the Horse Lubber for many years until I got the following letter from Bob Brady, author of the book *Hunting and Gathering* and one of the more interesting outdoorsmen in our section. Here's just what he wrote in an email to me received last week:

I was on an outing about 30 or 40 miles south of town and observed that there were thousands of jumbo grasshoppers crawling across the landscape. Hordes of them usually accompany

101

good summer rains. So, I thought I would collect a few and test them for palatability. I captured 15 in a few minutes. They are pretty easy to capture by hand because they can hop but only have vestigial little wings that do not work. They mostly crawl along the ground.

They are an interesting insect. A few get run over in the road and their fellows gather round them to cannibalize the remains and are subsequently run over and their fellows gather etc.

I don't think I ever saw a juvenile jumbo; so can't say much about their going from egg to adult. Kind of like jackrabbits in that regard. Ever see a baby jack?

Interesting that in the Bible, the Mosaic Law considered grasshoppers "clean" and fit for human consumption. Interesting that John the Baptist lived on locusts and wild honey.

So, I took the jumbos home and placed them into the freezer for them to chill out for about an hour. When I got them out of the freezer they were rigid. I broke off their legs and ran water over them and then salt and peppered them. Next, I dipped each one in egg white and then battered them in a Cajun mix for sea food, available at Wal-Mart. I then fried them in virgin olive oil until they were crispy.

I ate 14 of them. They were tasty and crunchy and the closest thing I can compare the taste of jumbo grasshoppers to is the great taste of fried okra.

I don't know if the capture of jumbo grasshoppers would be considered hunting or gathering, but likely the latter because of the relative ease of capture. I suppose a kid with an insect net could get them by the hundreds in an hour or two?

Let us hope that if space aliens invade Silver City, we can flee the city in the months of August or September, following a good summer monsoon. The landscape will be awash with readily available protein marching steadily, 6 synchronized paces at a time. To acquire, just smash one on the roadway and wait.

I don't know the species name of our jumbo grasshoppers. Maybe several species? I know they range from e. AZ to central Texas."

Did Bob Brady dine on the "deadly" Horse Lubber or a lesser hopper that resembles it? Is that "deadly" label so much stuff and feathers or did Bob Brady dodge a bullet? My "jumbos" sure looked like Horse Lubbers and the catfish liked them. Bob Brady did too. I think I'll stick with using them as bait.

This Christmas, the Gift of "Place"

Book authors are always being asked how they, and their writings, have been influenced by "place." The word has a boatload of definitions and meanings, but as queried above the author is being asked not about the place (in my case a little alcove off the bedroom) where he types out words and stories and books but rather a geographical area encumbered by its own cultures, climate, topography and critters.

Thus our "place" is an identifiable locale in the natural world, big enough and important enough that it has made a contribution as to who we are. Termed by one author as "the last best place," according to his book it is in Montana. Well, maybe.

My visits to Montana are few and brief......what do I know? Not enough to say anything against another state or region within a state, and yet, for me, I'd have to say this last best place is in southwest New Mexico, and as an outdoors man or woman I probably don't have to tell you, you don't have to be an author to see our "place" as a gift along about Christmas time each year.

Our place includes seven counties (Dona Ana, Luna, Hidalgo, Grant, Catron, Socorro, and Sierra) that total about 32,000 square miles. This makes up slightly more than one-fourth of the state and means southwest New Mexico is a bit larger than the state of Maine. Within this spacious realm we have just one city of size......Las Cruces, though at roughly 100,000 people it is dwarfed by El Paso and Albuquerque to the south and north on the interstate; I know people who have left Las Cruces because it was "too small" and there's "nothing to do."

But you're an outdoors person, like me, and you don't buy it. For us Las Cruces is plenty big already and, elsewhere in our place, there is all you could ever want to do.

Say you're a fly fisherman and you have just made the drive from Socorro to Las Cruces or Las Cruces to the Arizona line. The view is largely moonscape and if you're a newcomer you see no reason to stop and unlimber your rod. Most likely you would miss the Gila River headwaters in the 3.3 million acre Gila National Forest, just north of Silver City; over 500 miles of stream – browns, rainbows, bronze bass and the rare Gila trout – of classic fly fishing ambiance. It's a gift.

You may however prefer lake fishing for warm water species. Elephant Butte reservoir, the largest lake in the state, is 20 to 40 miles long (depending the input from the Rio Grande) and located about halfway between Socorro and Las Cruces. It's a zoo on three-day weekends like Fourth of July but take an ordinary weekday even in mid-summer and you will find this big lake far from cluttered and offering the kind of space and solitude and variety a fisherman can enjoy.

Country Sports II

I'm hardly an expert on "The Butte" and much of the time I've simply fished off the bank yet I've caught largemouth bass, smallmouth bass, carp, channel, blue and flathead catfish, white bass, crappie, sunfish, and a couple of stripers. I'm still waiting on a walleye.

Big game hunters can be busy nearly all year in this one corner of New Mexico. Because the topography runs from 4,000 feet to over 10,000 feet, and the precipitation from 8 to around 40 inches per year, a variety of game and habitat and pursuit is available. Elk, deer, bear, lion, bighorn sheep roam the forested mountains, while in desert/grassland terrain we have pronghorn antelope, oryx, ibex, and javelina. You won't find those last three critters in Montana. Feral hogs are showing up in places in southwest New Mexico, and meanwhile our wild turkey can be found at a variety of elevations and habitats. Legally, they are given big game status in New Mexico.

Southwest New Mexico is where the Rocky Mountains meet the Sierra Madre, This is a place where small game thrive. Our three quail – scaled, Gambels, harlequin or Mearns – can sometime draw in hunters from out of state (not this year), plus there's ducks, tree squirrels, bobcat, and a host of others, some of which, like the cottontail, coyote, and jackrabbit, can be hunted all year and, for residents, no hunting license is required. We also have interesting critters like the coatimundi which you hunt to see, not to shoot. Try to find one of them in Montana.

You may not be a hunter/angler at all. Southwest New Mexico, it is generally agreed, has a greater variety of birds, and better "birding," than any place in the state. The Gila River Bird Area, northwest of Silver City, is a good place to start. And show me a better canoe or kayak run than the Gila River from Grapevine Campground to Mogollon Creek, 42 miles of rapids, pools, and riffles through our nation's first designated Wilderness. Wilderness is part of the pageant of the American experience and on the Gila we have about 800,000 acres of it. It harbors a unique inter-face of human history and natural history and among the humans characters, notables, eccentrics and reprobates abound, as interesting and singular as any in the North American tale.

Among the characters is Ben Lilly, an indefatigable houndman and single-minded pursuer of bears and lions; notables include Aldo Leopold, avid hunter/fisher as well as visionary and wordsmith, the patron saint of American conservation who defined Wilderness (upper case) and acknowledged the influence of the Gila in inspiring his influential writings therein; eccentrics include Montague Stevens whose obsession, for a time, was devising a method of out-pursuing the grizzly bear with blood hounds and thus display himself, unintentionally, as a genius in training dogs and horses; while a reprobate, make a mark down by the grave of James Kirker, who made money trapping beaver but a lot more taking, and selling, scalps. All, and more, made our last best place home for a time; each wrote a book and/or had book(s) written about them.

This Christmas consider that your prize gift may not be that expensive item wrapped colorful and sitting under the tree. Rather, your best present may be the gift of place; it's free and waiting right out your front door.

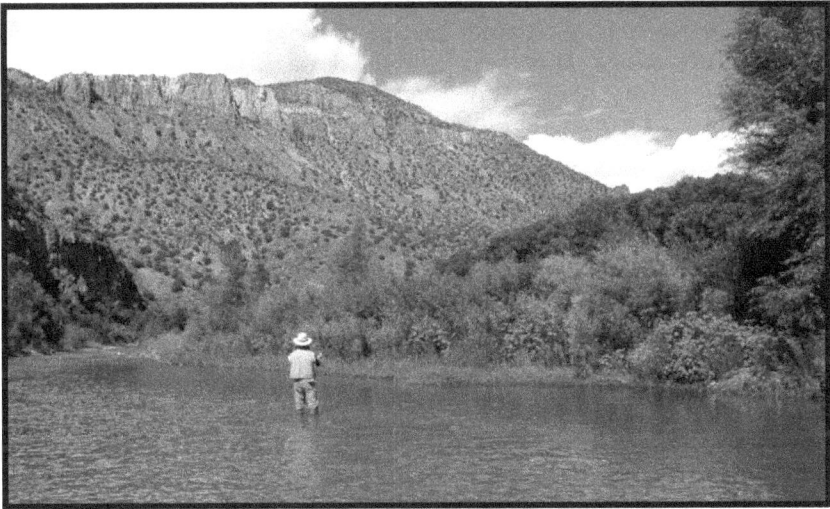

Photo by Jan Haley.

Kid Goat the Answer for Forest Travel

Surprise! My previous column on Gila travel management – i.e., the regulation of vehicular use within the 3.3-milliion acre Gila National Forest – did not diffuse the issue. Some folks, led by our local congressman Steve Pearce, are still vocal in favor of more motorized road access, and off-road travel for big game retrieval, wood and piñon gathering, or just for fun. Others want some roads closed, riparian areas protected, and generally a quieter forest.

I still think Alternative G, preferred by the Forest Service itself and New Mexico Department of Game & Fish, is the best compromise plan, albeit Pearce and the motorized access lobby seem determined to battle any new restrictions. However, both sides of this debate could benefit from what was born just two weeks ago in my barnyard – a kid goat!

Actually, Brownie, the mother, had two kids, but in this article I'm going to focus on the young male I call Camper, who will soon be castrated to grow up as a wether rather than a billy. Camper is going to be a pack goat.

The pack goat is a smaller version of the llama as a packer, with a better disposition. He is ideal for the backpacker who still likes to walk but who is tired of carrying 40-plus lbs. on his back. Under new forest rules, he can in part replace the all-terrain vehicle (ATV).

A wether like Camper makes the best pack goat. He's got the disposition of the doe but the size of the billy. But what makes a goat want to pack a load and follow you on wilderness trails? A goat, bonded to humans at an early age through bottle feeding or just lots of handling, has a dog-like loyalty. He'll follow you, with or without loaded panniers or a lead rope, and being a goat he can walk or climb most anywhere you can go.

It is said that goats will eat anything. This isn't strictly true, but they are very eclectic in their tastes and on a pack trip will feed themselves along the way. They mostly eat brush and browse, rather than grass favored by horses, mules and burros. Nonetheless, I always bring a little sweet feed along on our wilderness trips as a treat for our pack goats at the end of the day.

Range goats raised for meat, and dairy goats raised for milk, are often stubby in build and don't weigh much over 100 lbs. A good pack goat in fit condition can carry one third its weight roughly ten miles a day, though for the average goat carrying one fourth its weight is a more reasonable expectation. This means if you want to put your 40 lb. pack on a goat you need a big, leggy goat. Pack goat wethers are being raised today that are a minimum of 34" at the withers. My largest pack goat is a good three feet at the withers and weighs over 200 lbs. He can easily carry a 50 lb. load.

All the goat breeds have produced good pack goats but some have better reputations than others. Many Nubians are big and stout but they are notoriously lazy. Saanens tend to be big and leggy, an ideal pack goat build. They are reputed to be especially good in cold weather but tend to overheat in hot weather. The Alpine and Toggenburg breeds have both produced many good pack goats and goat packers are constantly working to breed them with more size. My own pack goats carry Spanish goat blood; this strain of open range meat goat is notably tough and agile. Breed or strain of goat is less important than the animals' eagerness to follow you down the trail. That's why you have to make a pet out of him.

Next to the camel, the goat can go longer without water than any other quadruped. I can recall making extended trips into the Gila Wilderness with my goats. It was hot and I would stop at every stream crossing to give them a chance to get a drink. The goats would go three or sometimes four days before showing any interest in water. On the other hand, a goat can overheat packing in hot weather. From time to time I will pour some water over their heads and necks to keep them cool.

Some folks I know in Magdalena went into the Gila on a slow rambling trip with a doe who was milking and a young wether. Not only did the goats pack much of their gear, the doe gave them a daily supply of milk that they either drank or made into cheese or pudding. They stayed 18 days! Thus, a goat or two can not only lighten your load, they can extend your time in the wilderness and provide fine companionship along the way. All while having a minimal impact on the environment.

Goat packing gear is remarkably similar to horse or mule packing gear except for the size. A pack goat can wear a goat halter but a stout, leather dog collar works as well. The pack saddles are cross-buck style, there is a saddle pad, and britching strap. Panniers are usually cloth and there is a tarp to cover the load. You don't need to know any fancy ties to secure the load. A goat will seldom try to buck off a load, but you'll want to use a lead rope to keep him from running off or peeling a load off in the brush.

Off-road vehicle use is coming to an end on our national forests, and for the health of the forest some redundant roads will be closed. Hunters will no longer be able to drive off-road to pack out big game. We'll all still use vehicles to access the forest. The smart outdoorsman will haul along a pack goat or two, to lighten the load and do the work off-road that is no longer open to the ATV. Whether it's packing camp, game meat, fuel wood, or piñon nuts. A kid goat like Camper may become a significant player in the future of Gila travel management.

Heterosis: A Most Interesting Can of Worms

"Heterosis: Increased vigor or other superior qualities arising from the crossbreeding of genetically different plants or animals. Also called 'hybrid vigor'." – The American Heritage Dictionary.

Bet you didn't know that! I confess I didn't "know" heterosis until a few years ago, and I've been breeding dogs, and livestock, and debating wildlife management issues for forty years. Getting an understandable definition down on paper helps; still, heterosis is a can of worms for sportsman, stockman, biologist, and environmentalist alike and at the root of some of the major natural history debates of the day, including locally, where it's at the heart of innovations and sometime arguments about cattle, dogs, lions, wolves and trout.

This piece is written by a non-expert and will raise more questions than it will settle debates. But one must be willing to open the can of worms to have any hope of sorting out its contents.

I recall a tour of a large Dona Ana County ranch. The owner had made use of a so called "Beefmaster" strain developed over many years for the West and composed of 50% Brahma, 25% English shorthorn and 25% Hereford breeds. The English half, I was told, contributed weight gain and quality of meat; the Brahma, heat resistance in a desert environment, toughness and survivability, especially at birthing time. But the local rancher had gone a step further with "a terminal cross with red Angus bulls," which contributed, I was told, "to improved demeanor, carcass qualities, and calf size."

Here was heterosis at work – several breeds, all cattle, but with very different traits arising from their respective histories in the disparate UK and India. Each was superior in its homeland; the right combination was an improvement on the original for the commercial stockman in the new environment of the desert Southwest.

I have done a similar breeding program with dogs, crossing greyhound with saluki in an attempt to develop a superior hare hound; the greyhound for pure speed, the saluki for "distance," heat resistance, and soundness at high speed over irregular terrain. The results have been generally good, with many of the hounds carrying both "bloods" exhibiting a combination of speed and endurance, coupled with a no-quit attitude ("hybrid vigor") that simply catches more hares.

Yet heterosis can leave the breeder scratching his head.

In the 1970s in Minnesota I started crossing rough-coated sighthounds – commonly termed "staghounds," with trailhounds of coonhound or foxhound breeding. It was a leap of faith as sighthounds and trailhounds, though both hounds, hunt very differently, the one hunting by sight, the other by scent. The offspring didn't all work out,

108

but for coyote hunting on winter snows in the north woods, the best of these hybrids could trail a coyote with their heads up, taking the scent out of the air like a good foxhound, yet with a sprint speed that would at times bring the coyote within view, and to bay, within an hour.

Yet when I brought two of these hybrid hounds with me to New Mexico they were failures. The vigor was there, but they were too slow to be coursing hounds and, in the new arid environment, lacked the "nose" to stay on a coyote track. Heterosis has its place but is not everywhere a panacea.

Recently, the New Mexico Department of Game & Fish revealed they would begin stocking Gila trout in the Forks area of the Gila, Sapillo Creek, and several other streams where rainbow and brown trout already live. According to Dr. Paul Turner, retired fisheries biologist at NMSU, it is believed the Gila trout evolved from rainbow trout coming up the Colorado drainage many millennia ago, then became isolated in the Gila region and developed their own distinctive traits.

"But as they are descended from rainbows, the Gila trout will crossbreed with them and produce fertile offspring," Turner said.

Will this crossbreeding, that is bound to occur, produce a superior trout through heterosis?

"That's impossible to say," Turner said. "It's unpredictable, but they should be healthy fish."

Turner said he believed it would make sense to henceforward stock only the native Gila trout in the Gila Forest, curtail the rainbow stocking, allowing the native trout to eventually take over in most streams, at least as a Gila trout phenotype if not in perfect genetic purity. I agree. And meanwhile the brown trout of the Gila drainage, which does not crossbreed with Gila trout or rainbows, could be left as naturally reproducing in some streams to provide their own brand of angling interest.

I'm told the opposite of heterosis, or hybrid vigor, is called "inbreeding depression." This is a cross so genetically close that offspring may result that are abnormal or unhealthy. This occurred in the case of the Florida panther. Considered a distinct subspecies of cougar, but imperiled by habitat loss, a somewhat famous houndman was dispatched to catch, collar, and provide information for study of the extant population. The results indicated the animal was indeed scarce, so much so that the population was showing unhealthy individuals with physical abnormalities that indicated inbreeding depression.

As there were no other "Florida panthers" to bring into the mix the U.S. Fish & Wildlife Service did the unthinkable – they dispatched the houndman to west Texas and eventually added western cougars to the Florida population. Of course they interbred; inbreeding depression was curtailed and heterosis produced healthy cougars. But the genetically

109

distinct "Florida panther" was gone and the critters are still imperiled by human population growth and habitat loss.

Here in the Southwest the restoration of the Mexican wolf subspecies is literally under fire, and the narrow genetic base that was present at the start of the program has gotten narrower due to poaching and lethal agency control. Some say inbreeding depression is a threat; others say it is already here. Would the population benefit from the heterosis that would follow an introduction of wild wolves from up north?

Some say, better we have no wolves at all, from north or south. Others hold on to the pure Mexican wolf subspecies ideal, albeit the animals that began the program were pen-raised and from genetically tight lines. Still others, including one prominent biologist/author, suggest we might need to introduce wild wolves from an unrelated genetic line that would invigorate the current population.

Is a deliberate infusion of heterosis in the future of Southwest wolf reintroduction? Perhaps we can crack the lid on that can of worms in a future column.

Juniper Creek: Canoe Run and Gator Tales

The Ocala National Forest. In acreage, it would fit into a corner of our own 3.3 million acre Gila Forest. But it feels surprisingly remote, being part wilderness and burgeoning with the plant life and fertile swamp waters of a southern jungle. You could get lost here, accidentally or on purpose, on a few hundred acres and not show up for years. It also ranks a permanent place in literature and outdoor adventure.

The Yearling, Marjorie Kinnan Rawlings' classic Americana of a boy growing up, took place here. Many doubt this, as Ms. Rawlings own place was further north at Cross Creek, and has been preserved there as a low-key tourist stop not far from ever-growing Gainesville. But she said herself that it was the wilder country further south near Ocala that was the inspiration and literary home of Jody and his ill-fated fawn.

The time was the late 19th century and the reader learns that the few homesteaders in the forest contended with a subsistence lifestyle, primitive adventures and wild animals. Surprisingly, as to the adventures and wild animals, the tourists of our time still do.

My wife and I had an adventure here in the fall of 1993. Visiting my cousin Dyer and his wife Pam, we had made a canoe trip down Juniper Creek. It's a leisurely run of about 7 miles through the heart of the wilderness; spring-fed and lucid as bottled water. For most of the run there is more shade than sun, not because of clouds but rather the overhanging jungle. It is beautiful and haunting.

We went in the fall on a weekday and saw just one other boat; we passed it early on and had the run to ourselves. I think that's why we surprised the big gator.

We'd already seen a half dozen, mostly little fellows, the biggest still smaller than a grown man. Then Cherie and I rounded a bend and there he was, sunning on the bank within reach of the paddle, and he had to be 12 feet long. Such and animal weighs more than 500 lbs. I was closer to him than I really wanted to be but there was nothing to do but hope he wasn't put into any sort of ill humor as we glided past. He was indulgent and remained motionless as Dyer and Pam floated by; we rounded the next bend and he was gone. But you don't forget that. And you know then why big gators have spawned so many myths, and a few scary truths.

Then, just last month, Cherie and I and Bud joined Dyer and Pam for another Juniper Run. We would look for raccoons and water birds and bass, gar and catfish, and of course we hoped to spot another big gator, though we knew there was one less along the run than when the year began.

In May, 2006, there had been a fatality here. A young woman had left her boat – the Forest Service tells you never to do this – to go snorkeling up a side channel. When she didn't return her three companions went looking for her. When they found her the gator still had her in his mouth. They risked their lives, pounding on the gator and gouging its eyes, before he let go and swam away. The woman was dead before they got there, from drowning, broken bones, and internal injuries.

Four days later a trapper got the gator – the pathologist said his teeth matched the wounds. He was 11.5 feet long and exceeded 500 lbs. By the time we all started our trip down Juniper Run the story was old news. Of course even without knowledge of the fatality, we weren't going swimming. But more than any other critter we wanted to see a big gator.

We were disappointed. We saw several gators each but none more than 5 feet long. Any gator is a sight but we wanted the myth, the legend come to life. Also, there were lots of big turtles, some wading birds, and some nice bass at the lower end where a guy in a kayak was having a blast catching and releasing them with a spinning rig. Everything was green and lush as I remembered it, and you could lean over the side and watch those bass in the water like looking down into a fresh-washed aquarium. But lacking a big gator, the highlight was the eagle.

She was soaring ahead of us for some time, at first at a distance and I thought it was a big turkey buzzard. But it was too big (probably a female as they generally out-size the males), and when she circled nicely overhead and landed on a snag, surprisingly close, I could almost measure the 7-foot wing-span and could see the white-feathered head and predator beak. I thought, "I'll bet she gets her share of those largemouth bass."

It was a delightful run in all and a great experience for young Bud who took the paddle in the front seat allowing his mother to sit on the cooler in the middle and enjoy the ride. There were lots of twists and turns but just enough current you didn't have to work too hard. There was always something around the next bend.

Four hours in all and we made the bridge and the pickup by the Forest Service. We were back at the headquarters where we started, winding down and having a soda, when one of those uniformed personnel stopped and asked how we had liked the run. I said fine but we were disappointed we hadn't seen any big gators.

"After the fatality," she said, "they went down in there and trapped out all the big ones. I think they removed thirteen in all."

This is where you just sort of hold your tongue. She was vague about whether the ones "removed" were killed or relocated but I had some thoughts I didn't express about the official policy of taking the animal out of the creek that had spawned all those memorable myths, legends and stories. And a few scary truths.

The big gators were gone because someone had acted foolishly. The gator removal certainly didn't equate to the woman's tragic death, but it augmented the loss. I contented myself in thought that some of the small ones we saw would eventually get big. And maybe some big ones would move in from elsewhere. I hope so. The big gator I saw in '93 was far superior to me in his realm. There is a beneficial humility whenever we humans are forced to stop and wonder at the natural world, and maybe even take a step back.

Photo by Dyer Michell.

In Pursuit of the Perfect Hobby

"A hobby is a defiance of the contemporary," Aldo Leopold wrote. "It is an assertion of those permanent values which the momentary eddies of social evolution have contravened and overlooked."

This perhaps explains the ongoing popularity of country sports that for most of us have lost their usefulness – gardening, homesteading, hunting and fishing. A recent Harris poll showed gardening to be the most popular hobby, favored by 14% or about 45 million Americans nationwide. Fishing was a close second at 12% or about 40 million Americans. I do both, but this popularity does not derive from necessity.

Yes, we make use of the crops we grow, the livestock we raise, and the game and fish we bring to bag. But as a practical matter we'd usually come out ahead if our time spent afield was used instead to garner wages, the money then applied to a similar quantity of meat and produce at the store. Yet values accrue with field sports, however impractical, and they are not for sale. Indeed, as a practical matter, I'm inclined to say that practicality is inimical to a good hobby. I found this out when I tried to be a fishing guide.

I've enjoyed fishing for a long time and I had come to have some success fishing with bait, fly, and lure in the waters of the Gila Forest. "Why not," I reasoned, "take people fishing for money!"

Stephen O'Day and I jumped through the hoops, got a guide's permit, and commenced to take people on pack trips into the Gila. My pack goats carried most of the load. We didn't have a lot of business but the business we had was good – our clients were nice folks, we always caught some fish, nobody got hurt, or lost, and the compliments far outnumbered the complaints. After O'Day dropped out with a temporary disability, my wife joined the team as the other guide. Yet after a few years I let that guide's permit go.

It wasn't the same, fishing for money. For one thing, I worried about the weather. When I go fishing, I take the weather as it comes, but with a client in tow, especially on a pack trip, the weather became a real concern. I felt a tremendous pressure to put my charge onto some fish. I usually succeeded, but I was always in fear I'd fail. When my client had had enough fishing for the day, sometimes I'd fish myself. But I didn't enjoy it much; and, if I caught the biggest fish, I felt bad about it. That right there should have tipped me off that I was not well employed.

Then, at the end of each outing, I'd find myself doing accounts to see if the trip made a profit. It usually did, but in satisfaction it amounted to poor wages. In the end, I find I enjoy fishing too much to do it for money.

Leopold spoke of both falconry and bow hunting as "perfect hobbies." He alluded to the difficulties involved and counted them as advantages.

The falcon, Leopold noted, requires months of training and in the end "may either 'go tame' like Homo sapiens or fly away into the blue," never to be seen again. Yet the hawk that makes a successful stoop at bird or hare becomes a "raptorial servant, and shares eons of evolution with his handler."

Leopold was a bow hunter. Not only that, he made his own longbows. He called it a "gamble," for while some of his inventions "cleave the sky with its shining javelin," others "burst into impotent splinters." Leopold wouldn't have it any other way. "The possible debacle," he writes, "is...an essential element in all hobbies."

I myself have spent years in the breeding, raising and training of hounds in hopes they can catch a hare. Some of them impress me as quintessential examples of the breeder's art – they are elegant, keen for work, and they can fairly fly over the ground. Yet most of the hares still get away.

And I'll make it tough on myself fishing. I learned to baitfish for carp long ago and caught them in good numbers. They always impressed me with their power and stamina; short of exhaustion they just won't quit. So, still fishing bait, I sought to land them on a fly rod. That's a tough proposition, but once accomplished I had to move on to a tougher one, fooling and catching a big carp with an artificial fly. I've done that now too; still, I could catch a lot more carp with bait. Seen as a hobby rather than a blood sport, something besides the usual grading of size and numbers drives this game of fishing.

Such pastimes as stamp collecting and the hawking of baseball cards are sometimes referred to as "hobbies." To each his own, but when juxtaposed to the natural lifeways of raising crops and livestock, or pursuing game and fish, stamps and baseball cards are milk-and-water affairs. Yet some of the best outdoor people I know are content to watch birds rather than hunt them, run rivers rather than fish them, and they can hike in contentment all day with neither rod nor gun nor dog and no yen for pursuit. I wonder they're not bored.

Just as well I don't promote my pleasures, however. I don't really want the competition anyway; the streams and coverts are already crowded enough. And, as Leopold wrote: "To prescribe a hobby would be dangerously akin to prescribing a wife – with about the same probability of a happy outcome."

The perfect hobby therefore must simply be the one that suits. And if a mere stamp collector can find contentment in a hobby, there's hope for all. Only the slacker, too dull or lazy to fulfill his idle hours, or the drudge, too busy to have time for them, is to be pitied.

A hobby is seldom necessary. But it can be terribly important.

"Kids" in the Wilderness, or, Hoods in the Woods

All through the summer of '95 we had been toying with the idea of starting a goat packing guide service. My prospective partner, Stephen O'Day, had been leading "troubled teens" on backpacking trips into the Gila Wilderness of New Mexico for several seasons. He knew the ropes of the outfitting business from the angle of planning, equipment, and handling personnel. My backpacking experience was made up almost entirely of solo excursions but I had the goats. Between us it seemed we might have an outfit.

October came around and Steve's usual assistant was unavailable for his final trip of the season. Our ultimate goal was to guide (hopefully) well adjusted adults, not the troubled youth of America, but this would be a good test of a goat packer's guide service. "You fill in," he suggested, "and bring a couple of the goats. If this works out we can handle anything."

A novice goat packer, I also had novice goats. Hilda, a 3/4 Alpine X 1/4 Nubian, was just large enough at nine months to fit a goat packsaddle. She'd been on one 3-day excursion and had done well but no more than ten miles had been covered round trip. On this trip she would be asked to go six days and 30 miles, plus put up with 9 "troubled teens" as well as two aging trip leaders. She was willing, but was she ready?

For her companion I picked Spike, 3/4 Toggenburg X 1/4 Nubian and just 5 months old. He'd worn a doggie packsaddle and had followed me around our 5-acre homestead, but I knew I was asking a lot of a kid that young and just one month removed from the day I'd had to castrate him with my sharpest knife. He was willing, but was he able?

This was a State Human Services program and not one of the boot camp regimes recently featured in the papers and seen on the evening news. True, of the nine teens, aged fourteen to seventeen, most had been in trouble with the law. The few who didn't sport a "record" were the product of what we used to quaintly call "broken homes." But each teen was there by choice. He was expected to help out, participate, stay with the group and not be too much of a pain in the *arse*. As leaders, Steve and I weren't looking to break anybody down. We were hoping to give nine kids a good experience in a roadless area, teach them some wilderness skills, and maybe even build them up a bit. Anybody who wouldn't help out, participate, stay with the group, or who proved to be a consistent pain in the *arse*, would be taken out to the nearest trailhead and picked up for a ride home. Simple as that.

We had one special incentive available to keep everyone together for the duration of the journey. At the end of this six-day hike up a wilderness stream in a spectacular canyon was a well known natural hot springs. These boys, being local kids, all knew about these hot springs

116

and they made us swear that we'd allow time for a frolic in the pool at the end of the trip. "You promise, okay man?" We promised.

Of course nothing like this can ever go as planned. Though it was early fall, we were less than 100 miles from Mexico and in the afternoon sun that first day it was unseasonably warm – close to ninety degrees. The dirt road going in was washed out and the big van had to stop well short of the trailhead. So the hike to the first camp on the San Francisco River took two hours longer than anticipated. We ended up making camp in the dark and Hilda overheated going in. I gave her what water we had and eventually put some of her load (about 15 to 20 pounds total in the panniers) on my backpack for the final descent but she still got too hot and finally lay down a quarter-mile from the stream. After a rest I nurtured her back on her feet and down to the cool flow in the canyon. She waded in like a Labrador retriever and drank deeply.

Spike meanwhile carried his 10-ound doggie pack with ease, never lagged behind, showed no effects of the heat or any interest in water, but ate like a horse, stripping great clumps of a variety of fibrous desert scrub all along the trail. Lesson number one for the novice goat packer: every goat is different; know each goat's capabilities in hot weather.

It never got that hot for the next five days. Indeed, we were blessed with the bright clear skies, crisp nights and warm days that make New Mexico the place to be in the fall of the year. And lesson number two for the novice goat packer came as we sought to cross the stream for the first time the next morning.

The book on goats, plus all the articles I'd ever read, said they have a natural fear and dislike of crossing water. Neither of my goats knew anything about crossing any stream you couldn't jump and I expected trouble, but at the first ford Hilda went in belly deep and out the other side like the whole thing was fun. Spike meanwhile was going nowhere near any flow of water he couldn't leap in a single bound and he couldn't leap this one. When I finally took him by the collar and pulled him through he bawled like I was waving my sharpest knife in his face. Lesson number two for the novice goat packer: every goat is different; know each goat's predilections on crossing streams before heading into the wilderness.

Throughout the trip, there were no great conflicts with the troubled youth we were leading. There was even some progress, but it took time. The first day the two unofficial leaders among the boys, Rico and Chuck (not their real names), decided they would take out on their own while the rest of us were still breaking camp. Steve got firmly in their faces and told them they were going with the group or they were going home. They dropped their packs, sat grumpily upon them, and waited for the rest of the group.

The rest of the boys were generally more compliant, but initially quite distant. It was clear they viewed the two trip leaders, the adults, as one group, and themselves, the nine boys, as another. We were not a team. But things got better after the football game.

At one campsite – it was the third day – there was a long, open sandy area underneath the big cottonwoods. We used a Nalgene bottle filled with water as a ball and had a game of tackle football. Rico and Chuck led the six biggest boys. Steve and I and the three smaller boys took them on. At one point Steve got a bright idea and said: "No matter who gets the kickoff, dog-pile Rico!" Chuck got the kickoff but we five all went for Rico and buried him. Everybody had a big laugh and even Rico got the joke. And the two fiftyish trip leaders and their three little guys won the game. But we didn't rub it in. Respect was earned all around. Divisions began to break down. Nine boys over time seemed less and less like young delinquents. Two trip leaders over time seemed more and more like a couple of guys who were kids themselves not so long ago.

Hilda and Spike worked some magic, too. Typical of goats, they would "horn in" at the dinner hour, looking for company as much as treats but making something of a nuisance of themselves and this was not part of the "trip plan." I heard some talk about "stupid goats," and "silly goats," and "why'd you bring them?" But Hilda and Spike like people and it's hard for people not to like them. By the end of the trip they were being scratched behind the ears by friendly boys who would offer to help feed them their grain in the evenings and pack them up to start the day.

Both goats made progress as packers. On the second day Hilda lay down again with her pack. I had suspected all along that heat was only part of her problem but I was at a loss to figure out what the other part was. I'd tightened her cinch by the book and it was no tighter than Spike's but on a guess I got her to her feet and loosened it a notch. You could see the relief come into her face. By all accounts her cinch was now too loose but she stepped out like a goat on a mission. With a loose cinch I had to be sure her load was perfectly balanced. I did that and she never got sore and she never lay down on me the rest of the trip. Every goat is different.

Spike continued with his great pace and frenetic energy and appetite, and by the third day was carrying as much weight as Hilda. And he was soon crossing the stream on his own. At the deeper fords he had to swim and he floated like a duck and paddled like a dog.

The boys stopped to jump off rocks and make a big splash at every deep pool, some fished for catfish and carp but the only catch was a big channel cat they fished out of some submerged rocks. Meanwhile, we were constantly reminded of what we owed our charges for the fairly good behavior......"remember man; you promised!" We promised.

The last morning came and the crew got through breakfast and broke camp in record time. We got to the hot springs at 10:00 A.M.; plenty of time for a dip. But the pool was taken......

......There she lay in the shallows, a most lithe nubile, bare-naked, sun-tanned brown as a berry and lots of blond hair everywhere it could possibly grow; a woman of a type that my generation would have called a "hippie girl." Nine troubled teens and two aging trip leaders had clearly been too long in the woods. We were struck dumb. But she was *nonplussed*. She stood in all her magnificence in the knee-deep water, gracefully shaded her eyes with raised hands, and said: "You want the pool?"

"We're a state program," Steve said, "and this isn't part of our contingency plan."

"I understand," she said. "Don't worry. I'm here all day."

She turned and made possibly the most awesome exit of a hot spring ever seen by man; certainly this man. Nobody moved or said a thing as she toweled dry and got into her clothes. Then Steve said: "Okay men...but steady..." and nine troubled teens descended into the pool.

All said, a good trip. Both the young and the not so young had learned from each other. Hilda had apparently forgiven me my errors, and Spike was a crackerjack of a pack goat at 5 months old. Two kid goats had won-over nine kid people. A pack goat guide service seemed like a real possibility.

But judging from the conversation on the way home in the big van, the novelty of goat packing will never be able to compete with a bare-naked hippie girl in a hot spring.

119

Adopt a Hog?

It is often said that the emotions of animals are more complex than commonly supposed; at the core of the animal rights movement is the notion of "sentient" wildlife. And I recall a book titled *The Secret Life of Plants* that claimed that even trees, shrubs and tulips have "feelings," responding negatively to inconsiderate care and bad "vibes." Maybeso.

It is certain that we humans carry complex emotions concerning the animals and plants that come under our care or control. And I would make the claim here that often these emotional responses don't make much sense.

A few weeks ago I wrote about the leghold trap controversy in New Mexico. My view was that these traps should not be banned though we might want to fine-tune the regulations and educate the public about safe release of non-target animals. I also admitted in the piece that while I wasn't a trapper I did set trotlines for fish. Predictably my leghold trap opinion pleased some, made others mad, but nobody got on me about being a trotline fisherman. Nor is trotline fishing an issue for humane groups in any state that I know of. A trotline is simply a trapline for fish – why is there an uproar in so many states over a coyote or skunk caught overnight in a trap while virtually nothing is said about a catfish or bass caught overnight on a hook? Clearly, most people respond differently to supposed animal suffering versus apparent fish suffering. Is this varying response logical?

Some will say yes, and explain that it's because fish are more "primitive" and have less "feeling" than animals. Tell that to a fish! And even amongst animals we see varying emotional responses from humans. Who knows how many thousands of "sentient" rats are trapped each year. I've trapped some Norway rats myself and while many are killed instantly I've had some drag the trap around till I tracked them down and whacked them on the head. But hardly anyone gets the vapors over rat trapping. True, rats are considered to be destructive vermin, but coyotes and skunks can be very destructive and a nuisance as well. A trapped rat is good riddance; a trapped coyote will cause many to call for legislative action (on behalf of the coyote!). Taken overall, it seems the public's response to the trapping issue is not logical.

Nor does the public's response to horses and hogs make much sense. Both are domesticated animals with a wild ancestry. Each can easily revert to the feral state. When that happens, one is esteemed, the other despised.

The general outline of America's wild horses and their now revered history is well known. At the close of the frontier West hundreds of thousands of wild horses ran wild on the range, descendents of Spanish barbs, lost cow ponies and plow horses, and cavalry mounts. There were so many of these feral equines they were abusing the range and in competition with cattle, sheep, and wild ungulates for feed and water. Over the first seven decades of the 20th century their numbers were brought into a rough balance with the range by horse hunters who captured them for remounts, or more often to sell at slaughter for horse meat or simply to feed the hounds. As of 1970 there were about 25,000 wild horses in the West, about right for the available range.

In 1971 The Wild Free-Roaming Horse and Burro Act was passed by Congress and signed by President Nixon, giving protection to a "living symbol of the American West." This law ended horse hunting and we've had an oversupply of wild horses ever since. Numbers have consistently exceeded 50,000 animals in spite of various horse adoption programs and recent expenditures of some $40 million per year by the BLM to get them off the range and into homes or ranches. Readers will remember reading about the big oversupply of feral horses a few years ago on our nearby White Sands Missile Range.

Contrast our modern response to wild horses with our response to wild hogs. It's jail time and public opprobrium if you're caught hunting a wild horse; it seems the hogs can't get no respect. Like the horses, the hogs were first brought over by the Spaniards. Also like the horses, some of them got loose and, being adaptable, easily reverted to the feral state. There are now feral hogs in at least 30 of the 50 states. A recent article in an Albuquerque newspaper detailed their abundance in several counties in eastern New Mexico, plus Hidalgo County in our own part of the state.

Needless to say, there has been no bill introduced into the U.S. Congress to protect these feral hogs as a "living symbol of the American frontier;" there is no "adopt a hog" program. Indeed, I know of no state that offers them any protection from hunters – no closed season, no bag limit, no restrictions on methods (guns, bows, dogs, traps are all legal). Currently (2014), and at great expense, feral hogs are being gunned down by the multiplied hundreds in New Mexico and Texas by buckshot sharpshooters firing from airplanes and helicopters. Try that, in any state, on the feral horse population and see how quickly you go to jail. Why are feral horses and feral hogs viewed so differently by the general public, the media, and the government?

Some would say it's because horses are more "sensitive." Try telling that to a pig! Perhaps the horse is potentially more "beautiful," but a big boar is just as impressive in its own way. The pig is arguably more intelligent. Both are interesting wildlife in limited numbers, potentially very challenging as game animals, highly edible, and both can become a destructive pest when over-abundant. Neither can be considered a native species in North America.

One extreme animal rights group says: "A rat is a cat is a dog is a boy," in an attempt to place all wildlife beyond the means of hunting or control. A more reasonable philosophy would view the coyote and the skunk, the bass and the catfish (and I suppose even the rat if you're a rat hunter), as interesting and worthwhile in limited numbers, a problem when over-abundant, and not beyond the realm of control, whether for sport or by necessity.

As for the equine and porcine races, I can see no logical reason for viewing, or managing, feral horses and feral hogs as either sacrosanct or despised. I have hunted feral hogs and would do so again. I shot a horse once but it was by way of necessity, not sport. Unlike hogs, it has never occurred to me "hunt" horses; that's my inconsistency but I wouldn't force it on the horse hunter. It seems it is as difficult to fathom human emotions as the emotions of the beasts.

The Last of its Kind; The First in Value

Well into his retirement, Sir Edmund Hillary opined in an interview that his own son along with a host of other young climbers of the day were "vastly superior" to himself as mountaineers, even in his prime. Well, today's mountaineer certainly has vastly superior technical equipment compared to Hillary when he made his great ascent of Everest. But I couldn't name Hillary's son or any of the other "vastly superior" climbers of the day and I doubt you could either. Meanwhile, most everyone knows that Sir Edmund and his Sherpa partner, Tensing, were first to climb the worlds highest peak (and make it back down) back in 1953. Their place as mountaineers in history and the public consciousness is thus secure.

Being first can make a place as well as a person extraordinary in the public mind. This can be seen in a brief history of forester Aldo Leopold and our own Gila Wilderness.

"In 1909," Leopold wrote in later years, "when I first moved to the Southwest, there had been six blocks of roadless country, each embracing half a million acres or more, in the National Forests of Arizona and New Mexico. By the 1920's new roads had invaded five of them and there was only one left: the headwaters of the Gila River."

In "Wilderness and its Place in Forest Recreation Policy," *Journal of Forestry,* 1921, he clearly defined his view of wilderness.

"By wilderness," he wrote, "I mean a continuous stretch of country preserved in its natural state, open to lawful hunting and fishing, big enough to absorb a two weeks' pack trip, and kept devoid of roads, artificial trails, cottages, or other works of man."

Elsewhere in the *Journal,* he indicates he thought the Gila headwaters not only the last place available, but arguably the best.

"The Southwest (meaning New Mexico and Arizona) is a distinct region. The original southwestern wilderness was the scene of several important chapters in our national history. The remainder of it is about as interesting from about as large a number of angles, as any place on the continent. It has a high and varied recreational value. Under the policy advocated in this paper, a good big sample of it should be preserved.

"This could easily be done by selecting such an area as the headwaters of the Gila River on the Gila National Forest. This is an area of nearly half a million acres (it would turn out to be nearly 800,000 acres), topographically isolated by mountain ranges and box canyons. It has not yet been penetrated by railroads and to only a very limited extent by roads.

"The entire region is the natural habitat of deer, elk, turkey, grouse, and trout. If preserved in its natural semi-virgin state it could absorb a hundred pack trains each year without overcrowding. It is the last typical wilderness in the southwestern mountains. Highest use demands its preservation."

In 1924, in response to Leopold's pleas, plans, and writings, the U.S. Forest Service administratively set aside nearly 800,000 of the Gila National Forest, off limits to roads, vehicles and "other works of man," yet open to camping, hiking, and "lawful hunting and fishing," as the nation's first protected wilderness area. It was a "primitive" concept that would grow in acreage and legitimacy thenceforth nationwide and culminate in the Wilderness Act, passed by Congress and signed by President Lyndon Johnson in 1964.

Today our nation's wilderness system totals over 100 million acres; the Gila Wilderness is no longer the nation's only wilderness, or the largest, but it will always be first.

But what of the Gila River itself; particularly that stretch noted by Leopold, "the headwaters of the Gila?" Here irony abounds. It may be just coincidence, but where in 1921 Leopold found that of six potential Southwest wilderness areas only one remained, today in New Mexico of six mainstem rivers (Rio Grande, Gila, San Juan, Chama, Pecos, Canadian) only one – the Gila – lacks a major water impoundment. The last of its kind in the state, the Gila ironically may well be worth more for being undeveloped. A recent study indicates that a free flowing river is also a bounty of financial return in jobs, direct spending, and economic growth which, like the river itself, can be a perpetual flow of dollars and water if we just leave it alone.

The economic study by Southwick Associates Inc., and commissioned by the small business group Protect the Flows, shows that river recreation – fishing, birding, river running etc. – along the Colorado River and its many tributaries contribute about $17 billion in direct spending annually in its watershed states – Arizona, New Mexico, Colorado, Utah, Wyoming, Nevada – and supports about 234,000 jobs in the same states.

Of more local interest, the study also shows the New Mexico portion of this economic benefit derived from Colorado tributaries, the Animas and San Juan Rivers in northwest New Mexico, and the Gila and San Francisco Rivers in the southwest quadrant, is significant.

The study does not delineate the economic value of the San Juan vs. the Gila. The San Juan scores well with its world class tail-water trout fishery. But the Gila also has trout, and 20 lb. catfish, and is the best birding area in the state. It's a horse apiece except for one thing: among New Mexico's rivers, only the Gila still flows free – the last of its kind.

The Gila is the last river in New Mexico that can teach what a natural river should look like; the "perfect norm" as Leopold said. Its qualities are both economic and aesthetic, proof that being the last of its kind can be just as valuable as being the first.

Wildlife Profile: Mexican Black Hawk

I suppose the proper name is common black hawk – that's how this bird is listed in my *Peterson Field Guide to the Western Birds* – but I think Mexican black hawk is a better name.

For one thing, this raptor is scarce and very limited in range north of the international boundary. It is more common in Mexico and south through Central and South America on down to about Ecuador. Plus "Mexican black hawk" simply has a better ring to it; this is a bird with its own esoteric characteristics and it is in no way "common."

This is a large hunting hawk. Wingspan is up around 4 feet, close to the red-tail hawk in size. Plus its wings are unusually wide, good for soaring and giving it a distinctive look in flight. The coal black feathering is set off by the obvious white band that rings the short, broad tail. Its legs are yellow-colored and unusually long for a hawk. Like the red-tail, the black hawk is considered a buteo or soaring hawk.

The first I heard of this bird was some 25 years ago and at that time the name Mexican black hawk was a bit of an irritation. There were some living and nesting in the San Francisco River canyon below Glenwood and the Forest Service closed the canyon off to public access about six months of each year so as not to disturb this bird. There was some rationale for this as 4-wheel drive clubs were having truck safaris and 4-wheel jamborees down there and indeed all the way to Clifton, AZ. There was concern that the roar and the road-making would impact black hawks, bighorn sheep, and other sensitive wildlife.

But all I wanted was to hike down there and catch some fish and there was some resentment that the bird – or was it the Forest Service? – was keeping me out during the best months of the year.

In time the closure was lifted, the ORVs somewhat restricted and, based on my casual observations, the birds flourished. Anyone observant who spends time down around the Mule Creek confluence is bound to see a black hawk or two.

Black hawks seem very particular about their habitats. They like water but you are unlikely to see one camped out around Elephant Butte Lake. Ospreys are fish hawks that like big lakes but the black hawk likes habitats along flowing streams and even a meager flow like the San Francisco or Gila Rivers will draw them in. When I lived along the Mimbres River I would see one from my front porch from time to time and that was a slim flow indeed.

Living along water, black hawks catch critters that live in or near the stream – fish, crawfish, snakes, frogs, muskrats and other small mammals. They soar and hunt but are also adept at simply perching on a snag then diving down to the catch. At different times I have seen them with snakes, frogs, and different unidentified mammals in their claws.

I consulted several bird books for this black hawk story and two of don't even list New Mexico as part of the bird's range, only south Texas and southern Arizona. And the birds were counted as "scarce" or "rare" in those sections. In fact, the black hawk favors our riparian habitats here in southwest New Mexico.

I've already mentioned the San Francisco Canyon. Two other hotspots are the Gila River bird area below the Mangas Creek confluence, and the Gila Lower Box between Redrock and Virden. These birds will go off to Mexico or further south during the colder months but even a casual birder can find them in the spring, summer and fall in the named places.

And they breed here, too. One time in spring on a canoe trip through the Lower Box we spent the afternoon on the beach underneath some big cottonwoods. We had pulled in there to get away from a bad wind.

Two black hawks had a nest above and they about drove us batty with their constant shrieking as they soared overhead. It was as bad as the wind, or worse, and as soon as the wind let down we were happy to move on and leave the birds to their family affairs.

I can't prove it, but I seem to find the black hawk more common now than when I first saw them 25 years ago. The canary in the coal mine will tell when the cave environment is suffering and the black hawk will tell us if we are doing a good – or not so good – job of protecting and enhancing our riparian habitats.

Down in the Gila Lower Box fencing has allowed the riparian galleries to come back remarkably in the last dozen years. The last time through there by canoe we saw at least a half-dozen black hawks.

On a tour of the U-Bar Ranch near Cliff a few years ago we were looking for willow flycatchers. A progressive grazing regime has aided their survival there. We saw some, but the biggest thrill for me was a good look at two Mexican black hawks, seen perched on snags at different times and places during the day. The black hawks tell me we are doing some things right along the Gila.

Recently, our local Gila River Festival drew some 500 people to celebrate the (mostly) free flow of the Gila River. The organizers picked the Mexican black hawk as the colophon of the festival and the bird was featured on everything from caps to brochures. It was an excellent choice.

Mysteries Not Solved; Columnist Eats Crow

Back in 2009, yours truly wrote a column announcing that the mysterious disappearance of famed desert wanderer Everett Ruess had been solved; not only had the remains been found and identity confirmed by DNA analysis, an eye witness report described Everett's demise in some detail. All this was based on a magazine article that I took as fact. Turns out, the story wasn't over. But first, here's my edited version of the Ruess story in 2009:

Everett Ruess was a different sort of mountain man – younger, and born into a toney California arts community rather than farm, ranch, or wilderness camp. Sentient, perhaps to a fault, he sought not to make a killing in gold but prospected instead for wild landscapes with bold explorations and a rich, sensual delight he tried with some success to pass on to others. The desert rat as artist. And then, age twenty, Everett Ruess disappeared into the canyon-lands of southeast Utah for 75 years.

His parents had money and social prominence – as a teen he had traded prints and artistic aspirations with the likes of Ansel Adams and Dorothea Lange. They were also feckless, indulging Everett's reckless wanderings from the age of sixteen. But when his occasional letters stopped coming entirely in the fall of 1934 a serious inquiry for Everett began. His last point of departure was Escalante, Utah and a search party on horseback headed down Davis Gulch into "the maze."

As reported in W.L. Rusho's book, *Everett Ruess: Vagabond for Beauty*, the search party found an old Ruess camp near Davis Gulch with two burros still healthy in a makeshift corral.. But despite this and other searches over a long period of years no trace of Everett Reuss was ever found.

Thirty-some years after the mystery began an eye witness surfaced. A local Navajo man, Aneth Nez, afflicted with cancer, consulted, and confided, with the local medicine man. Years before, he said, some 60 miles east of Davis Gulch, he had witnessed from Comb Ridge three Ute Indian youth run down and kill a young Anglo and steal his two burros. Nez reported that he had soon given the young man a Navajo burial in a nearby rock crevice along with the burro's riding saddle.

Nez was haunted by what he had seen, his thirty-some years of silence, and his participation in the burial. The medicine man told him his only hope for a cure was to get a lock of hair from the deceased and put it through a curing ceremony. This he did, finding the crevice and the remains still present; his demons exorcised as he lived another ten years. Before his death he passed the story off to his granddaughter, Daisy Johnson and her younger brother, Denny Bellson.

This might have been all just another unconfirmed tall tale but Bellson is still very much with us and the key to an article that appeared recently in National Geographic Adventure Magazine, authored by David Roberts. Following the directions laid out years ago by Nez, Bellson found the remains and the saddle in 2008 and promptly notified authorities. The FBI, Roberts reports, botched it, but forensic experts from the University of Colorado did not. Tooth examination and dental records, facial reconstruction, and finally DNA analysis eventually proved that Everett Ruess had been found.

So I wrote in 2009, but not so fast! More than one anthropologist was not convinced. The teeth, they said, indicated an older man with a Native American diet. And further DNA analysis by an American military laboratory convinced even the U. of Colorado and author Roberts that while the Navajo Nez may have indeed witnessed a murder, the remains found at Comb Ridge were not that of Everett Ruess. Mystery not solved!

I was also too quick to favor the conclusions of author Dick North in his book *The Mad Trapper of Rat River*. In condensed form the column I wrote in 2005 went like this:

Late in 1931, a young man calling himself Albert Johnson built a cabin along the Rat River, Northwest Territories, Canada, and set out a line of traps. Soon, Johnson was in dispute with a local Indian trapper over trapline rights in his Rat River locale. When the Royal Canadian Mounted Police showed up on dogsled to investigate the dispute, Johnson refused to communicate or open his cabin door to the officers. When they returned with a search warrant, he shot one of the Mounties through the chest, then escaped into the bush. The chase was on; it would last 48 days.

The Mounties pursued by dogsled, on snowshoes, and by airplane in their attempts to track him down. There were more shoot-outs; in one fire-fight Johnson killed Mountie Edgar Millen with his Savage Model 99, 30/30. Living on caribou meat and snowshoe hares, Johnson appeared super-human in his endurance, guile and woodlore; if he was mad, he was certainly not incompetent.

In the final exchange Johnson refused surrender and shot another Mountie, before going down in a hail of bullets on the frozen ice of Eagle River.

The Mounties had got their man, but who was he? The dead trapper carried no identification, and while it was generally assumed that "Albert Johnson" was an alias, the authorities showed little interest in tracking his history. They took pictures of the body, then buried the man, whoever he was. In subsequent years books and magazine stories reveled in the chase and the violence, but offered little by way of solving the mystery.

An exception was author North who eventually focused on a man born as Johan Konrad Jonsen in Norway in 1898 and immigrated as a child with his homesteader family to Williams County, North Dakota in 1904. There he took the name John Conrad Johnson. An errant, daring youth, skilled with horse, gun, and trap, he teamed with his older brother, Magnor, to rob a bank, horseback, in Montana in 1915.

Later arrested multiple times for horse stealing, he served time, was photographed with mug shots, then disappeared into the wilds of Canada about 1923. Was this the same man who called himself "Albert Johnson," the mad trapper shot down by the Mounties in February, 1932?

North was denied an exhumation that might have yielded positive DNA or fingerprint evidence. But he has compiled enough physical and photographic evidence that it appears likely he has got his man.

So I wrote in 2005, but not so fast! In 2009 an exhumation *was* conducted on the remains of Albert Johnson. A DNA analysis failed to match the DNA of North's Johnny Johnson and several other claimants. The identity of Albert Johnson remains a mystery.

Both of these mysteries may one day be solved and could lead to one or more columns. In the meanwhile however, yours truly must eat a small plate of crow.

Enviros Retreat on Issue of Population

Really, I'd rather write about trout fishing. Or predator calling, bird watching, homesteading, or even saving the roundtail chub of the wild Gila River. Anytime you write about population and growth you end up sounding like a scold, and half your readers will get riled, no matter what you say. But darn-it, trout, predators, birds, open space, endangered species and wild rivers are all affected, and depleted, by population growth. And I recently came across a most interesting document.

The Environmental Movement's Retreat from Advocating U.S. Population Stabilization (1970-1998) was published by the The Pennsylvania State University Press in 2000, part of its *Journal of Policy History*. Co-authors are Roy Beck and Leon Kolankiewicz, the former a journalist, the latter a biologist. Their 25-page monograph is measured in tone but devastating in its revelations and implications. Its abstract reads as follows:

"The years surrounding 1970 marked the coming of age of the modern environmental movement. As that movement enters its fourth decade, the most striking change is the virtual abandonment by national environmental groups of U.S. population stabilization as an actively pursued goal."

As early as the 1960s, the authors point out, major environmental groups had placed population stabilization on the front burner of core issues. Executive Director of the Sierra Club, David Brower, wrote in 1966: "We feel you don't have a conservation policy unless you have a population policy."

And the Sierra Club in 1969 urged "the people of the United States to abandon population growth as a pattern and goal…and to achieve a stable population no later than the year 1990." There was movement in that direction. By the early1970s the U.S. birth rate stood at 1.7 per family, well below the replacement level of 2.1, and legal immigration was less than 500,000 per year, less than half what it is today.

Yet, as the authors note, by 1998 the Sierra Club, Zero Population Growth (ZPG), and other major environmental groups had largely abandoned population stabilization as a goal, "but not because population growth had stopped or the problems it caused had been solved."

Indeed, between 1970 and 1998 the population of the U.S. would increase by more than 70 million people. It would increase by more than 33 million people in the 1990s alone. Yet few enviros noticed.

The authors write: "With the business and political establishments continuing to push for 'more growth,' and the environmental establishment now pushing for 'smart growth,' the special interest groups had succeeded in excluding 'no growt66h' from the range of acceptable, available options."

The monograph's analysis is detailed. But the reasons it gives for enviros backing away from the populations issues boil down to two related causes: the rise of the "New Left," and, "political correctness."

Called "Progressive Cornucopians" by Earth First! Founder Dave Foreman, the New Left was, and is, more concerned with "environmental justice" than conservation per se; i.e., any strict protection of land, water, wilderness and wildlife. Both justice and conservation are worthy goals, but the emphasis shifted for many conservation groups, which would now rather concentrate funds and labor on a toxic dump near a city than a wild river in the middle of nowhere. Foreman's own Earth First! group was hijacked by this very political turn-about.

The author's quote noted environmental journalist Mark Dowie: "The essential concern of the new movement is human health; wilderness protection and environmental aesthetics are worthy but over-emphasized values, often derided by anti-toxic activists as bourgeois obsessions."

Similarly, the author's note, ZPG is now more focused on "women's empowerment" than population stabilization or the birth rate/immigration rate *per se*. The authors say that political correctness began to surface as immigration by minority groups from third world countries became the primary cause of U.S. population growth.

"Of all the factors," the author's write, "involved in the environmental movement's retreat from U.S. population stabilization, the growing demographic influence of immigration is the single most important one." Thus, according the authors, the environmental groups "feared that immigration reduction would alienate 'progressive' allies and be seen as racially insensitive."

The result? Well, today's Sierra Club takes no stance on U.S immigration, currently running at near one million per year (legally) and at least a half million per year (illegally), though the club elsewhere acknowledges the injurious effects of such growth on wildlife, wilderness, open space and habitats.

The monograph notes that the Sierra Club favors "global" population stabilization as the long term means to stabilization in our own country. A more likely scenario is offered by noted historian George Kennan, who wrote that the current mass influx of immigration will decline naturally "only when the levels of overpopulation and poverty in the United States are equal to those of the countries from which these people are now anxious to escape."

Our future is clouded. Wilderness, wildlife, habitats, open space and agricultural lands – and thereby outdoor recreation – are under increasing pressure from seemingly ineluctable growth. Yet both the left and the right are disinclined to do anything about it; the right because they are "boomers" by nature, libertarians by choice, and actually like growth for business or ideological reasons; the left because they are so politically correct they haven't the gumption to face the issue. Yet both attitudes are self-defeating.

For example, the right would like to drill for oil in the Alaska National Wildlife Refuge (ANWR), where there may be 10 billion barrels in oil reserves. Production there would peak about 2025, we are told. Yet our nation is on course to add 100 million people to its population in the next 30 years. Assuming the boomers get what they want, how long would it take our scheduled population growth to eat up the savings and any new reserves found in the ANWR?

The left says no; improved conservation would save more oil than the ANWR could possibly provide. I favor this option myself, as do most sportsmen and conservationists. But how long will it take 100 million new people to eat up these conservation savings, and more? In either case, population growth soon consumes any benefit in either production or conservation.

Growth is destined to leave both the left and the right looking foolish and disappointed, their logic bankrupt. The environmental retreat from the population issues poses dire consequences, for the natural world, and every aspect of our economy and quality of life. We ignore these issues at our peril.

Water Transfers, A.K.A., Pipe Dreams

Note: Piping, pumping or otherwise moving large quantities of water, from the countryside where it naturally occurs to water-stressed boom towns fearful of losing their lifeline to perpetual growth, is an old money-making strategy in the Southwest. It often does create profit, for a few, and a temporary boost to growth, but invariable puts new stress on the life-ways of the rural areas from whence the water comes, as well as depleting life-sustaining aquifers, rivers, wildlife and habitats. The following remarks were presented in Albuquerque at the New Mexico Water Dialogue, January 14, 2010.

Long range water transfers – pipe dreams – such as the proposal to pump aquifer water from DeBaca County to Santa Fe, or the proposal to pump aquifer water from Catron County to the Middle Rio Grande region, or the proposal to pump Gila River water over the Continental Divide to Silver City or Las Cruces or El Paso, come under the general heading of water development. Water development is one of three variables that play on our worry that we have, or will have, a water shortage for a given use in a given place; the other two variables are water conservation and population growth. Whether news story or scholarly paper, the lead line on this topic will read something like this:

"With New Mexico's population projected to increase by at least 300,000 people each decade for the foreseeable future, water shortages and water wars loom on the horizon unless new water sources can be developed or conservation of available supplies becomes more efficient."

Sound familiar? What strikes me about these myriad scenarios describing our uncertain water future is that while water development and water conservation are always presented as mutable variables, where improvements or benefits can be achieved, population growth – the true source of the looming shortage and stress – is always presented as immutable, a given, an ineluctable force like the weather, like a hurricane, that you can't stop or even influence but can only react to it when it arrives. This is unfortunate as in the long run both conservation and development are incomplete solutions that must eventually be overwhelmed by growth, if growth is indeed ineluctable and perpetual as commonly portrayed

For example, Albuquerque, I'm told, has in recent years reduced per-capita consumption from about 250 gallons/person/day to about 150 gallons/person/day. This is commendable. But most of that growth of 300,000 people per decade as previously detailed is destined for the greater Albuquerque area. At that rate, how long till the growth eats up the savings?

As for water development, a look at the proposed water transfers mentioned earlier is instructive. These transfers in fact are booster projects and the results could be perverse. With the DeBaca County water aimed at burgeoning Santa Fe and the San Agustin water directed, presumably, toward burgeoning Albuquerque, these developments are billed as serving urban growth. I submit they are more likely to create it.

Once the water price is agreed upon, the contracts signed and engineering completed, bringing in a horde of new people to purchase and consume the water becomes more than a goal, it becomes a necessity. How else are you going to pay off your investment and scoop up the desired profit? Thus, in a rueful irony, that which was promoted as a means to meet growth needs for water, merely hastens the day when that newly acquired water is used up. That's how The West was won!

But where do you go for more water once you've drained hidden, pastoral DeBaca County, or the singular expanse of the San Agustin plains? And how do you justify transferring water from regions that are in hydrologic equilibrium – the idealistic goal everyone says they support – to distant boom towns that are unlikely to ever achieve sustainability because they don't know when to quit?

As for the Gila River proposal, I recall a meeting in Las Cruces more than 20 years ago when the lead planner for the Bureau of Reclamation sought to justify what was known at the time as the Mangas Diversion proposal. "We're a construction oriented agency," he said, and added, "New Mexico can't let that water just run downstream into Arizona"….it was the same old hash. Later, after two beers at Eddie's Bar & Grill, the lead planner was more insightful when I suggested his heart really wasn't in this one. "You know, Dutch," he said, "one of these days Senators and Congressmen from places like Ohio are going too figure out it doesn't make sense to spend large sums of the public's money to subsidize water and growth in the Southwest so the Southwest can attract more people from Ohio."

I call it the growth syndrome and much of the populace is in its grip, including many politicians, who typically favor growth in spite of all the trouble it brings, like water and energy shortages, resource fights, traffic, crime, dry rivers and dead fish.

Conservation is always good and, at times, water development still has its place. But we need to pay attention to the third spoke in the wheel. We don't want to build a wall around the place, but the first step in getting a grip on growth is to view it as a manageable dynamic rather than an ineluctable force. We should quit subsidizing it via thinly disguised booster projects. Conservation easements, open space protections, limits to numbers of new water or electric hookups, requirements that developers prove up water adequate to sustain their projects long-term; all these tend to squeeze growth without putting a freeze on the economy.

134

As well, we are told that over half of New Mexico's growth results from in-migration. Some companies are infamous for milking tax breaks, land deals and other subsidies from our local communities, then hiring the majority of the work force from out of state. We can and should insist on a preponderance of local employment.

As for DeBaca, Catron and Grant Counties, therein lies the resource sustainability we seek. We should be studying how they do it rather than bumping their customs, cultures, economies and environments out of kilter with long range water grabs and related pipe dreams.

Snowshoes: Winter Travel on Rawhide and Ash

There was a good flurry of snow in the Gila National Forest before Christmas this year. This put me in mind of a pair of rustic and archaic-looking aids to foot travel I have hung up on my library wall between shelves and racks of guns, fishing rods, and sporting books. Called snowshoes, mine are old-fashioned, of gut and wood, have an unusual history, and they're older than me. Other brands are new-fangled, a modern amalgam of aluminum, neoprene, and I don't know what-not. The variegated sizes, shapes, materials and styles are debatable if you have an interest in what's "best" but all can prove useful in taking you along on top of rather than sinking into deep snow.

When the snow is a foot or more in depth snowshoes become an aid in winter travel, on or off the trail. With snowshoes you can go places you never would on foot. Even a strong, enduring hiker will wear out walking in deep snow without snowshoes or cross country skis. And, on balance, I think snowshoes are a better bet than skis for wilderness travel in winter.

Where the snow is deep, light, and fluffy, snowshoes will offer better floatation than skis. That's one reason why cross-country skiers are largely confined to snow-packed trails. Also, snowshoes are much easier to maneuver when you leave the trail to bushwhack through the woods. Skis are faster on a trail and, some would say, more fun. Suit yourself. I like snowshoes because once you're mounted on a good pair and acquire some skills you can go most anywhere in winter on snow that you could traverse in summer on foot.

Snowshoe makes and styles have taken on a new dimension in the last twenty years. The traditional snowshoe of gut and wood is still made and used, but the new look in snowshoes has an aluminum or high-tech plastic frame with neoprene or some other artificial material for the webbing. I've never worn a pair of these "new look" snowshoes, but I've talked to those who have and I've seen them in use. They're exceedingly light, handy to use because of the small frame, and floatation is evidently quite good. But in sport, especially the country sports, I acknowledge a weakness for tradition and aesthetics.

Consider that the traditional handmade snowshoes still work well for walking on deep snow. Then consider that most of the time your snowshoes are not going to be on your feet at all but will be hanging decoratively over the fire place or on the wall of the den. What would you rather have hanging on your wall and honoring a rustic tradition – handmade rawhide and ash, or a factory imprint of plastic and neoprene?

To each his own, of course, but the traditional, Indian-made snowshoes come in three basic styles. The Bearpaw is a short, wide shoe (about 14" wide by 32" long) with a round, almost flat, nose and no

136

tracking tail. They're handy in the thick woods of the northern boreal forests but don't track as well as the two other styles.

The Alaska model (also called the Pickerel) is a long, narrow shoe (usually 10" by 56") that has very good floatation, a good turn-up at the toe to keep you from catching the toe in the snow, and is easy to use in open country. Because of the length of this shoe, they are less handy in the thick woods.

The Michigan style is a compromise at about 12" wide by 48" long. Floatation is good, there's a tracking tail and a raised toe for easy travel, and they're a nice, handy length and width. My own snowshoes that I brought from Minnesota in 1980 are Michigans and I got them in trade from a muscular old farmer named Johnson for a pretty good bolt action Harrington & Richardson .22. During The Depression though, Johnson had been a wolf hunter.

Times have changed; back then Johnson was a bush pilot as well as a farmer and in winter he would tie his (now my) snowshoes to the struts of the plane, his partner did the shooting, and when they'd get one, they would land on skis in the peat bog, strap on snowshoes and mush off and get the big northern lobo and tie the critter to the same struts as the webbed shoes. Johnson told me, "We got $50 bounty for the wolf and could keep and sell the pelt to boot."

Good money back then. Of course at about a hundred pounds apiece, these dead wolves could easily over-balance a plane in gravity to the ground and two wolves were about it, Johnson said. He told me, "We'd motor to the far end of the bog, head into the wind, and hope to hell we'd clear the trees at lift-off with both wolves aboard."

Either the Alaska or the Michigan would be a good choice for the New Mexico snowshoer. Snowshoeing is easier to learn than cross-country skiing. Step into the bindings, tighten up, and start walking. You will no doubt fall a time or two till you get the hang of it, but within an hour or so you will begin the slow, swinging gate that comes naturally with snowshoeing.

Don't be in any big hurry. When you are comfortable on the trail you are ready to venture off the trail and then, hardest of all, snowshoe up and down hill. Take your time and you'll teach yourself.

When I lived in northern Minnesota I used to follow the hounds in winter in pursuit of red fox and coyote. With the snow up to your crotch, the chase would sometimes go back into the bush where no skis or snowmobiles could travel. Without snowshoes, I never would have gotten to the bayed up hounds.

One time in Lake of the Woods County I went into a big chunk of thick woods on snowshoes, following hounds that had a red fox on the run. I left several companions on the road. They could circle this patch of woods on their snowmobiles, but they couldn't get back into the bush to follow the race.

137

The hounds chased that fox for the better part of the day. I heard the chase as the fox circled, and I got to see the red brush go by several times; indeed I could have shot the critter with my 20 gauge. But it was such a good race I wanted to see if the hounds could catch him.

They could not, and near the end of the day I came out of the woods with the beaten hounds. The boys on the road, with their pickup trucks and snowmobiles, all wanted to know about the chase. I told them what I had seen and heard and said that it was a great race. It seems they had missed out on most of it. I told them: next time, bring a pair of snowshoes.

You can find snowshoes for sale at local sporting/outdoor shops or online. And the Lincoln and Gila National Forests can tell you about snow conditions and trails.

Now's the time for winter sport and a good workout, riding the white stuff under snow-laden boughs on a cushion of rawhide and ash.

When the Trail Forks, Take the Other

I got a late start which bespeaks a lack of urgency and so I don't think I was expecting much from the fishing. And I don't like fishing on the weekends because that's when everybody else is out there. But it was a nice day and I needed to get out of the house. Turns out I was right about the fishing. But getting out was still the right thing to do for I caught something more elusive than a fish....

It wasn't at my first stop; I found half a dozen cars there at the trailhead. I don't guess all of them were fishermen – maybe none of them were. I guessed birders. Few birders bother with fish but half a dozen cars was too much. "It's Sunday," I thought, "and I asked for this."

I drove on to another trailhead that led to an equally pretty stream and was astonished to find the pull-off empty of cars. I rigged up as fast as I could, hoping to be well downstream before anyone else got there. There were tracks on the trail – several people and one of them had a dog – but they were from days past. I had the stream to myself and in spite of a late start I now had a sense of urgency and was expecting fish at the better spots. I knew the stream and just where to look.

The amenities of Indian summer! It means a short span of sun but a surprising warmth at mid-day. And a nice breeze such that when I'd take my pack off it would quickly dry the sweat on my shirt. I got hung up in branches at the first pool and lost my fly but it's a tight stream and that will happen. I told myself to slow down; I did, somewhat, and it wouldn't happen again. I wasn't catching anything but wasn't worried. The better pools were further down and I'd figured out that those who'd come in days before hadn't fished; they stayed on the trail and had left no tracks in the sand and mud where any angler would have stopped to cast and left their mark. Then the trail forked; I took the other.

That's when it hit me. This was a stream not far from town and here I was on a visible trail following a lovely stream on a weekend and even in the open sandy spots there were no signs of human passage. Of course it didn't mean that no one had ever been down here, just that weeks must have gone by, enough time for old rains and sifting sands to obliterate the last human passage. There were deer tracks, fox tracks, bird tracks, I saw two javelinas, but as for people I had found a trail not taken.

Remoteness, and a lack of competition, are always a pleasure, generating at once a controlled eagerness and the welcome knowledge that one need not race another angler to a pool. I anticipated trout.

I carefully cast and dapped and drifted and jigged a beadhead nymph in all the good looking spots – the deeper runs, deep pools swirling around big boulders, whitewater and slow water. I got no takes let alone any fish on line and did not so much as see a fish of any species in water

139

clear enough that something piscine should have showed up if any were there.

This had happened at the same stream a year ago; I think I wrote it up in this column. I reported that I had fished hard for two trout but one of them had jumped five times! There had been an ash flow since then but also the long hard cleansing rains of summer. Some trout should have moved up from below, or down from above. But I couldn't raise one to save myself. It was getting bad enough that a tug on the bottom was starting to feel good.

Deep down the canyon I stopped for lunch. I ate a can of sardines with my fingers and on a hunch switched to a Pistol Pete – black and grey hackle with a red tail and a spinner – and when I was done eating I smeared my fishy fingers over that fly. I had used sun screen that morning, possibly a turn-off to fish, but now covered that up with the smell of sardines all the way from Norway. A trout is not a catfish but even sight feeders are sensitive to smell in the water.

Just below the log where I sat for lunch I found some fast water descending into a swirl around a rock then tailing off into a quiet pool. I picked the quiet pool because overhanging branches made the faster water hard to reach with any sort of cast. I looped a roll cast into a high arc and between the branches. The fly made I thought too big a "plop" on landing but the lone trout living there didn't think so and took it like I'd hit him in the face. He didn't jump five times – just once – but was big enough to pump the rod for a while and then he lay in the shallows between my ankles.

I didn't actually catch him; he flipped the fly as I was reaching for the release. But I had touched him, with my feet, so I counted coup on a rainbow about a foot long.

I didn't stop to fish on the way out. The trout have not returned to this stream and the odds were slim I would better my take on waters I'd just fished. And I wanted to end my efforts on a high note, that one fish having taken on big proportions.

It was a bucolic retreat and I took in the sights along a faint trail that took me on foot, leisurely, back up the canyon to the truck. For the first time I noticed pines and willows and wildflowers and butterflies that had survived cold nights and colors on canyon walls. At one point I was taken aback by a set of tracks on a mud flat. It took me a moment to realize they were my own; I had fished here just hours ago. I peered at my own sign, my smile mirrored in the adjacent waters.

Country Sports II

AGRICULTURE,
HOMESTEADING,
COUNTRY LIVING

Mr. Ott and the Pursuit of Old Yeller

We called him Mr. Ott and he was a cowboy. That meant something different – "cowboy" – at the time of this story, the early 1960s, than it does today, for Mr. Ott at that time was seventy-something, born in the 19th century, and had spent "his whole life a-horseback." .He was short, bowlegged, wore his spurs it seemed everywhere but to bed, and his stilted walk in high-heeled boots had him looking like he was always just two steps from a fall. But he didn't fall and was pure grace on a horse because he was a cowboy.

Otto Reagan was the whole name. That might not mean much as a name, except he was the adopted son of a rancher whose name is a legend to this day in the south Texas brush country – Rocky Reagan. That summer, early 1960s, my cousin Hodie Soule and I were know-nothing teenagers from New York State who somehow –– the details are not important to this story – found ourselves as ranch hands on Mr. Rocky's 41,000 acres that straddled the Rio Nueces mostly in McMullen County, Texas. Mr. Ott was the foreman of the outfit. He was tough, funny, profane and fair. We three lived at what was called the Ray Ranch, a line camp, little more than a shack, perhaps 20 miles from the nearest town (Three Rivers, TX).

We sure tried to be ranch hands. Real cowboys we'd meet on the rare trip to town would say: "What can these boys from New York do, Mr. Ott?" And Mr. Ott would say: "Why, these boys will do whatever you ask 'em to, but they're so green the goats have 'em nibbled about down to the nub."

Truth was, we stumbled often enough to give Mr. Ott stories to tell to the end of his days. We learned, fast as we could, how to bridal and saddle and ride a horse. Horsemanship was a work in progress though, and the more we learned and better we rode the better we understood how inscrutable horses can be, how big and fast, and how much it hurts when a thousand pound animal gallops under a stout mesquite limb, you forget to duck, and he peels you off.

"Everyone who rides has gone to ground," Mr. Ott said. "it's a lesser number climbs back on and keeps a-goin'"

That challenge was pretty clear, and we also learned to milk goats, butcher goats, fix windmills, brand calves, burn prickly pear, and then the river came up one night and flooded the countryside. When the water went down we had 3 weeks of work ahead, fixing and rebuilding fence blown out by flood.

This was good news from our view for some of this downed fence was so remote and boggy we had to go a-horseback to get there. Me and Hodie liked that. So we rode, the three of us, and on a mule we packed staples, and wire, and post hole digger, and fencing tools and an axe. Once there, Mr. Ott said, "I'm going to make a little round and see

144

what's got out. You there, Hodie, you dig us some good deep post holes and make sure you get 'em in a straight line. Dutch, you take that axe and cut you some mesquite posts – it'll take ten or twelve – drag 'em back in here with your mare, and the two of you set 'em in and tamp 'em down like they're set in cement. Before you're done I'll be back and I'll help you string the wire."

Well no way would we let the old drover get back before we got done and Soule got the diggers and the dirt started to fly and directly he had 10 post holes dug. And I got the axe and the chips started to fly and directly I had 10 mesquite posts cut. And we used Redwing, my mare, to skid them in; we set the posts and when Mr. Ott rode up me and Hodie were seated and taking in some shade.

The old cowman couldn't quite believe it but he looked down the row of posts and it was purely straight. And he leaned against a couple of posts and they were like set in cement. And then he stepped back and looked up and his eyes got big and he said, "Lord God, boys; you put them posts in upside down!"

And sure enough, with about half the posts, we'd put the skinny end in the ground and the fat end up in the air. He didn't make us swap ends on any but by the end of the summer the whole town of Three Rivers knew the story about those post hole diggers from New York.

It was toward the end of the summer when we started to hear about Old Yeller. This wasn't a dog or a dog story, this was a wild bovine who had eluded good cowboys on at least three gatherings and got spookier every time. Old Yeller could run like a deer, had some wide and wicked hooked horns looking like a corriente steer, only she wasn't a steer; Old Yeller was a cow. And she had a reputation.

Eight or ten cowboys were there to gather this pasture with us and I got paired with Mr. Ott and early on that day I said, "Mr. Ott, if we see Old Yeller do you want me to rope her?"

"Lord God, no! You'll have a wreck and injure a good horse. We'll never get her in the brush. But if we can get her crossing an opening, you give that horse some rein and she'll run up and flank that outlaw and you keep her running straight and I'll be on the other flank and we'll just see about Old Yeller."

Well it was late in the day and oh-my-gosh there she was..... a rangy, rough looking old lemon-yellow cow and she fled into the woods like the feral stock she was and the brush started poppin.' Some of that brush poppin' was me and Mr. Ott, trying to keep up. We lost ground in the brush but suddenly Old Yeller ran out of woods, out in the open now of a grassy flat with a few prickly pear here and there. There was room to run.

I have never felt such acceleration on a horse; in fact Redwing did it all; I just managed to keep my seat. And then we were alongside and Redwing gave Old Yeller the eye and the old wild one didn't like the looks of things but it was too late; from the other flank Mr. Ott threw a loop on the run, got one horn and the muzzle. It was imperfect and precarious and Old Yeller was bad to fight and Mr.Ott said, "Throw your rope!" I uncoiled a loop, threw it, missed, but when the loop hit the ground Old Yeller stepped in it. She was stopped long enough as two other cowboys arrived and they didn't miss and that quick Old Yeller was strung out and a caught cow.

Some years later a friend and I went to visit Mr. Ott, now retired, at Callaham. He was recovering from pneumonia and a hospital stay and every little bit would cough and expectorate into a fruit jar. He couldn't laugh much with that lung disease, but he smiled broadly when I reminded him of our summer at the ranch, cousin Hodie, and our pursuit of Old Yeller. He called my friend "Pretty Lady" and said it sure was good of us to stop by.

"What Am I Bid For...a Pig?"

I thought about it for a while and then my son Bud confirmed that this was the fourth year in a row we had headed out for the Grant County fair grounds to bid on one or more pigs for his 4-H "market swine" project. We're still far from experts in the porcine field of animal husbandry, but it seems we've learned a few things along the way. Since Bud just turned 12 that means we started when he was barely nine. That first year he had a partner.

He and his friend Sam would each bid on a pig in the spring, they would raise them together at our place (pigs are social animals and "raise up" and eat better with company), then the boys would show them at the fair come fall. Each had hopes of making the auction sale, where the real money is, but we reminded the boys that even if they ended up with pigs the judge didn't care for they could still get packer price for their animals. With the parents paying for the feed that base price would still yield a hefty nest egg on a two-hundred-plus pound animal. Especially when you're nine years old.

Well on the day of the pig sale at Cliff, Sam and Bud were off at the Tour of the Gila bike race. Meanwhile Sam's mother and I each bid on a pig at the fairgrounds. We had no idea what we were doing and it showed. I'm always nervous at auctions (anything that makes me have to think fast makes me nervous) and we ended up with two healthy but rather shapeless Hampshire barrows at the minimal price of $75 each. Neither one of us wanted to take a chance on one of those $300 piglets when we didn't know what we were looking for, trying to anticipate what some judge might like 6 months hence.

The summer passed and the boys fed their pigs, "Ribs" and "Bacon." Then they overfed their pigs. In spite of a good exercise program, by September Bacon was already over the 280 lb. limit and Bud's pig, Ribs, was less than 10 lbs. under. We got some hasty advice from a knowledgeable neighbor and put each on a crash diet. Ribs made the sale at 269 lbs. but Bacon, with the shoulders of an ox, ballooned well past 300. He was sold on the hoof at private treaty.

Meanwhile, Ribs, still shapeless, did not even get a polite glance from the judge. But, to Bud's credit, his pig handled well in the ring and we later found a buyer at packer price plus; I think it came to .75/pound. That was just over $200 for a nine year old boy. My kid had earned money in the livestock business, put it in the bank, and we both knew a little more about pigs than we had six months before.

The next summer it was "Rocky" (a Duroc) and "Hamlet." (another Hampshire). Sam was no longer in 4-H but Bud and I paid more for these two, got better pigs, did not overfeed, and really worked them, walking

147

them through the pasture daily to build up that muscle definition the judges like. We did better all around.

Still, neither pig made the auction sale. But Rocky at least got a look from the judge and, as always, there was an eventual sale available at packer price. Rocky was sold, Hamlet fed us, and Bud said something like, "You know, Dad, I'd have to do a lot of yard work to get as much as I can from a big ol' pig." He was only a little sobered up when I reminded him that his parents had paid for Rocky's feed.

Last year we became bold. We paid $300 for a Duroc gilt that our knowledgeable neighbor helped pick out, and bid half as much for a nice muscled- up Hampshire barrow. They both looked like prospects and, based on our apparent increasing knowledge, the cheaper Hampshire impressed us as maybe even better than the gilt. Then, halfway through the summer, he died.

Left with the Duroc gilt, Bud put in a lot of time on his only prospect, knowing some of the other kids had a half dozen pigs, or more, to throw into the ring. I thought our gilt was good, but probably not good enough – muscled up nicely but a bit too short-coupled and blocky to make the auction. I warned Bud not to be too disappointed if his $300 pig wasn't quite a champion.

But pig judging goes by trends, as much as female fashion or beauty, and our judge liked our short-coupled, muscular pig. "Loins," as we called her, made the auction sale (a 2nd place in her class) and went for $2100.00. I told Bud, "Son, you are now in better financial shape than your father!"

And so the other day we were off again to Cliff to bid on a pig or two. It was mostly Hampshires and Yorkshires; only one of our favorite Durocs was there and he was no prospect. We surveyed the crop ahead of time and marked down three "Hamps" we particularly liked. It shows that we've learned a thing or two that a couple of these pigs we picked went for the highest price at the auction. Too high for Bud and I; I went all the way to $400 for "the pick" before bowing out to a bolder bidder. It was fun, and Bud was a real help with what he's learned. I still get nervous over all that fast talk by the auctioneer, and the need for quick decision with big bucks involved, but I've yet to buy something I didn't really want.

We ended up with a nice Hampshire gilt for $225, with a muscle groove down the spine and "dimple" between the hips and a promise from a friend that he'd find us a Duroc to keep her company. We're learning, Bud and I. Still, it will always be a bit of a crap shoot when the pigs come into the ring and the auctioneer says, "What am I bid for .....?"

148

Organic vs. Chemical Ag – Part II

Last March I wrote a column on organic vs. chemical agriculture. In the column I blasted the "conservative" journal *National Review* for what I saw as a fountain of misinformation contained in an article by John J. Miller entitled, "A Food Movement Makes a Pest of Itself." The basic contention of Miller was, organic yields are about half that of "conventional" farming which makes liberal use of commercial fertilizer, herbicides and pesticides. This is bad, it was claimed, on two counts.

Besides the obvious inefficiency, a low organic yield (if true) would require the farming of more wild or otherwise uncultivated lands; the resultant loss of habitat would have a marked effect on wildlife, and hunting, fishing, bird-watching, and other recreation associated with undeveloped land. All this makes the debate of great interest to conservationists and country sports enthusiasts like you and me.

It didn't take me long to research information demonstrating the high yields and environmental benefits possible through sound organic farming (like Mr. Miller, I was able to find sources that pleased me). I wrote the column and sent a copy to Miller and to the Hudson Institute, the conservative think-tank where Miller had gotten most of his information.

Mr. Miller never responded, but I got a prompt phone call from Alex Avery who, with his father Dennis, has dominated the chemical side of the ag debate on a national scale for decades.

Mr. Avery was very polite, articulate, and not surprisingly had his argument down pat from long usage. He readily conceded that modern organic agriculture can equal or exceed the grain yields of chemical ag "on a field-by-field basis." However, he said, on a "system-wide basis," organic yields would trail by "25 to 40 percent."

"Why?" I wanted to know.

"Because," he said, "the organic farmer must let a portion of his farm lie fallow each year to put nitrogen back into the soil."

There is something to this. The organic farm typically is not straight grain, say corn. It is grain and hay and livestock; when a given field is in hay, say alfalfa, it's not producing any corn. The same-size chemical farm next door, meanwhile, plants every acre to corn every year – the overall corn yield is higher than the organic farm though the yield per acre for corn may be the same on both farms.

I countered that the hay field is not really fallow, though it will be plowed down at some point to put the green manure into the soil. The hay itself is harvested, or pastured, or both in one year; the hay and livestock may yield more profit per acre than the grain.

I didn't see a clear winner at this point and we went on to the wildlife/habitat issue. Mr. Avery repeated the inefficiency claim; that organic farming would lead to expanded cultivation of wild or uncultivated lands, a net habitat loss. I disputed his interpretation of "inefficiency" and said, "What about the Everglades?"

He conceded that fertilizer run-off from sugar cane fields had caused eutrophication of the Everglades, abnormal plant growth was choking out fish and wildlife; but, like a good libertarian, he said that those highly subsidized sugar cane growers should be allowed to go out of business. On that we agreed. But I pointed out that it is the chemical ag inputs, not the subsidy, that causes the eutrophication.

Frankly, I expected Alex Avery to surface as little more than an irritating polemicist. But he was quite charming, in a contentious sort of way, very knowledgeable (though, like me, with a bias) and the conversation got me to looking further.

First I got a copy of the Rodale Institute "Farming Systems Trial." This document details a long-term experiment on the Rodale Farms in Pennsylvania where three adjacent plots have been farmed conventionally (chemical ag), with manure-based fertilizer, and with green manures like alfalfa, clovers, beans, etc., for 15 years.

The result: "After a transition period of about four years, crops grown under organic systems yield as well as and sometimes better (particularly during drought) than crops grown under the conventional system; organic techniques significantly improve soil quality, as measured in structure (tilth), total soil organic matter, and biological activity."

And through the Rodale website I corresponded with Klass Martens. This upstate New York farmer has been getting astounding production of corn, organic yields topping 200 bushels per acre. Further, he does it by a system that hammers the final nail in the chemical ag argument.

Upstate New York is a cold climate (I know, I grew up there). Still, Martens is able to "double crop" year by year. I'll let him describe it:

"On a well managed organic farm, soil is kept covered with legume cover crops in the fall, winter and early spring before land is prepared for planting. Often these (cover) crops are interseeded into the (grain) crop so as the crop matures and is harvested, the cover crop is already established. This provides a large amount of extra nitrogen....

"A common rotation would be Year 1: wheat underseeded with clover; Year 2: corn; Year 3: soybeans; Year 4: spelt (interseeded at soybean's yellow leaf stage or sown immediately after soybean harvest in year 3) underseeded with clover; Year 5: vegetables such as sweet corn which are harvested early enough for a cover crop to be grown."

Thus, even on a straight grain farm, with no livestock, fields can be farmed organically and consecutively, year by year, while maintaining fertility with green manures. The argument --"you need to let land lie fallow" – is defunct. And you get 200 bushel to the acre for corn!

Organic farming could feed the world as efficiently as chemical ag, without the damage to habitats and the environment. But Martens warns: "There is a portion of our modern society that organic agriculture can't sustain. That is the multinational chemical companies and the large international grain traders. Our factory system of animal production would also fail and would have to be replaced with much smaller and more diversified units.

"The costs of food production that are now being externalized would have to be paid directly by consumers instead of indirectly through farm subsidies, environmental damage, health care costs, and massive imports of cheap energy."

Whether farmer, homesteader, hunter, angler or conservationist, the organic approach awaits our future, a function of the "right livelihood" Wendell Berry articulated some years ago.

Bonding With a Kid (Goat)

Two weeks ago I offered a general interest report on goat packing. This week it's time to look specifically at how to turn a baby goat into a friend who will carry your pack. This comes about because we have two new kids on the place. Kid goats that is. They really caught us by surprise.

Gwyneth is our doe. She's out of a Spanish buck and a mostly-Alpine mother; she's well built and has good height (at least 30" at the withers) so while not a pack goat herself she has the size and conformation to produce young wethers that can carry most of your gear on the trail.

I knew she was pregnant, but not this pregnant! In the past she and our other does have been consistent in dropping their kids the last week of February or the first week of March. But Gwyneth gave us two nice black and white males a month early, which shows how much I was paying attention to her condition.

Delivery was uneventful and she didn't need any help. But I got her a shot of oxytocin from the Vet to make sure she was cleaned out properly. Then my son Bud and I each took some time to hold, handle, pet, talk to and generally try to socialize the two kids. That's a key factor in starting right with pack goats.

The thing about a goat is, he will bond to you, and follow you around like a dog if you raise him up right. That's important in a pack goat as you want him to keep up on the trail, willingly, not having to be dragged along like a recalcitrant burro. The first few weeks are crucial.

The surest way to bond with a goat is to become its mother. You do that by separating the kids from the mother at birth; you milk the mother morning and evening, and bottle-feed the youngsters at least 4 times during the 24-hour day.

Once you have a baby kid goat looking to you for milk you have a bonded goat. All this is very labor-intensive, however. Some folks I know have tried an in-between approach. They allow the kids to nurse initially from the mother. But a few days later they begin to separate the doe from the kids during the daytime. They then bottle feed the kids morning, noon and evening, returning them to the mother at night. They only do this for a week or two. They then let the mother back with the kids full time; just that short week of bottle feeding has bonded the kids to you.

With good handling a kid goat can become a pet even without bottle feeding. I have a wether named Buford who's about 8 months old. He's part La Mancha and part Boer; he comes running when he sees me and he would climb in your back pocket if you'd let him. I got him from some folks out on the Mimbres and I asked them if he was bottle-fed. "No," they said, "but we held him a lot when he was little."

So that's what you need to do with the young kids when they are still at the milk stage. Spend time in the pen with them, especially the young males, as they will grow larger than the does and make the best pack goats. Hold them, talk to them, make friends. And young kids, being playful, can be a lot of fun.

My first two pack goats were Hilda and Spike. They weren't related but they were about the same age. As baby kids they loved to jump up on things. I found it great sport to get down on all fours, so my back made a table about two feet off the ground. Those two kids would come running, jump up on my back, do little pirouettes, then jump off. Great sport! And it helped us to trust each other later, out on the trail.

Sometime in the first three months you will want to castrate the young buck and make him a wether. I always used to just cut the cojones off, spray the wound with disinfectant, and let the little guys get over it. But others in the family got on me about that, called the method barbaric, so now we use those special rubber bands you can buy at the feed store. In any event, unless you plan to use him for breeding, you want the young billy cut and the sooner the better.

At three months or so is a good time to get a collar on the young wether and get him leash trained. If he likes to be with you anyway, leash training comes easily to the young goat.

At 6 months to a year is a good time to get him used to a pack. Unlike a young horse or pack mule, it is seldom that a young goat will try to pitch the pack off. For a half-grown goat I'll use a dog pack first, then graduate to a real goat pack with sawbuck and panniers. I use jugs of water to give them a load, not too much a first, just enough to put some weight in the pack. Then take little hikes. If you have an older, trained, pack goat to work with it helps. Goats are very herd oriented and the young goat will want to keep up with the older one. Out on the trail they will try tricks like maybe rubbing the pack off on a tree. Just walk them through things, discipline gently as you would a good dog, and don't work them too hard. Try to make it fun for all.

Crossing streams is a trip; most goats detest water. But even more than that they don't like being left behind. If necessary, take him by the collar and strong arm him across. Try shallow streams first. He'll soon learn a stream crossing is nothing to fear.

A good pack goat is a fun companion, will go places a horse or mule can't go, and will take that 40 lb. backpack off your back. Not every young pack goat works out but the ones that do are well worth the time of training.

For further information, look up "pack goats" on The Web, and get a copy of *The Pack Goat* by John Mionczynski.

Dateline Cliff: The Fair by the River

The Grant County Fair, held each year in Cliff, New Mexico, can sure take up a week of your time. Oh a visitor can pick a day, drive out and spend a few hours watching the livestock shows, or the rodeo, or take in some rides at the carnival, then leave for home whenever he likes and call it good. But if your kid has two pigs entered in competition you're in for some daily chores, a lot of 60-mile round trips from Silver City (two a day), and a disconcerting view of the Gila River along the way.

Disconcerting? Well, every trip to the Fair takes you over the river bridge at Cliff; you can't help but slow up and take a look at the flow, and think: "There's some big ones in there, if I only had the time!"

It starts on a Tuesday when you load the pigs. My utility trailer could haul them, if pigs would leash train, and could jump like goats. They can't, so you have to borrow a stock trailer, starve the pigs that morning, then later in the day lure them into the low-rise chute with plenty of grain. A hungry pig will sell out for grain every time and we got our Duroc barrow and Hampshire gilt loaded and driven to the Fair. On the way we crossed over the river. The flow was high; too muddy for bass or trout but I already had the fever thinking about the possibilities for catfish and carp.

Wednesday son Bud got to take off school to weigh his pigs into the competition. You know who had to drive him out there. Each pig just barely made the minimum of 200 lbs., not a good sign as they would look small in comparison even in the lightweight class. Then we had to shear and smooth their hair down with clippers, shampoo and condition them to bring out muscle and sheen. They looked better – quite good in fact – but so did everybody else's and theirs were bigger – most of them – by 20 lbs or more. Meanwhile the Gila River was a mere walking distance away but there was no time to think about that.

Thursday Bud showed his pigs; the Duroc show, Hampshire show, and gilt show. He showed them well. Unlike last year, though, he was overmatched by superior stock and won nothing. This all took most of the day while the river flowed, still high and muddy, not far away.

Friday was the lamb competition. It figured to last till early afternoon, and afterwards, we were told, we could hunt for buyers and fill out disposition of sale papers for our stock. I was out there early to feed and water pigs then, once my chores were done, saw an opening to try my luck along the river.

The water was still murky, though down some, but the catfish didn't mind. I caught two middling-sized channel cats at the first hole. It was a cloudy morning, looked a little rainy though it never did, with no wind. I had hiked in and was of course beyond the roads and it was utter silence and solitude as I watched these tough little fish bend my pole and move

154

the line in the water. I was bait fishing with a fly rod and that made it sport and I beached each fish and let them go.

Things slowed up after that. But I worked several miles of river downstream and found good pools along the way and by noon had some lunch and three more channel cats under my belt. None was over about 14 inches though and I wanted more to brag on than that. So I took my time there after lunch, for this was a pool known to harbor carp. The gentle current and backwash swirl looked ideal and I was fully prepared for a 30-inch fish.

I was had. A small fish, probably another channel cat, kept stealing my bait; I not only never got him caught, when he was done my worms were gone. I was now out of bait with maybe an hour left before I would necessarily head back to the Fair to sell our pigs and buy a lamb. I sure didn't want to get caught late with no buyers left and me having to haul those pigs back home.

I always carry a fine mesh net and it wasn't far to the next hole. I caught three crawfish and a hellgrammite in short order and put the hellgrammite on a #6 hook. I put the creepy thing in some good looking water, knowing I didn't have long to wait.

I didn't wait long. Nothing beats a hellgrammite for bait and a strong fish grabbed it straightaway and swam upstream with the bait. I lifted that 9 ft. rod and nailed him to the hook.

For a while he felt like a trophy but that was my fly rod taking every pull, tug, and run of the fish and putting it all with feeling right into my hands. On the beach he was stout and muscular and glistened a silvery sheen. And I'd like to say this channel cat went 20 inches but it was probably more like 19. Fishing is such a benign state of wishful thinking; in subsequent recounts I probably did round it off to 20 inches, bragging on my best fish of the day to anyone not too bored to listen.

Nineteen or twenty, the fish went back in the water and I made long strides for the truck and a return to the Grant County Fair. There I sold one pig for $200 to a neighbor, bought the other one – our own pig – for the same price and our own use, plus a leggy lamb with a broad back from a kid Bud knew. Bud got the pig money ($400 in all) and this plus the lamb made two kids happy with a proper monetary reward for their six months of livestock care, feeding, and knowledge gained.

It would be two more days before the packer would come get the stock. Of course I had to make two trips a day to the fairgrounds to feed those pigs until the packer picked them up. But all said it wasn't a bad week. After all, I did manage to steal away for half a day of my own pursuit, catching six channel cats on a fly rod while doing my time at the Fair by the river.

Back into Wilderness with Pack Goats

I can't recall the exact date, but the middle of the night, first week of March, 2009, was not an opportune time to be birthing goats at our place.

The snow fell heavy and wet, turning everything outside to slush and mud. The nanny, Elizabeth, was having her first experience as a mother; meanwhile, Cherie and I had been spending most of our time at an Albuquerque hospital seeing our son through a slow recovery from a serious illness. When I got home that night to Grant County, I thought: "Best check on the hounds, chickens, goats, etc., before I see about some supper."

I knew Elizabeth was expecting, but not so soon! When I opened the door to the goat yard she already had a pair of them on the ground, in the wet snow, because the billygoat, Charlie, had pushed her out from under the lean-to. Some father! The kids didn't look too good, sprawled out on the ground and covered over with a wet snow, and Elizabeth was a picture of a nanny in distress.

I got the three of them in the barn and onto some dry straw. Once the little guys (I checked that part out straightaway) were dried off with a towel they perked right up, got to their feet, and began to nurse. Elizabeth, whom I had named for……..I can't recall……..was suddenly a picture of pride and satisfaction. I thought: "I'm back in the pack goat business."

I have been using goats as pack animals on and off since 1995. But I was left without a packer when my wonderfully tall, strong wether, Henry, died unexpectedly in 2008. Henry stood over three feet at the withers, could carry 50 lbs. all day long, and on a pack trip followed me around like a dog. Out on the trail there was nothing of the "reluctant burro" attitude about Henry. I figured to do as well with my new guys nursing Elizabeth. I promptly named them Henry II and Scuttlebutt.

The trick to raising a good pack goat is to get them bonded to you at an early age. The surest way to do this is to bottle feed the little beggars. That is also the most time consuming however, and you end up not only having to nurse the kids with a bottle, you than have to help keep the mother milked down on a twice-a-day milking schedule.

With a sick kid in a far-off city I knew I had more important things to do. And I knew I could gentle these two kids by another method because it worked with Henry I.

Every morning, after feeding, I'd let little Henry II and Scuttlebutt out of their pen. I'd lay in the grass and let them sniff around me, climb on me, and try butting me with their budding horns. I'd talk to them, pick each one up and hold him in my arms, and when at a few weeks they got old enough to eat some grain I would feed them out of my hand. They were soon as playful as a couple of puppies.

156

At one month I castrated them with a rubber band. This process takes about two weeks. They didn't like it much at the time but after the first day ignored the squeeze and, being just goats, never associated the initial discomfort with me. At three months they were weaned, growing like weeds (their father, Charlie, I'm sure weighs at least 200 lbs.) and as friendly a pair of black and white Spanish goats as if I'd raised them in the house.

Big Jon Finn bought Scuttlebutt, though the goat continued to live at my place, and from six months on we periodically worked the goats, first with a dog pack, then with a cross buck and empty panniers, then with the panniers having some weight. Nobody complained or failed to keep up so last week Jon, Bud and I lit out for four days in the wilderness on our first real camp-out with our new goats and with Bud in full good health once again.

We headed up a reach of the Gila River with I'm guessing about 25 lbs. on each goat which means Henry and Scuttlebutt were carrying more apiece than Jon, Bud, or myself. This of course is the whole idea of having a pack goat.

I feared a jackpot at the first crossing as goats are known to hate the water but with a firm hand on the collar they made it across without a major revolt. By the third or fourth crossing it was plain to them and us that river crossings were not to be feared. We hiked in about 4 miles and in spite of being just over a year old and about three-quarters grown our goats never faltered or lagged behind and we made a good camp in the canyon with plenty of shade and fishing holes within an easy hike upstream or down.

The weather held nice with plenty of sun but a lot cooler than in town. We tied the goats to a picket line at night but otherwise they wandered around camp and fed themselves and each day they followed us like dogs as we hiked the river and fished. Big Jon Finn with his deadly night crawlers got a 19-inch bass while Bud and I, respectively, got a 17-inch chub and a 17-inch rainbow on flies. Those were the biggest but we all caught bass and trout and chub and while the goats didn't help us catch the fish they weren't any bother either.

We saw just two other people in the wilderness. They remarked, "Hey, those are goats!" Indeed they were and on the fourth day we hiked out and again the goats carried most of the load while we all dodged two big rattlesnakes along the way. I figure Henry II and Scuttlebutt will mature at around 200 lbs., will carry about 50 lbs. apiece if need be, and even now as youngsters I can safely say they have us back into the wilderness with pack goats.

When Hay Harvest was a Country Sport

Having half a dozen goats, I have to keep hay in the barn. I do have some acreage where they can pasture at certain times of the year and, on the trail, as pack goats, they easily feed themselves in the forest. But in this arid climate it's easy to overgraze and strip a pasture, even with a few goats.

So hay is a staple and every month or two I stop by the feed store and load (and later unload) the trailer with 5 or 10 bales of alfalfa. They are 3-twine bales and so plenty heavy – at least 100 lbs. apiece – but, within limits, I don't mind the work. It takes me back to the days when I was employed as a professional harvester of hay.

It was the 1970s and I was a new resident of northwest Minnesota. This was way up there in Lake of the Woods County, near where Minnesota, Ontario and Manitoba merge; the human population was sparse, wolves, moose, deer and jackrabbits roamed the admixture of northern hardwoods, boreal forest, and broad flat farm fields. I worked for several of the better farmers in the region, including Bert and Randy Bergan, Ike McNeil, and especially George Swentik.

George farmed several thousand acres, all without a sack of store-bought nitrogen, potash, or phosphate; he fertilized with plow-down (green manure), controlled weeds with tillage, and pests with crop rotations, including summer fallow when the soil was worked on a given field but no crop was grown. Hay (mostly alfalfa) was a large part of this farming mosaic, as feed for his 100 head of beef cattle, as plow-down, and especially as a cash crop. George put up anywhere from 60 to 80 thousand bales a year, much of which he sold by the semi-load to dairy farmers in southern Minnesota who journeyed north a long way to load up with the best for their cows.

Into this large farm operation in 1971 wandered yours truly, who was trying – but only rarely succeeding – to write and sell hunting and fishing stories to the outdoor magazines. I didn't know a disk from a harrow, but, to make up for all those rejected manuscripts I hired out to George at $2.00/hour for "whatever needed doing on the farm." I survived only on blind luck.

Farm work, they say, is statistically the world's most dangerous form of industrial labor. I dug post holes, drove truck, plowed fields and did most every other thing you can do with a tractor, and somehow avoided ever turning a load (500 bushel or 30,000 lbs!) of wheat over into the bar ditch, or rolling the tractor, or getting my pants leg caught in the PTO (power take-off) which can maim you for life. I proved a fortunate if not particularly skilled farm hand, except for the hay harvest where I shined.

That figure of 60,000 to 80,000 bales mentioned earlier was not a misprint. George had literally thousands of acres in hay, and with two cuttings from good soil and the right amount of rain there were many tons of high quality protein growing in the fields each summer that had to be converted to rectangular bales weighing 75 to 100 lbs. apiece. This took a string of hay trailers – more than a dozen – each one 16 to 18 feet long with strong decking and 4" x 4" tamarack stringers that would support as many bales as a pair of skilled stackers could build up without losing the load.

It also took labor, which primarily meant myself and the Becklund boys, Gayle, Boyd, and Bruce. Gayle was the oldest and most experienced in farm lore and plenty stout, probably 6 feet and 190 lbs. Boyd even bigger – six-two and well over 200 lbs. and bull-strong. But over time it was the two scrawniest among us, me and Bruce – both about five-ten barefoot and 160 lbs. soaking wet – who got the job of stacking those trailers on the move, as the bales came up the chute, endlessly, from either a twine-tie or wire-tie baler, one of which George always kept working albeit the other one might be in the shop.

George taught us how to stack a trailer, an intricate process of building tiers of bales up and up such that they "tied in" as the load grew and with the top layers "weaned" to a peak that, done properly, held even a 10-tier load secure as it went down the road to the barn or a waiting flat-bed semi.

It was savagely hard work with the all-day lifting and heaving, sweating and scratching while wrestling with each bale, and swatting at horse flies, some of them the size of your thumb. Their bite, when successful, would pick you right up off the ground.

So we made a game of it, Bruce and I, and early on we thought 100 bales and a good secure load was an accomplishment. Then we built up to 125, then 150 (at 80 lbs a bale that's 6 tons!) on a trailer. As the stacks got higher word got around and people took to stopping along the county road to watch us work.

One day on a lark, me and Bruce stacked a trailer with 200 bales. It held together but didn't last long because Boyd and Gayle gave us the red-eye when they had to lower the load several tier to get it under the high wires and out of the field.

And one time, so help us, me and Bruce trailed and stacked 3,009 bales in a single day, working virtually non stop from 10 a.m. to 10 p.m. when darkness finally came and rising humidity made the hay to "tough" to bale. We knew it was 3009 bales because the counter on the baler said so. I've never heard of its equal and it meant we were not only skilled but tough as a boot. It prompted one bystander to comment to George:

"You really must have to feed those two guys?"

"Hardly at all," George said. "You give those boys a can of sardines and a banana and they'll go all day."

Alfalfa, averaging 15% to 20% protein, is still the premier livestock feed and the best of green manures when its stubble is turned in as a natural fertilizer. Even people have turned to alfalfa tablets as a health and nutrition supplement. Haying can be brutal work, but I recall the days we turned that work into a game, making the harvest of alfalfa a country sport worthy of memory.

Organic Farming: When Organic Wasn't Cool

Picture organic farming……..

Stereotype #1: the organic farm is relatively small (closer to 100 acres rather than 1000 acres). Stereotype #2: crop yields on the organic farm, like for wheat and oats, are about half of those achieved by those farmers using herbicide, pesticide, and store-bought fertilizer. Stereotype #3: due to the scanty yields, the organic crop is expensive at both ends – production by the farmer; purchase by the consumer. And yet………

I arrived in Lake of the Woods County, Minnesota, in 1971. What I wanted to do was make a living writing and selling outdoor stories to the "Hook & Bullet" press. I did over time see my byline here and there in the outdoor media but it was no "living" and I quickly offered myself up as farm labor to help pay the bills. I was readily hired; surprising as I owned up right off that I had never worked on a farm and didn't know a live furrow from a dead one. I worked for three farms through the 1970s; all three had the local reputation as owned and operated by "good farmers."

Bert and son Randy Bergen operated one of the larger farms in the county, surely over 1,000 acres. Very workmanlike and efficient, up to date on technique and equipment; when the local paper, the Baudette *Region*, wanted a farm quote for a story they'd often go talk to Bert.

Ike McNeal was an old-time producer who used to farm with horses. He kept his 200 cultivated acres in good shape and told me he "made money every year" with one 50-horse Massey-Ferguson tractor that was almost as old as him. The Bergen and McNeal farms both routinely used store-bought fertilizer plus herbicide and/or pesticide when needed. The third farm did not.

Farming several thousand acres was my neighbor George Swentik. Like Bert, Randy and Ike, wheat and oats were standard cash crops on the Swentik farm. But George also reserved a significant portion of his land to alfalfa, clovers and other legume hay crops that he sold in bales by the truck-load – flat-bed 18-wheelers – to southern Minnesota dairy farmers. And because he periodically plowed them down or tilled them in, these "green manures" allowed him the option of not using, or having to buy, store-bought fertilizer, which came in 50 lb. bags holding precise ratios of nitrogen, phosphorus, and potash.

I remember those bags oh so well! Each spring I hefted fertilizer, a bag at a time, by the multiplied ton for Bert, Randy, and Ike. As hard, physical labor it was on a par with stacking hay, but lacked somehow the undeniable panache that attended the hay harvest. Fertilizer in bags is just hard, dirty work!

In contrast, recovering or advancing fertility by the organic approach can not only restore soil, it can yield some nice days on the tractor as

161

well. I recall the late summer, circa 1975, when George set me to plowing down 160 acres of alfalfa in one remote field surrounded by Minnesota wilderness near an almost-gone community called Carp. It took me the better part of a week to turn that field with a three-bottom plow but I was hardly bored.

Wildlife gets used to the all-day pounding of a working 60-horse diesel tractor. Plowing disturbs and reveals innumerable mouse nests and that first evening two red fox came out onto the field, followed the tractor in the dead furrow, and snapped up mice as their terrain was altered.

The next evening a coyote joined the mouse hunt. He was a little less bold than the fox, followed the same dead furrow but further back, and over the course of the evening this coyote got his share of fat mice that the fox had missed.

The third evening a timber wolf stepped out of the woods and onto the field. He kept his distance, had no interest in hunting mice, but he was the first Minnesota wolf, though not the last, I saw in the wild. Deer were common, and one evening a bull moose came to the field to graze. It may be wishful thinking but I've come to believe that field was so productive of wildlife due in part to George's organic approach to farming. But was it organic farming?

In the decade I worked as a farm hand I never once heard George say the words "organic farm" or "organic farming" or "organic farmer." Organic agriculture was not yet cool. Or clearly defined. George controlled weeds with tillage, got fertility from green manure, and controlled pests with crop rotations. It was simply "smart farming" and was "better" – for the land, for the wildlife, for farm economics.

How about yield? .In the café, shooting the breeze, the good local farmers, including George, could report an average of 40 to 50 bushel/acre for wheat; 75 to 90 bushel/acre for oats. George's grain harvest sold at the same grain elevator at the same price as that of Bert, Randy, and Ike. And one year it all came together.

"I had some land in green clover and red clover and I plowed it down as summer fallow," George said. "I worked it in good and planted to wheat and oats and the measured yield that next fall was 80 bushel/acre for wheat and 131 bushel/acre for oats. This was on a little over 500 acres so it weren't no garden plot."

So much for stereotypes!

George Swentik is now semi-retired, raises some hay but that's about it. I now know the difference between a live furrow and a dead one and in retrospect think I learned some other things as well on the farm in northwest Minnesota, back before "organic farming" was cool.

Of Pigs, Trout and Big Box-Mart

You raise a son and you can't help but hope he will like the things you do. It's a chance you take because he may grow up to be a fine young man – maybe even finer than yourself at that age – and yet have entirely different interests. I like hunting and fishing and the rural life, but this is an age of video games, MP3 players, and something my own kid wants called an X-Box. I often have no idea what he's talking about.

We live on 12-acres with guns, hounds and fishing rods, a garden and farm animals. But how do you keep the boy down on the farm after he's seen Big Box-Mart?

This year my own son Bud had every reason to be discouraged by country living. He's in 4-H and had raised pigs for the County Fair two years running and had yet to get a ribbon let alone make the auction sale. Then, when we bought him two more pigs this spring, his barrow up and died from no apparent cause. And at the time he seemed like the better pig.

At the shooting sports this summer Bud had periodic trouble with his gun, lost confidence, and seemed destined to drop from the fifth-place finish he'd achieved at the district-wide contest the year before.

The drought hurt the fishing through the spring and early summer, and when it did start to rain it wouldn't stop and the rivers and streams turned high and muddy. My luck fishing was not impressive, his was worse the few times we got to go together, and last time out we hiked to a waterfall that had never failed and we both got skunked. Under the circumstances, it would be easy to see an 11-year-old lad turn from rural pursuits to the instant gratification of videos games, and ever more frequent trips to Big Box-Mart.

Still, he retained his work ethic with his remaining pig, a Duroc gilt. We bought a high protein product and he adjusted her feed periodically through the summer to get her big, fleshed out, but not so fat as to lose her form. He walked her every evening to muscle her up and get that big, round muscular butt and groove and dimple down the back and rump the judges like. By fair time she looked like she had a chance and his pig and the show were very much on his mind, Big Box-Mart or no. He wanted to win and admitted it and we had to caution him that the competition would be stiff and "those other kids have good animals too, Bud, and they have not been idle with their pigs."

In the Duroc event the barrows and gilts went against each other and the kids drove them around the ring and showed them off. The judge liked Bud's gilt right away and pulled her aside. Not quite as much as he liked one of the neutered red swine, but my wife heard one old timer in the stands say, "That judge will always take a barrow but that gilt is the better pig."

Maybeso. Or maybe not. Regardless, Bud got second overall among the Durocs – first among the gilts – which put him in the auction where on Saturday he showed her off again…… this time alone. The bidding was fierce and all hyped up by the callers and the auctioneer and Bud was nervous as any businessman on the ragged edge of a big-bucks deal. In the end his Duroc gilt went to a most generous soul for $2,100.00.

Earlier, in mid-summer, his best pig had died and he couldn't hit the bulls-eye with his gun. We got a new gun and got sighted in just in time for him to place second in the district shooting contest. And now with his surviving pig on the way to the packer he was in better financial shape than his parents. I suppose he'll want to spend some of his fortune on that mysterious X-Box but we told him at least half would be locked into his college fund. He said he was good with that, and showed some emotion when he said goodbye to the animal he'd worked so hard with and that had got him all that money. And he said, "Dad, I think I'll use some of the money to buy another good pig next year."

The streams are clearing now too and a couple of days later I snuck off to fish. I wanted to take Bud, to make it up to him for getting skunked last time out, but it was a school day. Of course I went to a different run of water. And every time I caught one I wished it was him that was having all that fun on the end of the line.

Oh, I've had better days, but I got 8 rainbows that jumped a lot, and 5 bass that fought well for their size. I got most of them with a Pistol Pete, but several on a bead-head wooly bugger, and on the way back to the truck tried hard for a fish of size. I had a few garden hackle and my theory was a big nightcrawler would draw a bigger fish than any fly.

Well my theory was flawed and small fish kept beating any large ones present to the worm and they were stealing my bait every time. I was out of time and nearly out of bait when so help me I caught a 13-inch rainbow on the last half of the last worm in the box. He jumped like the others, only bigger, and like the others was returned to the stream. Restored, I headed for the truck thinking, "If Buddy could catch one like that, on fly or bait, he'd go to Big Box-Mart for fishing gear instead of videogames and an X-Box his old man missed by two generations."

Home, he asked me how I'd done. I told him I caught 13 fish, most of them jumped, one was longer than a foot, and they were all still in the stream. And he said, "When are *we* going fishing again, Dad?"

Scythe: Hand-tool of Use and Satisfaction

I used to be a deckhand on a crane boat. This was in upstate New York on the famed Erie Canal and a deckhand on a crane boat gets assigned all kinds of labor. One day they set me to work clearing brush along the river with a scythe.

I was initially befuddled by the tool, a lengthy, twisted and convoluted contraption straight out of American Gothic. In a time of chain saws and various motorized brush-cutters, it seemed hopelessly antiquated. I knew chain saws and brush-cutters. But this scythe chopped erratically and soon wore me out though I sported my prime of nineteen years.

Ol' Fred, the craneman, could hardly believe my ignorance; once again he had failed to comprehend that I had not, like him, grown up farming with horses. He took the scythe and began to mow.

It was a revelation. With no more effort than sweeping the floor he efficiently sliced through great sheets of grass, weeds and brush, wielding an elongated instrument made for his hands and frame and seemingly no heavier than a broom. Then he handed it back to me.

"You don't chop, you sweep," he said. "Keep the blade parallel to the ground. Keep it close to the ground on the backstroke as well as pulling through. It's sharp; it'll cut without much effort. You told me, kid, you could paddle a canoe all day. This is easier."

Well it took a while to get the hang of it but he was right – pull through easily in a stroke level to the ground and with a sharp blade and the grass, weeds and brush magically sheer and lay in neat rows wherever you go. Logically, the body begins a rhythmic shift of weight from right to left and the blade does the work. The long handle means you don't have to stoop to work; this saves your back. An occasional brief stop to sharpen the blade was all the rest I needed.

"You're gettin' it, kid," he said.

Scythes have been around a long time. One source I looked up said the two-handed scythe began to replace the single-handed sickle in the twelfth century and was the tool of choice for grain, grass, or hay harvest until the 1850s when the McCormick reaper began to take hold. For grain harvest a version called the cradle scythe was preferred.

I saw one of these once at the Farmer's Museum in Cooperstown, NY. I can't picture it exactly but it looked like the usual scythe but with an extra long blade and four short wooden posts arranged along the cut so that as the grain fell it was "cradled" momentarily whence the laborer gave a little flip at the end of the stroke. This caused the cut of grain to lay out straight and bunched in what is known as a swath or wind-row.

The grain could then be more easily gathered in sheaths and stacked in shocks whence it dried before being thrashed, either by hand, or in

165

later times by a thrashing machine or combine. It is said that a good scythe man could cut, cradle and wind-row more than an acre a day.

I am told that there is an American style scythe and a European style scythe.

The American version is the one you see in antique stores and old movies, at the Farmer's Museum in Cooperstown and perhaps at the Farm & Ranch Heritage Museum in Las Cruces. It's the one I used along the Erie Canal. There is the long, rather stout wooden limb (called a snath), twisted so as to place the two handles in such a way as to allow you to sweep the blade parallel to the ground. The blade is 24" to 30" long and is rather heavy as well, weighing one to two pounds.

The European style is recommended in some current supply catalogs. I have yet to handle one myself, but the European model is described as having a lighter, straighter snath and a lighter blade. It may well have advantages for today's homesteader who is looking for a smaller hand-tool to replace that noisy, smelly, unreliable weed-eater in trimming brush and weeds around the place, rather than a larger scythe to swath an acre of grain per day.

Some year ago some folks here in Silver City owed us for some eggs and goat cheese they'd taken home. Instead of payment they suggested a trade for a scythe. I looked at the scythe, noted what good shape it was in, and readily agreed.

Since then I have used it only occasionally, but usefully every time. After our hand-harvest of the corn it is an easy matter to sheer off the corn stalks with the scythe and haul the remnant vegetation to the goats and chicken flock.

After the summer monsoons I get after the heavier weeds and mow them down with the hand-tool. These shuckings, too, go to the goats and the chickens.

My wife is vigorous in her pursuit of weeds around the place. She wants everything trimmed and uses one of those gas-powered, string-cutter, weed-eaters. But the weed-eater is noisy, smelly, and needs about $80 in tune-up costs every year. I'm thinking she could do as well – even better – if she learned how to use the scythe.

The scythe is not noisy, smelly or polluting. It is wonderful exercise and wrestling with a weed-eater can't compare with the rhythmic conditioning one gets in scythe work. But the tool must be kept sharp.

I have merely honed mine with a whetstone. I am told however, that a good scythe requires periodic "peening." That is blacksmith talk for flattening the blade with an oval anvil and ball-peen hammer. Then you give the final honing with the stone. I still have much to learn in scythe work.

In a 1979 essay, Wendell Berry wrote: "(The scythe) is the most satisfying hand tool I have ever used." And Berry is a student of farm tools of the hand.

166

The next time that damned weed-eater won't start, give it the boot. Transfer the cost to fix it to a tool that is ready anytime you are. Google "farm scythe" and you will find supply houses that still handle this tool for the ages.

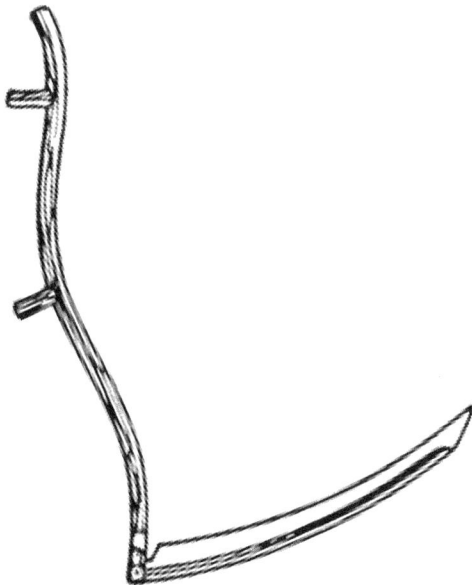

Some Thoughts on Spanish Goats

Long before I had any interest in goats I lived amongst them for several months. This was in south Texas down along the Nueces River and at the ranch I worked on that summer there were a number of animals that, for me, were a lot more interesting than goats. Like horses, and beef cattle, and alligators, and alligator garfish, and 50 lb. catfish, and hound-dogs and coyotes and golden eagles and quail. Any and all these critters had a lot more to offer than the ragged band of some 120 goats that ranged about the line camp where I lived.

For one thing they smelled (I learned later it was just the bucks that had the odor). It wasn't a bad smell really, but you knew by the smell, or lack of smell, when the goats were in close by the windmill getting a drink, or out on the range. Also, there were a couple of does I had to milk, since we were 25 miles from the nearest store, and on occasion we would butcher a kid. I liked the milk and the cabrito (still do) but the milking and the butchering were chores, not like saddling up, working cattle, or fishing for those big catfish.

Nonetheless, when you live with 120 goats for several months you remember certain things about them. They were medium sized – I'd guess they averaged 28 to 32 inches at the withers, does to bucks – and they were tough. They lived entirely off the desert scrub where they ranged, and stayed fit and healthy on the diet. They could run and bound and climb in a way most dairy goats cannot. And they did a good job of fending off the coyotes. I don't believe any of these goats had lop ears like a Nubian, but many had semi-erect ears that they would carry folded forward, as if they were shading their eyes, and some had prick or fox ears like an Alpine. They had coarse, straight, longish hair; more hair than most dairy goats but not like that of the Angora or Cashmere. The does had horns that most resembled an Alpine's. But the few old bucks in the herd had great horns, long, curved, scimitar-shaped racks; these bucks could scratch an itch on a hip just by cocking their heads. They came in all colors but parti-color (black with white patches) was the most common. I asked the foreman one time what kind of goats they were and he said they were "meat goats." When I asked the breed he said: "Spanish."

I left the ranch, years went by, and goats scarcely crossed my mind. Then a son was born, and to give him better milk than money could buy we got an Alpine/Nubian doe named Jesse. She was wild as a March hare but I tamed her down by keeping her in a pen without food till she'd eat out of my hand. She was bred to an Alpine buck and had two doe kids, Gwendoline and Hilda. Raw goat's milk proved even better than advertised and Jesse produced enough for the whole family. I kept Hilda and traded Gwendoline for a mostly Toggenburg buck, Spike, four months old. I castrated this buck. Then, after reading the book *The Pack Goat*, I put modest loads on Hilda and Spike and took them on several trips into the mountains. I begin to realize that goats are useful for a lot of things and that they are every bit as interesting as horses, coyotes, and maybe even hound-dogs and 50 lb. catfish.

I began to think about breeding, raising and using pack goats. All the information I could find said I needed big, leggy animals. So I hunted for goats with size. I bought an Alpine doe named Paint who stood 32 inches at the withers and looked promising for breeding. Then a woman from Reserve, New Mexico, called and began talking up her Toggenburgs. They were registered, she said, and she milked them twice a day and used the milk to bottle feed beef calves. She said the calves grew better on goat's milk than the milk of their own mothers and by weaning the calves on goat's milk she had cow's milk to sell. She said these Toggenburgs were "money makers any way who sliced it." I told this woman I wanted a couple of goats for packing into the wilderness and asked how big her goats were. She said they were "pretty good sized."

I met this woman outside Silver City and she had a four year old buck and a six month old buck for me to look at. The older buck was smaller than my newly acquired Alpine doe. The buck kid didn't look too promising either but I felt bad about the long drive the woman had made and, though I'd made no promises, I gave her $30 for the young buck. When I got him home he was smaller by several inches than my mostly Toggenburg wether, Spike, who was a month younger. The young buck from Reserve went into the freezer – not a bad trade at $30. The woman from Reserve had the right idea for her business, raising small goats that didn't eat much but gave lots of milk, but my goat herd hadn't grown at all.

I kept looking. One day, the man who'd sold me my Alpine doe, Paint, told me about a guy named Raines who had some goats near Virden, New Mexico. I called and asked about these goats and Mr. Raines said he had some kids he could sell that were "mostly Spanish." I told him I wanted goats for packing and asked him how big they were. Sure enough, he said they were "pretty good sized."

This didn't sound like a good recommendation to me and I recalled the Spanish goats I'd known in south Texas which weren't real big. But on a hunch I went down there.

Mr. Raines had about 15 does, about half with kids, on a pasture right on the state line between Virden, New Mexico and Franklin, Arizona. Turned out these goats really were "pretty good sized." The does were sized about like Hilda, running perhaps 30 inches at the withers, and the lone buck who ran with them was built like a jeep, had to be at least 3 feet at the withers, and had a great Spanish rack, long, curved, scimitar-shaped horns that allowed him to scratch a hip just by cocking his head. He was one of those bucks that when you got in the pen with him you sure hoped he was friendly.

These goats were all parti-colored (white on black) with longish hair, coarse but straight. They had semi-erect ears that they would move around in various positions but which they usually carried folded forward, as if they were shading their eyes. Except for averaging a larger size, they very much reminded me of a bunch of goats I'd known in south Texas many years before. Mr. Raines said the buck was "half Spanish, half Toggenburg." I must have looked disbelieving as this big buck did not have Toggenburg horns, hair, color, or ears. Mr. Raines added, "He don't show the Toggenburg except it helps give him his size." He said the does were all "pure Spanish." The whole bunch, buck included, looked "pure Spanish," to me, but assuming the buck did have some Toggenburg in him, this made the kids on the pasture "mostly Spanish," just like he'd told me on the phone.

I looked at these goats and I knew I was going to buy a couple of them. True, I could not recall that anyone had used Spanish goats for packing before, at least not in the USA. And I knew I was looking at goats raised on range; they were bonded to open spaces, not people. But they were alert, active, agile, and just had a great "look" to them. And anything out of that buck ought to have size. Whatever trouble I might have turning them into pack goats, I knew they would not be barn potatoes.

We herded the whole lot into a pen and roped and tied a four month old buck and a nine month old wether (needless to say they wouldn't lead). I paid Mr. Raines $35 for the buck and $50 for the wether. I named the wether Franklin and the buck Virden; we lifted them into the pickup and I took them home.

I never did try very hard to tame Virden. Since his only purpose would be to breed does I didn't really care if he bonded to me or not. As it stands he'll follow me around but always keeps an arm's length away. With Franklin I did the same thing I'd done with Jesse – I kept him in a pen without food till he got hungry enough that he would eat out of my hand. It didn't take very long. Even a range goat who's never been handled will sell out for grain and some good alfalfa hay. Once he was coming to me to get fed it wasn't hard to get him to lead, accept a pack, and all the rest.

I took Franklin and Spike on a four day trip into the Gila Wilderness when Franklin was about 18 months old. It wasn't a hard trip but it included a 1500 foot climb out of a steep canyon on a warm day. I knew Spike was up to it but it was the first real test for Franklin. He did fine. He was by this time just as tame as Spike. He carried his load (about 35 lbs.), never lagged, hung around camp, and just basically did his job. With maturity I figure he'll be up to a 50 lb. load – maybe more – and some hard hiking.

Meanwhile, I bred Virden to Hilda. Out of that breeding I kept a wether named Calvin. He's about 30 inches at the withers at ten months old, was bonded with grain and alfalfa just like Franklin. He's been on day hikes and it looks like he, too, will make a pack goat. He may never be as big as Franklin (36 inches at 24 months), or Virden (36 inches at 18 months) but I figure most anything I breed to Virden will produce wethers that will reach the 34 inch height *The Pack Goat* author John Mionczynski marks as the desired minimum for a mature (4 year old) packer. Size isn't everything in a pack goat of course, but so long as Virden's around it's one factor I think I can call a given at my place.

One question still begs to be answered: What is a "Spanish" goat? Well, the original Spanish goat would have to be the Spanish Ibex of the Pyrenees. This wild goat may well be the progenitor of what we call the Spanish goat today. In *The Pack Goat*, John Mionczynski has an interesting comment on the Spanish goats of Catalina Island, off California: "These goats, left to free-breed by the Spanish in the 16th century, remained until the 1980s as a clue to the appearance and gene pool of the Spanish goat of the days of exploration....[they] bore a hearty resemblance to the wild Spanish Ibex."

There appears to be a true-breeding strain of Spanish goat called the Murciaga. At a filling station a few years ago I met a rancher who had a whole stock trailer full of these uniformly compact, russet-red goats.

These speculations aside, I think it safe to say that the so-called Spanish goat of the American Southwest (which, incidentally, easily outnumbers all the dairy goats in the nation) is a type rather than a breed. One rancher, Mr. James Barton of Sonora, Texas, told me: "The goats we call `Spanish' are descended from goats the conquistadors brought over from Spain. Some went wild and evolved through time into a tough, range goat that we raise today for meat and hair."

Mr. Barton raises both Spanish and Cashmere goats and he said the two "breeds" are closely related. "Some Spanish goats will grow that special hair, some won't. The ones that do we call Cashmere."

Of course, ranchers have been constantly refining the Spanish goat to improve their meat or cashmere producing capabilities. The latest trend is to cross South African Boer goat with Spanish goat to get a faster gain on kids raised for meat. Mr. Barton recognizes the qualities of the Boer as a meat goat, but maintains that the Spanish goat will always have its place.

"The Spanish goat is like the Texas longhorn," he said. "He'll do better on less than any of his kind. Without supplemental feeding, the full-blood Boer won't hold up under our range conditions. The Spanish goat will [hold up]; he's not out there waiting for a handout."

Mr. Barton said his own Spanish goats average about 200 lbs. for the bucks, about 150 lbs. for the does. There are larger breeds than the

Spanish meat goat, but 200 lbs. for a mature buck or wether is within the range desired for goats that pack.

Like the Spanish goat, the pack goat may be seen as a type rather than a breed. To date, quality pack goats are almost entirely of the dairy goat breeds, or mixtures thereof. But it will be interesting to see if the tough, resilient Spanish goat of the American Southwest becomes a part of the mix that may eventually produce a new breed: the Pack Goat.

Photo by Jan Haley.

FISHING

Angling for the Gila's Native Fish

Books, articles, columns and reports on sport fishing in the Gila River drainage of southwest New Mexico invariably involve the pursuit of non-native species, one or more of which are now present over all of the upper Gila watershed. Indeed, there are currently more non-native species (at least a dozen) than native species in this section of the drainage. Among these non-natives, the most popular with anglers include: smallmouth bass, channel catfish, flathead catfish, brown trout, rainbow trout, hybrid trout (rainbow mixed with cutthroat and/or Gila trout), and carp.

This column is one of the few outlets in New Mexico outdoor writing where incidents of catching the Gila's nearly-forgotten native species are noted. I've related some anecdotes and experiences but I've never taken a comprehensive look at the Gila's native fish as sport. So let's see what we've got for native species in the Gila; find out which ones you may fish for and how; and consider, how do these fish compare to the more popular non-natives as game fish?

A 2007 report from New Mexico Department of Game & Fish lists the following native fish species as occupying the New Mexico portion of the Gila historically: longfin dace, Gila chub, headwater chub, roundtail chub, spikedace, loach minnow, speckled dace, Colorado pikeminnow, Gila topminnow (all these are "minnows" though not all are minnow-sized); desert sucker, Sonora sucker, razorback sucker (sucker family); and Gila trout *(Salmonid)*.

That's 13 species. However, the authors note that neither the pikeminnow (which may reach 50 lbs.+) or razorback sucker has been documented in New Mexico, albeit it is considered they may well have entered our state "seasonally" in historic times. Anyway, they are not here now and five of the "minnows" are minnow-sized leaving us anglers with six native fish (three chubs, two suckers, and a trout) as possible game. Let's throw each one a bait, lure, or fly and see what we find.

Regarding the chubs, the species are a sticky wicket for the laymen angler who tends to lump them all together as "Gila chub." The true Gila chub (Gila *intermedia*) in New Mexico is found only in the upper headwaters of Turkey Creek, also in a scattering of similarly isolated locales in Arizona. They are fully protected at both the state and federal level and reach, at best, 10" in length. I'm sure they'd take a small fly but they're too scarce and too small to draw any serious angler interest and are, like the Chihuahua chub of the nearby Mimbres River, a scarce novelty that the average angler and general public knows hardly at all.

The roundtail chub (Gila *robusta*) and the headwater chub (Gila *nigra*) are another matter; they can reach 20" in length and, more-so than the Gila chub, have that streamlined, athletic look that says "game!"

They used to be one species. I've seen pictures of both and have caught a good many and, to me, they still are one species (I can't tell them apart). I'm sure modern genetic analysis comes into play (too much knowledge can be a dangerous thing), but a main-line difference seems to be, if a specimen is found in one of the forks of the Gila it's a headwater chub; if found downstream in the mainstem Gila it's a roundtail chub. Otherwise, to me, the separation of this fish into two species is the creation of a distinction without a difference,

These chub are not uncommonly caught in all three forks but appear now rare in the mainstem Gila; the roundtail variety only is being considered for Federal ESA listing. Both are on the New Mexico "State Endangered" list.

I've caught roundtail/headwater chub to 16 inches. They readily hit fly, bait or lure and fight like a wild trout...for about 20 seconds. At that point the chub seems to say: "I can't get away; may as well turn on my side and go ashore and get someone to turn me loose." And it works; they seem to know they're "endangered" and can't be kept!

So the roundtail/headwater chub is worthy, game to a point, and hopefully can find some population recovery below the forks. You probably wouldn't keep one even if it was legal (they have those difficult floating bones like a sucker) but the males are wonderfully colorful with bright red fins during the spring spawn.

We are left with the desert sucker (*Catostomus clarki*) and the Sonora sucker (*Catostomus insignis*) and the Gila trout. The suckers resemble one another and I confess that for years I never knew or cared which was which. But they're really quite different. The desert sucker has a "flat" mouth it uses to scrape algae and other plant life off of rocks and the bottom; the Sonora sucker's mouth looks like the end of a garden hose and they go after insects, "bugs," and various other aquatic life of similar size and thus the Sonoran sucker is the angler's choice.

Both suckers are said to reach 30 inches in length but a 2-foot Sonora sucker is the largest in my record book (my son, Bud, has caught a 26-inch specimen). Bait works of course but what's neat is the way the Sonora sucker will take a slow-drifting fly and then battle you all the way to the bank. They fight like a carp, with great strength, long steady runs, and lots of endurance. Neither sucker is endangered but if I'm going to kill a Gila fish to eat I'll start with a catfish and leave the suckers with their floating bones alone.

The Gila trout (*Oncorhynchus gilae*) is now merely threatened rather than endangered (under ESA rules and definitions) and you can fish for them in roughly a half-dozen streams in the Gila National Forest. Since they readily breed and hybridize with rainbows and cutthroats some have said they are simply a color phase of *Oncorhynchus mykiss* and we should leave it at that. But I was up Black Canyon the other day and caught four of these "lesser rainbows" and while they didn't jump they

177

were at 10" the most frenetic, fast in the water fighters I've known. Even a 19" brood-fish of the species hooked at the forks one day nearly climbed out of the water to get my wooly bugger and tussled like a foul hooked eel till finally beached..

It must be noted that some fishers have no use for the Gila's native fish; the chubs and suckers are "trash" – in their view – while the Gila's native salmonid "never gets any size" (not true). Conversely, some biologists would like to eviscerate the Gila of all non-natives; they "pollute" the biome and "don't belong."

The resolution (if there is one) of that debate awaits another column. For now I'll simply say that I believe the non-natives are here to stay (though perhaps under a different management regimen), while the sport fisher should be happy to add the roundtail/headwater chub, the Sonora sucker, and the Gila trout to their game list.

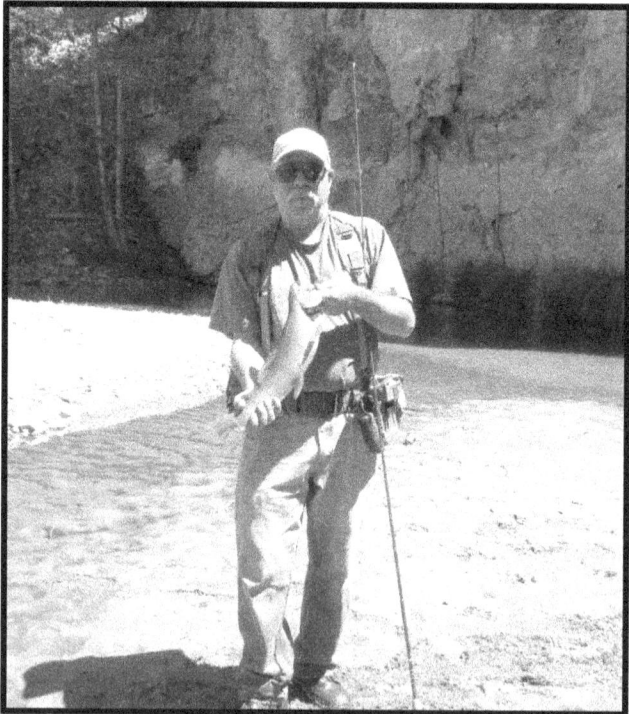

Gila Trout.

Good Time for Armchair Fishing

Winter has not only arrived, it has set up camp. Here at the place we have seen a low in the single digits on more than one occasion and snow is piling up in the high country of the Gila National Forest. The water is too cold for catfish or carp and the streams too high and muddy for bass and trout. The weather is great however for armchair fishing. Three recent publications come to mind.

Instinctive Fly Fishing by Taylor Streit (Lyons Press, 212 pgs. $24.95 hardcover) comes well recommended simply by the reputation of the author – the man is one of the best known anglers in the Southwest. In this book he attempts to cast through the windy mythology and overdone technology that clouds the sport to help you improve your game and better enjoy fish on a fly. He succeeds admirably.

Streit writes that he has been a fly fisher for 35 years but it was only when he took up guiding as a profession that he, by necessity, really learned how to catch trout.

"Twenty-five years of guiding," he says, "have shown me that the keys to fly fishing success are usually just common-sense rules of Mother Nature: keep the sun at your back and your fly in the water; and think like a predator."

My sentiments exactly lo these many years, but Streit has thought of some things I hadn't.

For example, I've been inclined to keep the sun at my face, to avoid my shadow on the water. Streit points out that you want the sun shining in the fish's eyes, not yours; of course you avoid the shadow of a slanting sun by getting low on the bank as you approach and cast. All that goes with "thinking like a predator." A good angler is a hunter with a rod instead of a bow or gun.

The author agrees with all of us that a hatch stimulates the angler as well as the fish, but he says that matching the hatch is overdone:

"I remember one still and misty morning on a lake in southern Colorado when a huge midge hatch came off. They were rising everywhere, but I was having little luck getting any of them to see and take my minuscule imitation amongst the gazillion flies. I switched to a black Woolly Bugger, dragged it in front of those rising fish, and caught one after another."

Streit has an interesting casting tip. The number one fault in the usual casting stroke is breaking the wrist. Lay the index finger rather than the thumb along the top of the handle, he says, and it immediately firms up the wrist and the stroke. He suggests this approach also improves accuracy, but says it will short you on distance when you want a longer cast. I've found I can cast a similar if not particularly impressive distance whether the finger or thumb is on top of the handle, but Streit is right that

179

the finger grip does reduce the tendency to break the wrist; although, I hasten to add; nobody should take casting lessons from me.

The book is simply filled with useful information, clearly presented, that serves to de-mystify fly fishing. What Streit ultimately wants to pass along however, is not a whole new set of rules or instructions, but a mindset that will have you hunting trout instinctively and successfully. This book is a good first step. Step two, Streit would agree, is to take the information with as you spend a lot of time along the waters.

If *Instinctive Fly Fishing* is a literate "how-to" book, *Flyfisher's Guide to New Mexico* by Van Beacham (Wilderness Adventures Press, 434 pgs, $28.95 softcover) is its "where-to-go" equivalent. Within its pages, the author covers literally thousands of miles of streams in the Land of Enchantment.

There is nothing fancy here. In orderly fashion the author, another northern New Mexico fly-fishing guide, takes you to the myriad waters of the state, tells you how to access them, reveals what fishing you'll find there, the particulars of the habitat, and how to fool the local fish.

The chapter on southwest New Mexico is written by yours truly; revealing where-to-go is a thing one does with mixed emotions. In short, this book tells you where they are. It's still up to you to catch them, and both Beacham and I hope you let most of them go.

Streit and Beacham are both good writers, and better fishers than most of us in our dreams. The best of information however, needs a respite such as that provided by the evocative volume. I recommend *Holy Ghost Creek* (University of New Mexico Press, 126 pgs, $23.95 hardcover) by Frank Weissbarth.

This slim book is a collection of essays that subtly trail the author's adventures seeking wild trout in the small remote streams of northern New Mexico. He likes the same kind of water I do.

"Solitude and fine fishing can often be found together on small streams," Weissbarth writes. "They seldom coexist on big rivers."

In one essay, the author perceptively explores how the hunter, or the angler who hunts fish, sees the world as the non-hunter does not, and suggests that "when the last hunter or fisherman passes from the scene, a large segment of the natural world will pass from human sight."

Elsewhere, Weissbarth says: "There are things beneath the surface of the river I will never know. There is not time enough to learn them and the river is always changing. But sometimes, in a rare day, for a few moments or hours, the barrier between water and land vanishes and I see the trout in their watery world ...."

What else the author sees at Holy Ghost Creek, and other streams in the northern part of the state, can be found in an evening of good armchair fishing. It will be time well spent in winter, till the insects hatch and the fish start to feed come spring.

Flies, Wet and Dry, in Arizona

If you have a kid in school, you want to take advantage of "fall break." Coming as it does in mid-October in southern New Mexico, it is the perfect opportunity for family time in the great outdoors. You don't want a chance like that to get away.

Two years ago this family took fall break to tour southwest Colorado and northwest New Mexico. We didn't hunt or fish but saw some great country and I wrote it up in this column. I hope some of you have had the chance to follow our footsteps there.

Last October we went to the Deep South – Georgia and the west coast of Florida. We hunted (wild boar) and fished (snapper and redfish) and took a canoe trip. We found great sport and I hope my write-up caused some of you to travel and try something like it.

This year it was a trip to the White Mountains of Arizona. That's just a few hours from where most of us live; sometimes we overlook the obvious in outdoor sport.

Springerville, Arizona, sits in a bowl (called Round Valley) of mountain grasslands at 7,000 feet just over the New Mexico line. Greer, Arizona, is in the White Mountains at 8,500 feet and not far away. Between the two run the headwaters of the Little Colorado River. We rented a cabin near its banks on the X Diamond Ranch.

On the X Diamond you can fish a mile or so of private water or hike upstream into a portion of the Apache National Forest. Generally, there is a fee on the private reach but not this time. "There's not much water in the stream this fall," our hostess said. "It's so low I'm not going to charge you the rod fee."

That sounded like a roundabout way of saying, "Don't be surprised if you get skunked." But with a free stream and nobody else fishing I was going to give it a go regardless. Young Bud was game, too. "I can't wait to try fly fishing," he said.

The Little Colorado was indeed low, but I've caught lots of trout in smaller streams in the Gila National Forest. The water was icy, as was the air and with all wading gear at home we had no option but to wade wet. We came to the first crossing and stepped into the flow. Bracing what! And just below was a little pool easing under an overhang of brush. I tossed a nymph in there and got a hit but never had him on.

Bud and I had been doing some practice fly casting in the side yard. The next pool provided an opening and Bud stepped up for his first attempt at catching a fish on a fly. Like most any beginning fly fisher – and many veterans for that matter – he spent too much time false casting and not enough time with his fly in the water. But he snuck up on the little pool like I told him to, got his fly to the water without splashing the surface, and it wasn't his fault that nothing would take.

181

At other pools he showed he could make a decent roll cast, before cold feet sent he and his mother back to the cabin. I carried on for another hour. I found some deep water behind and below some beaver dams. With fall colors all around and the sky still clear blue, I got two small rainbows on a wooly bugger and a brown about a foot long that got loose in the shallows before I could get my hand on him. Well, I would have turned him loose anyway.

Numb feet sent me back to the cabin for lunch. But toward evening I went alone upstream. I found a nice run just below where two flows came together; there were rising trout there. I confess I have gotten complacent on my local waters, content to catch most everything on flies that sink. But this seemed a classic rise. I tied on a parachute Adams, cast upstream; it floated downstream and I got a nice rainbow on the first pass. I had largely forgotten the pleasures of trout that come to the surface to take the fly. But my catch soaked my fly and thereafter it wanted to sink. I reached into my vest for floatant, then remembered I didn't have any; or, if I did, it was home in an alcove with hip boots and waders.

Upstream I found another beaver dam. The wind was up again but whenever it slacked and the surface calmed, trout would rise on the pond. I false cast to dry the Adams, then lofted it out there. The white "parachute" stood out on the surface and I guess the fish could see it from below because before it could sink a nice one rolled next to the fly, missed it once, then took it down. This was the best fish of the trip, near 15 inches, with nice rainbow colors, and it hardly mattered that the wind subsequently came up, ruffled the surface, and I never saw another rise.

The next day was warmer, still sunny, with less wind early in the day. We went for a horseback ride, another first for Bud. It lit him up, riding through the pines. After lunch, and a nap, he was ready to try the fly rod again. We hiked back up to that beaver pond. I'd told a big story about that 15-incher the evening before and said I anticipated more of the same. Plus I'd picked up some floatant. "When the wind was down, they were rising everywhere," I said.

But they weren't this evening. Bud and his mother shared a rod and both cast well enough, I thought, to fool a rising trout. And when the Adams didn't work they tried the wooly bugger. None of us could get a hit with flies wet or dry, even with the pond flat calm.

When the wind came back near dark it got cold and Cherie hiked back to the cabin. Bud and I lingered along the stream, and found a rising fish in some slow water underneath some leaning trees. I saw no way to cast to this fish, so I floated the Adams down the chute, feeding out line to avoid any drag on the fly. Bud watched my strategy, and when the fish hit, said, "It worked, Dad!"

Bait Fishing with a Fly Rod

I haven't been fishing this winter but that doesn't mean I haven't thought about it or looked for an excuse to write about it in this column. It all came together with the latest catalog that arrived in the mail from Frank Amato Publications.

The Amato book list is so much identified with fly fishing that I had to do a double take when I saw among his new offerings the title *Bait-Fishing for Trout* by one Terry Sheely. I determined it was a real how-to book on the subject, not a joke, and the author apparently was still alive, he and his book seated and holding their own midst volumes by Steve Raymond, Harry Murray, and Frank Amato himself; anglers who wouldn't admit to bait fishing trout since grammar school.

I haven't read *Bait-Fishing for Trout* so this is not a book review but I am intrigued by the various debates that arise whenever anyone mentions or writes about bait and flies in the same conversation or paragraph. What's the fuss all about?

Modern sport fishing began shortly after World War II with the advent of spin casting which allowed even a novice to throw a lure 100 feet or more without much fear of a backlash. Since then the typical angler grew into the sport by bait fishing as a kid then advancing to spin casting with artificial lures at a roughly young adult period. Some then "advanced" from spin fishing to fly fishing and it is fly fishing that gets most all the press; by the numbers, fly fishing books simply overwhelm anything to do with bait or spin fishing every year.

But as to the fishing, the fly fisher is a rarified minority. According to the U.S. Fish & Wildlife Service, out of some 35 million American anglers, about 3 million are fly fishers. That's not quite 10%. And bait fishermen are still the most numerous of the fresh water fishermen (apparently, many anglers forgot to "advance"). So if fly fishing has a rarified quality that produces many books and some literature, and if at the same time bait fishing attracts more anglers and produces more fish, why not combine the two approaches at times by bait fishing with a fly rod?

The sport offers a nice blend of fishing pleasures. Even a medium grade of fly rod has the flex to magnify the power and animation of the fish and the resiliency to wear a truly big fish down. A 4 to 6 wt. graphite rod, 8 to 9 feet, can handle anything available in the local area, the 4 wt. for trout and bass in streams, a 5 wt. or 6 wt. for catfish, carp, or stripers in larger waters.

I have a lower grade Orvis rod that initially was a disappointment. Granted it was one of their cheaper models; still, it was an Orvis, 9 feet and 6 wt., and I expected a snappier backcast and subsequent "shoot" of the line. I eventually caught on to the fact the rod had a very slow tip and with practice and a slowed rhythm I learned it would throw a fly with a decent loop and distance. But it was better than decent at casting bait.

Here the slow or soft tip was a benefit as I could toss out a nightcrawler, crawfish or hellgrammite to a soft landing without the bait coming off the hook. As to casting bait with a fly rod, the roll cast is the standard throw; with practice it can achieve surprising distance and one becomes adept at placing a real fly in the right spot with a soft landing. For stream fishing I like to use the bait with no sinker; roll cast a quartering throw upstream into the current; keep an almost tight slack as the "fly" comes down stream and watch for the take. For a really long cast, use a weight, pull out a length of slack line, and let the sinker carry the cast to that distant pool.

In 2010 on a Gila canoe trip I stood on a high bank and eyed a distant pool that had all the habitat to house a big catfish. With a crawfish I caught myself for bait, and a sliding sinker to give the line some extra throw weight, I lofted the bait a good 30 feet and centered the pool. When I hooked him he bowed the rod like a fish a yard long. That's the fun of a fly rod, and the challenge. I did have to work him in and out for some time but that cheap Orvis put a relentless spring and pull on the line and I never let the fish rest. He came to the beach in 20 minutes at two feet long instead of three and later that day fed three over the campfire.

It was indeed a catfish and a flathead catfish at that. The manager of a catfish farm in Mississippi told me the species was too predatory – read cannibalistic – to raise commercially but, he said, "There's no finer eating fish swims fresh water."

The artificial fly or lure will never equal the real thing the fish normally eats in his home water. It may look real and, manipulated by skilled hands, may act real, but the live reality, properly hooked and presented, is the ultimate attractor and to boot it smells right to the fish. I'll always prefer the challenge of artificial flies for bass and trout but I'll never be too proud to see the advantage to bait for catfish and carp whenever the water's murky, and the special pleasures to be had fishing that bait with a fly rod.

.

Farm Ponds and Fabulous Fishes

At first glance, to a fisherman, a pond might seem less impressive, and less productive of fish, than a lake. And more prosaic than a stream or river. On second glance, that may just depend upon the pond.

First I guess we'll have to take a stand and distinguish between a pond and a lake. I was going to say something like 60 surface acres seems a good separation and after looking around I'm thinking that's pretty close to good. Henry Thoreau after all called his favorite water "Walden Pond"; he wrote that it was 61 surface acres in size, and it's a good thing for him he called it a pond because "Walden Lake" doesn't quite get it. Walden Pond is cool; Walden Lake? Golly, I don't know if Henry would have ever found a publisher!

Anyway, I'm here to say that for this story a pond is a small lake of less than 100 acres whose waters are essentially still rather than flowing like a stream.

In a chapter in *Walden* called "Higher Laws', Henry takes on the subject of hunting, meat eating, animal rights, etc., and while somewhat ambivalent throughout the discussion, he has clearly got the vapors about killing and/or eating animals, the main objection being that hard labor caused him to have to eat "coarsely." The coarse part of the meal, of course, being the flesh of animals. But for Henry, animals apparently were on some other level than fish.

"Fishing," he confesses, "still recommends itself to me." And the best fish in Walden Pond he describes like this: "I am always surprised by their rare beauty, as if they were fabulous fishes......it is a wonder that they are caught here, that in this deep and capacious spring.....this great gold and emerald fish swims.....Easily, with a few convulsive quirks, they give up their watery ghosts .....like a mortal translated before his time to the thin air of heaven."

Written by a true transcendentalist; keep the meat, free the spirits; no catch-and-release angler was this bard of Concord! And the great gold and emerald fish native to this "deep and capacious spring" is not the largemouth or smallmouth bass, though they too can in some waters sport "great gold and emerald" colors, but the chain pickerel, a lowly species, as generally conceded by today's angler. I can't recall that I've ever seen a pickerel story written up as a feature in one of the *Hook-and-Bullet* magazines; no *Pickerel on the Fly* on your bookshelf or mine. Yet with Henry Thoreau as companion and scribe, fishing in a farm pond named Walden, this still-water pickerel is a rare pleasure and stimulates a precious literary legacy.

I've read Henry's Walden Pond book early in life and again, later, in college, and every few years even now. But I've never fished its waters. My first experience fishing someplace like it was the Vanderkamp Pond

185

in upstate New York, north of Oneida Lake, on the fringe of the remote Tug Hill Plateau. My cousin Hank was part of the family that owned The Vanderkamp; several hundred acres plus the pond that I'm guessing was close to 100 acres itself.

Whatever the size it was full of a very game fish that jumped, some weighing several pounds, and because it was a private pond the fish were seldom fished and vulnerable even to young teens who were just winging it on this new species – largemouth bass. Our weapon of choice was the Hula Popper.

I wonder if they still make that plug? A short, fat cigar stub in size with a hairy hula skirt round the middle; you'd throw it out there on the edge of the cattails, give it a "pop," then see how much patience you had as you waited for a big largemouth to blast it off the surface. Fewer pops was generally better but the temptation was great to keep it moving if you didn't get a hit right away and then the popper was soon off the habitat and a bass would rarely venture beyond his cover.

We got good at "edging" that cover though and caught some beauties, some real bruisers, in spite of ourselves, and the fishing was invariably good 'cause me and Hank were the only ones using it........the name Vanderkamp soon became Abandoned-kamp in our lexicon and remains so today though our time there is long past. Anyway, it was quite a pond.

We have a number of ponds in southwest New Mexico, like Bill Evans, Bear Canyon, and Lake Roberts. These sometimes produce well, and sometimes not, but they're likely crowded on the weekend. So I'm going to write about a little 15-acre pond I know that's private and nameless and rimmed with big shade trees. Despite its small size it's got some nice largemouth, big bluegill, and the odd warmouth bass.

The warmouth bass looks a lot like a rock bass but is prettier – reddish-brown streaks along the lateral line, yellow belly and orange spots on the dorsal fine – and is actually a member of the sunfish family. They get up to 2 lbs. or a bit more and the one I caught on my last trip to this small water was over a pound with a lot of "pull." What they do when hooked is get that wide body broadside to the angler and the direction of the line and "fight big." I was using a 4-weight rod and started with a Pistol Pete and it was too heavy for the leader. So I switched to a smallish wooly bugger and my landings improved though I think I only landed four fish, the warmouth the biggest.

Stephen O'Day and son Bud used spinning outfits and easily caught more than me and it was a lovely day and I got a bang out of that warmouth bass on a fly. I hadn't caught one of those in years, and this pretty fish and place and day offered up a good example of farm pond fishing. Henry caught it just right: "I am always surprised by their rare beauty," he said, "as if they were fabulous fishes."

186

Behold the Not-So-Lowly Carp

I was fishing the Rio Grande down along the levee near San Marcial, back when Elephant Butte was filled to the brim. I had my fun catching a nice channel catfish but it couldn't compare to the half-hour battle the guy downstream was having with the biggest bass of his life. Or so he thought.

The fish finally broke the line, but by then he was exhausted in the shallows and this ol' boy and his kid were able to splash in from the bank and beach him. When it turned out to be a carp rather than a bass the man's verbiage was unprintable, and embarrassed his young son. With the parting shot – "trash fish" – he tossed a ten-pounder into the bushes.

An "exotic" imported from Europe, the lowly carp doesn't have many friends. Maybe it's the inelegant bugle mouth, or the debatable reputation as a bottom feeder. Regardless, few fish in New Mexico are more wide ranging, or get bigger, and while they seldom jump, no fish fights harder pound for pound.

We make curious mistakes sometimes. The largest American carp on record (74 lbs.) is bigger than the largest muskellunge (69 lbs.). Yet the muskie is a piscatorial icon with a restricted range that only an elite handful have ever caught. The carp is a ubiquitous commoner and, ironically, is often derided for being so successful.

By my experience a 5 lb. carp will easily outlast a 5 lb. largemouth bass, and often a smallmouth bass, on similar tackle. Only the propensity of the smallmouth to jump gives it the nod as "the gamest fish that swims."

The carp makes bait fishing fun again precisely because he is so sensitive to baits improperly placed, or heavy line or big hooks, or the sight or sound or smell of the angler. There is a dilemma in carp fishing. Light gear is more likely to fool him but that makes him hard to land. The carp is bull-strong and will break you off or run your spool if not worn down by deft play of rod, reel, and line. Yet use heavy tackle and you may not get a bite.

In fly fishing for carp (more on this later), you will find the carp as spooky to a bad cast as a wily old brown trout.

I began to specifically direct myself to carp a few years back on the Gila River. My son Bud and I planned to fly-fish that day for smallmouth bass but when we got to the stream we found it high and muddy. A purist fly-fisher would have gone home but we turned some rocks in the shallows, caught hellgrammites with a fine mesh net, and switched to split shot and #8 hooks. Both carp and catfish can find a bait in any sort of water and we were now fly fishing with real flies. I tightened up on something big at the first deep pool.

With a 5 wt. rod and 6 lb. tippet he played me more than I played him; if he had chosen to head downstream the fish would have easily run my line and all the backing. But he chose to circle the big pool. Still, it took me 90 minutes with my old fiberglass rod bent like a hoop to beach him. I let him go with a new respect for carp.

A week later, using a crawfish and modern graphite spinning rod, my son Bud, age eight, landed what looked like the same 30-inch fish in the same pool in 20 minutes! Showed the old man up and this time we took the prize, and a kid's memory for a lifetime, home for supper.

The surest way to catch carp is by chumming, not permitted in designated trout waters but otherwise ok. Here's how:

Buy two cans of corn and soak half of one can the night before in liquid raspberry Jell-O. At the water chum out a couple of handfuls of the yellow corn, then thread two kernels of that raspberry corn on a #8 hook. Use light line (about 8 lb test) and a small sliding sinker; a carp is wary and if he feels weight he'll likely drop the bait. Use a rod with a soft tip (a fly rod is the most fun) for easy casting and to lessen the chance he'll break you off. That yellow corn will draw a school of carp but they'll zero in on those two kernels that smell like raspberries. You can only hope the biggest one in the pod gets there first.

The latest thing in carp angling is straight fly fishing. Where you find them in clear water you can sight cast to feeding carp. Far more wary than a trout, you must get the fly in the water well ahead of the approaching fish. A beadhead nymph gets to the bottom quicker and the bead acts as an attractor. A 1X to 3X tippet (roughly 6 to 8lb test)) is about right.

Carp that are cruising slowly, nosing the bottom from time to time, are the ones you look for. These are feeding fish and the carp, with its relatively small stomach, is feeding much of the time. So you spot a feeding carp and cast not to where he is but to where you think he will soon be. The cast must be delicate or you'll spook him and the whole pod. Then, as he approaches your sinking fly, "crab" that nymph along the bottom with a hand-over-hand strip to give it life; when his nose goes down and tail goes up it's tight lines and you better have a good drag on your reel. I lost one on a fly last summer that would go a dozen pounds when he ran me into a backlash and broke me off. Yet the next week I caught another better than two feet long on a prince nymph and 4 wt. rod and felt like a hero.

It is true that carp can live in polluted lakes and rivers where other fish can't but remember it is us not the carp that fouled the waters. Carp don't prefer pollution or silt, they are just more adaptable than their brethren. From good water carp meat is savory and here's how you get around the bones.

Skin and filet the carp as you would a big catfish or bass. Cut out the dark meat along the lateral line. Put the remaining white meat through a

188

hamburger grinder or mixer; this renders the fine, floating "Y" bones unnoticeable. Add a good mix of seasoned bread crumbs, like making a meat loaf, then bake as a fish loaf or fry as fish patties.

"Exotic," unloved, this is a powerful fish that will test your skills on bait or flies and can grow as long as your leg. They are here to stay and may be found in most of New Mexico's lakes and rivers. Behold the not-so-lowly carp.

A Big Fish, Or, A Big Fish Story?

People will do a lot to get their name in the books as the record holder of a certain species of fish. Any species of fish. I myself recently talked the New Mexico Department of Game and Fish into including the carp as a species worthy of record. Now, if you catch a monster carp in New Mexico, have it weighed on an approved scales, have the catch certified by a Game and Fish officer, and you may see your name in print with the state record bugle-mouth bass.

I may make a run at that state record carp myself. And I'll try to resist the temptation to cheat. Apparently, that can be quite a temptation; like I said, people will do a lot to take hold of a record. Witness the on-going muskellunge controversy.

The muskie is a high-profile fish. Like the largemouth bass, the holder of the record for the biggest muskie can expect not only fame, but a fortune as well in endorsements and related compensations. One who was aware of this was Arthur Lawton.

Arthur Lawton and his wife Ruth went after big muskies with professional zeal and an almost religious fervor from the late 1940s through the early 1960s. Their locale was the Thousand Islands region of New York State. They were well aware that others in that region, most notably a one Len Hartman, as well as anglers in other muskie hotspots in Wisconsin and Minnesota, were after the same prize.

In September of 1957, years of almost daily fishing paid off. Arthur Lawton apparently landed a 69 lb. 15 oz. monster muskellunge, apparently had it photographed, and weighed and witnessed on an approved scales, and submitted the catch as the new record for the species. He was subsequently approved as the new record holder for big muskies and held the title for 35 years. Then, although nobody caught a bigger fish, he lost the title to a 69 lb. 11 oz. muskie caught by Louis Spray of Wisconsin. What happened?

Well, the Lawtons were long since gone, but one John Detloff of Wisconsin, and the Wisconsin-based National Freshwater Fishing Hall of Fame, began an investigation in 1992. They had a photo of Lawton with several big muskies strung out on a pole, one of them the supposed record-holder, and analysis of length and girth concluded the fish could not have weighed anywhere close to 70 lbs.

I remember seeing that photo in the *In-Fisherman* magazine and I agreed; the fish was no record. With no Lawtons around to defend themselves the record was abrogated in 1992 by the "Hall of Fame" and International Game Fish Association and given to Spray's huge but perhaps still slightly smaller fish.

But something was still fishy. The new record muskie was from Wisconsin, as was Detloff, Spray, and the Freshwater Fishing Hall of

Fame. Did they do a number on the deceased Lawton to take the record from New York and give it to the cheese and dairy state?

One who says "maybeso" is Larry Ramsell, a leading muskie historian. Ramsell originally agreed with the determination to remove Lawton's muskie from the record books. Now he has done his own investigation and is having second thoughts.

For one thing, more than one witness to the weigh-in of Lawton's muskie is still alive and they say it was an honest 69 lbs. 15 oz. As for the photo of Lawton with several muskies hanging from a pole, Ramsell says it may have been taken weeks earlier; two other photos, of poor quality, show a single fish that is far larger. This was the record fish, Ramsell says, but the photos were lost, or declined for being fuzzy, by the "big fish" associations in 1992.

I see two possibilities here, neither of which speaks well of the often over-zealous quest for record fish. Either Arthur Lawton perpetuated a fraud in 1957 and got his come-uppance in 1992, or, he was the greatest muskie fisherman who ever lived and got robbed.

For now, the record rests with Spray and Wisconsin. At least a portion of it. The International Gamefish Association thinks both Lawton and Spray told "stretchers" and perpetrated frauds in their attempts to score big with their best fish. They have the record holder as Cal Johnson (deceased) and his 67 lb. 8 oz. muskie caught near Hayward, WI and dating back to 1949! And the great state of New York still believes in Arthur Lawton's fish.

Even the Lawton 1957 muskie controversy is new compared to the fuss over the record largemouth bass.

In June, 1932, a 19-year-old farm boy named George Perry caught a 22 lb. 4 oz. bigmouth bass from Montgomery Lake, Georgia. Despite controversy, the record has stood for more than 70 years.

Perry only had one lure with him at the time, a Creek Chub Wigglefish. He had the fish weighed, measured, witnessed and notarized in Helena, Georgia, but if a photo was ever taken of the fish it has not survived. Thus the controversy.

A few years back *In-Fisherman* did an investigation of this long-standing record and concluded it was probably legitimate. There was no big prize money awaiting a record largemouth bass in those days and the disingenuous Perry would have had little incentive to cheat.

Huge prize money and endorsements await the angler who legitimately breaks the Perry record, however. Most serious observers say it will be worth at least a million dollars to the angler. It almost happened just weeks ago.

Mac Weakley of Carlsbad, CA caught a 25 lb. 1 oz. largemouth from Dixon Lake. However, he foul-hooked the fish on the side of the face. That is a likely disqualification and Weakley did the right thing; he not only made no claim to the new record, he let the fish go.

191

So did Cale Sanders of Roswell, who broke the New Mexico state smallmouth bass record at Ute Lake, just weeks ago on March 31st. Sander's bass was 24" long and weighed 7 lbs. 3 oz. and broke by 5 ounces the previous record from Navajo Lake set by David Young in 1999.

Sander's fish was kept alive in an aerated live well through two weigh-ins; he is now back in Ute Reservoir and presumably will get bigger. If you catch him, I hope you treat him the same way Cale Sanders did.

As for that new carp record, some claims are bound to come in this summer. Carp can get as big as Arthur Lawton's muskie, so anything is possible. The officer in charge though, better double-check everything if the carp angler claiming the big fish is an outdoor writer – you know how those guys will stretch the truth to make a story.

Fishing Locally for the "Exotic" Brown Trout

It was just a few years ago that the word came to me that brown trout had colonized a high country stream in the Gila Wilderness. My friend had been in there, expecting rainbows (another non-native fish), but ended up catching brown trout instead. This fellow is a fisheries biologist as well as an excellent fly fisher and I had to believe him, though we both knew this stream as extremely isolated and holding only rainbow trout in the past. How did the brown trout get in there?

Of course I had to go see for myself. I got a late start, took the wrong trail initially, finally arriving at the stream with less time awaiting me than I'd planned. I caught a few rainbows, proving that species was still there. At other pools however, the trout were so wary I simply could not sneak up on them, or my less-than-perfect casts spooked the fish. These wary fish looked like brown trout in the water but I couldn't say for sure without bringing one to the bank.

I did finally hook one, but lost him early in the fight. Over the years since my technique has improved apparently because I have caught a number of brown trout in this "rainbows only" stream. The mysteries remain. Brown trout have invaded this stream, but how did they get in there? Were they stocked by a wildlife agency........very unlikely. Brought in and released as an outlaw introduction? That's my best guess. Time will tell, or maybe not

I relate this quizzical speculation to illustrate two points about the brown trout – strictly speaking, they don't belong here; and, they can be irritatingly hard to catch.

The brown trout of the USA (*Salmo trutta*) is among our "exotic" wildlife, meaning it was brought in from another continent. Importations date from the 1880s. Some came from Germany and one still hears the phrase "German browns." Others came from England and many of those stocked in western states came from Loch Leven, Scotland. The species rivals the rainbow in size, is somewhat better adapted to warmer, turbid waters, and once stocked browns more than rainbows may "take hold" and become naturally reproducing in a given stream.

This is the case in our own Gila National Forest where browns have not been stocked anywhere in decades. Yet they persist in the three forks of the Gila River and a number of other streams in the wilderness.

Trout are seen as the most aesthetically pleasing of all fresh water fish by many anglers, and many anglers would yield the final accolade to the brown. The name "brown" hardly does it justice, though the fish's back and sides do show the warm brown of fall colors. Black spots, mixed with brick-red spots, highlight the back and flanks and these spots are generally encircled by white halos. The belly often trends of into a butter-yellow. A flamboyant God painted the wild rainbow and the wild brook trout; a more subtle artist conceived the lovely brown.

The first fish I can remember catching was a brown trout, on Chittenango Creek in upstate New York too many years ago. Yet I haven't written much about browns in this column as for a number of years I never caught any. I was either in the wrong place or they were too smart for me.

Then, last October, I caught one on the Little Colorado River in eastern Arizona. The ice broken, I caught another one this summer up one of the forks of the Gila. It was about a foot long and, born and raised in the stream, carried all the colors described above. A few years ago I caught two browns out of the Bow River in Alberta. None of my four browns had great size, and you may go to your favorite stream next week and catch four in one day. But I'm just happy to be a brown trout fisherman once again.

As to techniques, browns are known as being perhaps more piscivorous than other trout, though any trout is more inclined to eat fish as it gets older and bigger. But tradition favors streamers for brown trout. I caught all four of my brown trout below the surface.

Yet in a hatch they will readily rise to small dry flies. The smaller ones may not be that cagey but the larger browns are almost fool-proof. Tradition has it that once you find the tippet delicate enough to fool a big brown, it will be so fine it can't hold the fish.

Serious brown trout anglers often fish at night. Big hair bugs, wooly buggers and strong leaders a large brown would dope out easily in the daytime may completely fool the same old boy at night. It's half-blind fishing; you can't see the fly but the fish can. I need to try it myself.

The brown trout does not interbreed with our native Gila trout or cutthroat trout but is seen as a competitor with native fish and thus some biologists want them gone. Their range has shrunk in the Gila forest as non-native trout have been removed to make way for Gila trout in some cold-water streams. If a new plan to remove non-natives on behalf of roundtail chub goes through (more on this in a later column), brown trout in lower elevations of the Gila drainage could be eliminated as well.

In northern New Mexico browns are being removed in places on behalf of the Rio Grande cutthroat subspecies. All this is fine up to a point, but I recall my father telling me about a 5-lb. brown he landed on Butternut Creek, New York, that rumor had it had fooled other anglers for years. He talked about that fish for the rest of his life.

Many fish managers today get the vapors over "non-natives," but I hope the brown trout has a place in the future of the Gila drainage. It's been with us here in southwest New Mexico for 100 years. With its singular beauty, wary reserve, and game fight, it is a naturally reproducing resident of our nation's first wilderness, albeit it arrived by "unnatural" means.

Carp at the Butte with Hook & Bow

My wife and son find me rather "Scotch" about spending money and I suppose when it comes to what I regard as luxuries it's true...... I'm tight as the bark on a tree. And despite the moniker "Dutch," I am in considerable measure of Scotch descent. So when this Elephant Butte carp shoot came up we had a brief debate whether to reserve a room in one of those cheap, quaint, old-timey 1950s motels at Truth or Consequences (my choice), or, that fancy, well known inn by the lake. They won. So Bud and I headed out the day before the carp shoot with a reservation at the "better" place.

We needed a room because the carp shoot was for the TV show "Wild New Mexico" and the launch was scheduled for "sunrise." That's early this time of year and we were coming from Silver City. Nobody likes to begin a two-hour drive at 4 AM just to arrow some carp. So for convenience we went over the day before and I told Bud, "We'll fish carp off the bank in the afternoon, stay over, and be handy for the sunrise launch the next morning. With luck we'll take carp with both hook and we'll arrow a couple to boot."

"Yeah, I want to shoot one, Dad, with a bow."

We set up our fish camp near the dam-site about 4 PM and got a rod apiece in the water; one 9 ft. spinning rod with a "bait walker" reel, and a 7 ft. bait casting outfit with a clicker on the open spool. We chummed out some corn, put corn on the bait casting rig and a lively nightcrawler on the spinning rod, and waited. Waiting is the nature of bank fishing for carp and soon Bud said, "I see some fish."

Sure enough, you could sit up on a rock above the rods and see a few carp cruising the bay. They'd disappear, then after a while they would surface again. Some were small but we saw two that would go 30 inches or so. "I hope one of those big ones cruises by one of our baits," I said.

But we waited. And waited. When we finally got bites we couldn't hook them. I got one on, battled him for five minutes, and he slipped the hook. Finally, one took the corn bait on a good hook-up. It was a strong tussle but in the end I beached a 25-inch fish. I let him go and said, "Bud, you take any bites from here on, whichever rod gets lucky."

He did and before we quit to find the motel he landed two nice carp about 22" each, both caught on the casting rod. After a slow start we'd got our sport from carp off the bank, albeit nothing 30-inches long.

Bud and his mom were right about the inn. I still like quaint 1950s motels, but we got a nice room where we could see the lake, cleaned up, the meal was excellent, and we could look through the window of the hotel restaurant while we ate and watch cottontails as big as jackrabbits frolic on the grass. Later we watched "Sports Center" on ESPN and saw the highlights as the good-guy Cavaliers beat the hated Pistons. All said, lakeside luxury was worth whatever extra we paid above my "Scotch" limits. Bud was pretty proud and said, "Guess you're glad we stayed here instead of downtown, huh Dad?" Indeed!

We were at the launch at sunrise. They had two boats for 8 people and a bow fishing rig for each boat, 35 lb. compound outfits with the cord attached from the fish arrow to a spinning rod with a closed faced reel. A new system to me but it worked. Guide JR McManus can find any species of fish in the lake. He took us to the east side and there were carp everywhere, spawning in the shallows and circling in the bay. None let us have any easy shots.

Nonetheless, New Mexico Game Commissioner Jim McClintik got six fish and everybody else got one or two in a morning's work, including Bud who took a two-footer on a good long shot and got another hit with a head shot. He was sure proud to have scored with the men with bow and arrow.

The only disappointment was the lack of large carp. I've seen 3-foot carp at the Butte but nothing close to that on either day of this trip. It seems the big ones keep to themselves, and whether you're bow hunting or rod and reel fishing you have to do some scouting to find them. They're worth it. Any carp 30" or better is a trophy.

I believe the carp average larger in the Gila River than at the Butte or the Rio Grande, probably because they are less populous and have less competition for a better food source. That's something Bud and I will keep in mind as we take our own bow fishing rig to the river waters.

For the record, the carp were spawning at the Butte the last week of May with the water temperature at 68 degrees. You can take them from a boat or wading the shallows on the east side of the lake (no hunting allowed on the west side). And you can take them with rod and reel off the bank all year long.

Some fish, these carp; big as stripers and a lot more plentiful. I think we did it just right, bank fishing with rod and reel one day and bow hunting the next. Make it a two-day event and stay over. But Bud reminds you, for full enjoyment, don't be "Scotch" like his Dad; and stay at one of the "better" places!

A Dry Fly, a Streamer, and a Nymph

With fires raging in the forest and the streams drying up it perhaps makes more sense to write about fishing than to get out there and do it. So, here's an age-old discussion about trout flies.

Fly fishing writers are forever going on about fly selection, as in that famous phrase: "match the hatch." That catch-all (no pun intended) verbiage makes sense when there is a hatch going on but I would put it down as limited advice. Especially for the Gila Forest angler. Most of the time in our local waters there is no visible hatch going on; hatching aquatic insects may not be ready to come to the surface and thus remain cryptic, or do so sporadically or in insufficient numbers to rouse the fish to rise, *en masse*. Regardless, the writers are persistent that the food the trout or other fish eat must be imitated or "matched" by the fly. Well, maybe.

To test this theory I picked three famous flies, well regarded by a preponderance of fly fishers, including myself, to try to get a feel for whether they work as advertised, why they work (provided they do), and whether they in fact imitate literally one or more aquatic insects or other trout food. Of the three, one is a dry fly, one is a streamer, and one is a nymph.

For a dry fly I will investigate the venerable Adams, and its popular sequel, the Parachute Adams. The Adams is sufficiently "classic" that it has its own lore, a story of a one Judge Charles Adams who was having the devil of a time fooling newly introduced brown trout in northern Michigan, circa 1922. He implored his fishing buddy, Leonard Hallady, to tie him a fly that would trick these trout. Hallady complied and produced a brown and gray hackle fly that he named after his friend, the judge. The lore does not tell us what particular insect Hallady thought he was imitating, nor can we say for sure how closely today's Adams resembles the prototype it's creator first took from workshop to stream.

We can safely say his creation catches discriminating browns and other trout, then and now, lives on in variations by other fly-tiers, and we can add that the Adams remains generally speaking a non-descript brown/gray fly that, according to a cadre of Internet fishing writers I researched, "resembles a variety of mayflies" as well as "other flies with upright wings."

Thus the drab Adams is certainly not an attractor, nor does it precisely imitate a specific fly, as does for example the look-alike elk hair caddis, or some of the hopper imitations, that do rather look like grasshoppers. Nobody really knows why the plebian Adams works so well.

A variation is the Parachute Adams, which is the classic Adams with a tuft of white hackle atop the brown/gray original. To me, like the original, it only vaguely resembles a real mayfly, but the white "parachute" makes it more buoyant and serves as an attractor, both to the hungry trout and to the fisher who wants to see his floating fly. When I use a dry fly on our Gila Forest streams it's usually a parachute Adams.

The summing up? As imitators I'd give both the Adams and its parachute derivative a "B" at best; as fish catchers they get an "A."

It seems the Royal Coachman was originally a dry fly, still venerated in lore but seldom cast by today's angler. But with different dressings and a layback pattern, though similar colors, there came to be the Royal Coachman streamer. Thus this Royal Coachman sinks and, as a streamer, is designed to imitate some sort of minnow or tadpole or crawfish or other aquatic life other than some six-legged insect. I have a couple of Royal Coachman streamers in my fly box. They are relatively large and easily my prettiest fly. For that reason alone it is easy enough to pick one out of the crowd and tie one on from time to time. Sometimes they catch fish; I've caught trout, bass, and chub out of the Gila River with my Royal streamer. But carrying all the colors of the flag, I can't say this fly resembles anything I've ever seen in fresh water.

What would stimulate a cagey wild trout to belt something that must appear inedible, even to a fish? Couldn't say. Regardless, my Royal streamer is proof that fish will take a fly by attraction, or even provocation, as well as imitation.

For a nymph I'll look no further than the one I use all the time, the Prince Nymph with the gold bead-head. On the Net, where one site sells these little hummers for as little as .75 cents apiece, they say it "imitates a variety of stonefly and caddis fly nymphs." They also say that "it is the green peacock herl with its efflorescent qualities that makes it so alluring." This is the fuzzy body of the tied fly (nymph) but a look at some photos of stonefly and caddis fly larvae failed to turn up this green fuzzy body although, like a stonefly nymph, the Prince Nymph does sport a two-forked tail.

Then there is the gold bead head which gets the fly down near the bottom. "In sunlight the gold bead acts as an attractant," the experts say and I agree. But, neither the stonefly or caddis nymph generally sports a gold-colored head shining in the sun and standing out from a darker body.

And what about the two white lay-back wings of the Prince Nymph? These stand out from the green herl and brown hackle and give the fly much of its distinctive appearance. They no doubt appeal to the fish too but, again, where in nature is the white-winged nymph with the shiny brass head we're supposedly trying so hard to match?

The gold bead head Prince Nymph looks like an aquatic insect larvae all right; but, to me, more like a breed of its own, more commonly found in the angler's fly box than swimming live in the water. Once more, we have a superior fly that works well but, at best, only dimly approximates in appearance what actually lives in the water.

Maybe I'd catch more fish if I paid more attention to "matching the hatch." I've certainly got a lot to learn. Meanwhile, I'm pleased I seem to do all right with these "generalist" flies that somebody smarter than me dreamed up and learned to tie that I can buy off the Net at Cabelas or Orvis for less than a dollar apiece.

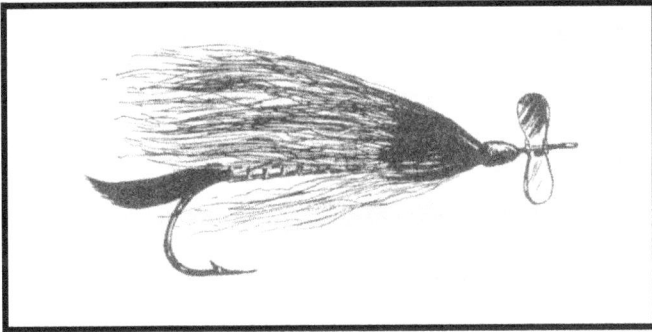

The Gift

It was memorably cold at night. Both mornings, just before sun-up, my sweaty socks, hung out to dry in the juniper branches, were frozen stiff. It was early in May and in elevation our campsite wasn't but 200 feet higher than the home place of 6200 feet. But at the north end of the Gila National Forest when the sun went down the temperature didn't just descend, it dropped out of sight. It was hard to imagine it would be seventy-something by noon.

We were there to blast and cast; just me and Bob Brady, blast a turkey or two if we could get up early enough. Cast my new fiberglass rod, too. Fishing in the Gila drainage had been poor of late, due to ash flow from the fires, but Lord knows this particular implement was too expensive to just leave in the case. We knew there were a few turkeys in the canyons; we weren't so sure about the fish in the stream.

The fly rod was something of a story unto itself, a good story from my view, and like all good stories it has a touch of irony at the end. It was a gift from a conservation group made up mostly of fly fishers, apparently for services rendered for six years as an erstwhile member of the New Mexico State Game Commission. I figured to get the boot from the new administration in Santa Fe and I was right. But it was a nice surprise consolation to receive this rod from fellow fly fishers.

I question whether I was worthy of such an elegant gift, but I suspect they did it because as a Game Commissioner I was rather more interested in fish and fish management than most; the subject had received scant attention at Game Commission meetings, compared to the furor over big game controversies (like the booming elk populations) and predators (like wolf depredations). The irony was that they gave the rod to someone who didn't always agree with wildlife agency or company or conservation group policy re: usefulness and status of non-native sport fish (like smallmouth bass), which according to some, "don't belong here."

Early that evening we drove close to the running water of one of the forks of the Gila River and using both artificial flies and real hellgrammites we caught between us I'd say seven or eight smallmouth bass, all small; i.e., under a foot long. But they were fun to catch on my high-dollar rod which was light of weight and easy of flex and valued on the market and among veteran anglers at far more than I could ever afford myself.

At first I didn't get it. Opening the box I put together a 7 ft., 3 piece, 3 weight outfit that, because it was fiberglass, seemed unnecessarily "retro" and dated as soon as I strung it up. Glass is heavier than graphite but lacks the gut to produce a fast tip that might send a fly on a low rapid arc to great and impressive distance. Like in *A River Runs Through It*, the movie. Glass rods were overtaken by graphite more than 30 years ago. So why would a state-of-the-art outfit like Scott of Montrose, Colorado want to redress old technology?

Precisely because the "slow" tip of the glass rod allows the fisher to feel the rod "load" on the back cast, for better control on the forecast, and with most applications on most water, accuracy and touch are more important than distance. That's what I felt with the first use of my gift rod.

Back at camp we hit the bedrolls early for Bob thinks that to awaken at 4:30 a.m. is sleeping in. We were calling turkeys, us sounding like hens, at first light. A veteran turkey hunter, Bob could make the odd, throaty sound of a hen calling for a gobbler by rubbing what looked like a thick pencil dipped in chalk onto a small, framed piece of glass. And down in a deep canyon we got two gobblers to respond ("gobble") and one to come part way to our stand. My first turkey hunt, I got a taste of the anticipation the hunter feels when he has a 25 lb. bird coming in. But he didn't come within shotgun range.

At camp there was time to kill and so we strung out lunch and a knap; Bob thinks fishing in the middle of the day is a waste of time in this country and he's probably right. So we hung around camp and waited on the sun to slant such that we would find us some shade upon the waters and then down into the canyon we went. Bob can hike better than me but he waited on and we took turns at the first pool and I got lucky and hooked the big one there, on a brown wooly worm, #10 hook, 3x tippet.

Well, I couldn't call it a trophy. But, a 15-inch stream-born smallmouth, caught on a hand-made, 3 weight glass rod built to have a touch and a feel, is a big fish. For me anyway. Yet I could control him with that light outfit and I got him in after a great and inspiring struggle which is how I know he was 15 inches (Bob had a tape.). I let this wild, albeit non-native fish go and wondered if the conservation group or our principal wildlife agency would approve of the fish or the fisherman or the rod or the release.

Bob approved and caught a couple more smaller ones himself and all told we got near a dozen and while I got the biggest he caught most of the fish so we both had something to cheer.

And the turkeys I suppose cheered too – in their own way – as they toyed with us again the next morning. Hidden away under a tree and crouched in camo, we saw herds of elk, deer, and javelina, hawks, eagles, blue herons, coyotes, and later, a coatimundi on the road. So we came home with memories rather than meat, and speculated on the irony of use and the prospects for survival, or even revival, of an out-of-range game fish, and a fishing rod that, in retrospective, fishes a lot better than its owner.

Find the Water, Find the Fish!

I recall it was late June that the first decent rains began here in the southern half of the Gila country. The weathermen, and women, offered their usual pessimism about "don't expect an early monsoon season," and "we expect below average precipitation this summer" but, in fact, it's been wet all through July and August, the Gila River, the Mimbres, and a myriad of tributaries have been running consistently above average, and even the creek by the house has flooded several times and each time left us temporarily stranded. Meanwhile the fishing has changed with the rising waters, offering both challenges and opportunities.

It was certainly a challenge back in June when my son Bud and I packed in for three days when it was still dry. We camped along a good trout stream. But it was so low and warm the fish were dormant. We could scarcely raise a bite and even carefully presented nymphs produced only a few very small trout. Last week when I went in there I hardly recognized it as the same stream.

The water was high enough that you had to be careful crossing or you might slip down with the current. A good flow can revive a stream but in this case it also meant high, murky water – almost muddy – okay for catfish and carp but not good for the trout fisher with a fly rod. I almost turned back to try and hunt up a stream where a fish could see a fly.

But I kept hiking, drifted a #12 beadhead Prince nymph in all the likely pools and runs, got a few hits and by noon had landed a few of those same-looking very small trout. After fishing out a good pool with no results I stopped to eat a sandwich in the shade and reconnoiter.

I reckoned with the high water there had to be bigger trout in the stream. I considered I needed to try a larger, attractor fly. Or, better yet, that live grasshopper I could see on a weed stalk not far from where I sat and ate my lunch. I fished my fine mesh net out of my pack and soon had that hopper impaled on my #12 nymph. I fished the same pool that was empty of fish before lunch, drifted my "fly" on an almost-tight line with an upstream quartering cast, but the pool wasn't empty anymore. Now it produced a nice 13-inch rainbow that couldn't resist a Prince nymph with a live grasshopper attached. For fish, smell and taste is part of the hunt, for trout and bass as well as catfish and carp.

I hunted hoppers but could find no more of any size. But there were hellgrammites in the stream; I turned over a bunch of rocks and eventually got three. They, too, may augment a Prince nymph and before I got back to the truck I had two more good rainbows, one of which stretched to 16 inches, jumped, and tested the resilience of my 3-wt rod.

Returning the last hellgrammite to the stream, I was pleased. high water had replenished a nearly dry stream, brought some good fish in from somewhere, and in spite of a muddy flow I had found a way to catch them.

The Mimbres River is a variegated mix of public and private land, and stretches that flow perennially, intermittently, or only during flood flows. A few weeks ago it trickled, briefly, all the way to Deming on the desert, but just last summer during drought my son Bud and I were disappointed to find a long dry stretch well up into the forest.

"No problem this year," Rex Johnson told me a couple of weeks ago. "I was in that same stretch this spring and it had a good flow and was well supplied with browns, though they weren't easy to catch."

We went there. There was plenty of water and it was clear enough you could see fish; there could be no excuse here for dipping down to use of live hoppers or hellgrammites. They weren't all browns, but they were predominate and therein lies a tale.

It's a tale with a mystery I cannot solve. Traditionally, at least for the last 100 years, the Mimbres was all rainbows – at least if you're counting gamefish – and nobody knows how the browns got in there over the past dozen years. Or they're not saying. We do know it wasn't any agency stocking; indeed, officialdom deems all trout as non-native to the Mimbres (this is disputed by Rex and others) and would like them removed on behalf of the native Chihuahua chub.

I'd like to debate the Mimbres as an historical trout stream in a subsequent column; for now both browns and rainbows are in there and we did all right. At least Rex did. He had those browns doped out with a non-descript wooly bugger and more than doubled my three brown trout. After switching from a nymph to my own wooly bugger my 14-inch rainbow proved the best fighter of the day – fast, enduring, and a leaper. But Rex soon caught a fat 15-inch brown to claim the trophy of the trip which he of course released.

All said we caught more than a dozen trout on big, fuzzy flies. A sneaky approach was necessary, especially for the browns, and they responded best to an upstream cast and a nearly-tight line on the drift. And if you didn't hook him on the first hit you just as well go to the next pool. At least the browns were that touchy. And all this where a year ago there were no fish because the "river" lacked the water to even float a juvenile chub.

An improbable uplift in the desert, where some good trout waters can nourish anglers one year then literally disappear the next, the Gila watershed provides a fresh hunt for the angler seeking gamefish every season of the year. This summer the rains came. Don't pass up any possibility. Find some flowing water and you'll likely find some fish.

Fine Line Equals Fine Fishing

The standard outdoor story or column is filled with information that generally fits under one of two headings – "how-to-do-it," or, "where-to-go." This column is usually a poor choice for that sort of information; I'm not inclined to give away what little where-to-go knowledge I have and I'm not smart enough to presume to tell other hunters or fishermen how-to-do-it.

Other people are smart enough however, and two books in my library open an interesting discussion on light versus heavy line for fishing. I've touched on this issue before but these two writers offer a perspective we can all learn from.

Lunkers Love Nightcrawlers has the look of a home-grown, self-published book. Written by George Pazik, *et al* – the *et al* being the editors of *Fishing Facts* magazine – it showed up in my used book shop and I expected some very common information on worm dunking. But these boys are no ordinary worm dunkers.

They have rightly discovered that even in worm fishing – or perhaps especially in worm fishing – a natural presentation is paramount. Thus they use nightcrawlers as fine art, using small hooks to skewer the worm at the very tip so it waves in the water like a real nightcrawler floating downstream. Further, they have rightly discovered that the lighter the line used, the more naturally the worm floats, and the less likely the fish is to see the line.

So they recommend 6 lb, or 4 lb., or in very clear water even 2 lb. test monofilament for worming for bass. Even big bass. To the skeptic who says a big fish will break such fine line they say, not if you're a good fishermen.

They have done some interesting experiments to prove their point, too detailed to itemize here, but the sum of it is, if you take your standard bass rod and reel with 4 lb. test line, and hook it to a stump, you can't break that line on a steady pull against the rod, regardless of your strength and even if you bow the rod into a full hoop. I've tried it and they are right. Since you can't break 4 lb. line, even pulling on a stump, why use heavy line, even for heavy fish?

Of course we've all had bass and other fish break line on us, even line much heavier than 4 lb. test. But, as the authors note, this is invariably due to controllable factors – poor knots, nicked line, or dropping the rod tip so the fish can jerk a straight pull on line. Nicked line and dropping the rod tip are easily corrected. A poor knot is trickier but the authors can help with a new knot (at least it was new to me).

The authors took Trilene 12 lb. test and found it actually broke at 14 ½ pounds on a straight pull. They tied and tested an improved clinch knot 10 times and found the knot broke at anywhere from 6 to 10 lbs. So the standard improved clinch knot weakens your line by 25% to 50% or more.

The authors took the same line and tried and tested the Crawford figure eight knot 10 times and found it broke right at 14 lbs. each time. The figure eight knot loses little or nothing in the listed strength of the line and the book shows you how to tie it. The message is clear: when bait fishing, use small hooks, light line, flexible rods, and hook the bait so it moves in the water like an unattached natural lure. Pazik convinced me that light line makes a difference in bait fishing, whether the goal is bass, trout, catfish, carp, whatever, and they think it's because the fish can see the heavier line and are spooked.

Harold Blaisdell disagrees. In *The Philosophical Fisherman*, Blaisdell considers the importance of light line in fly fishing as well as bait fishing. He likes light line, or leader or tippet, but says it's not the view of the line that spooks the fish, but rather what the heavier line does to the bait or fly to make it appear unnatural in the water.

He notes the innumerable times he has been dry fly fishing and the fly floats near the feeding fish and the fish ignores it time and again. Then he changes position, or gets that just-right, dead-drift float, and the fish rises and takes the fly. Obviously, the tippet didn't just become invisible to the fish; rather, on the good float the fly finally passed by appearing to float naturally, as if unattached to the line, and so the fish was fooled into a take. The same principal would apply to nymph fishing.

The lighter the line or tippet, Blaisdell says, the less influence it will have on the bait or fly, the more natural it will appear and the better your chances of fooling and hooking the fish.

I think Blaisdell is right. If I can see the line or tippet at 10 feet (and I usually can) the sharp-eyed bass or trout can certainly see it at a foot. But he usually doesn't care about sight of the line itself, he only cares if the line or tippet makes the bait or fly appear false.

Blaisdell also notes that when fishing an attractor, such as a lure in spin casting, a popping bug or streamer in fly fishing, light line is less important and may not matter at all. The fish strikes the attractor in anger; he is less fooled than aroused and throws caution to the winds.

Light line makes a big difference in bait fishing and dry fly and nymph fishing. Both books are recommended, and you need to learn to tie the Crawford figure eight knot.

A Question of Fish and Birds

It was commented at a lecture at the recent Gila River Festival that there are more bird watchers in America than hunters and fishermen combined. Any of these statistical summaries can be suspect, but since this speaker was not apparently attempting any political point against the consumptive outdoor pursuits I'd be willing to say he may well be right. Or close to it.

One reads that hunter numbers are down to about 15 million, with fishing sporting at anywhere from 35 million to 50 million participants. Some say the number of anglers is declining, too. And all this in the face of an overall national population increase of about 3 million per year.

I'd guess that the fisher numbers are so variable because lots of kids fish but don't get a license and so are hard to count. And lots of saltwater fishing doesn't require a license, so the U.S. Fish & Wildlife Service (or whoever gathers the numbers) can be imprecise or variable in their estimates.

Against these numbers the speaker said there were "about 55 million birdwatchers in the USA." Since no form of bird watching I know of requires a license I'm not sure how they get that estimate, but it's a modern era with computers and spread sheets and "extrapolations" and other things I don't understand so I'm not going to argue.

I will say that at the Gila River Festival all the bird watching tours were well attended while the only fishing outing, offered by me, was attended only by myself and my son. Others came along with us, but it was for the hike, and the discussion of river ecology and watershed health; Bud and I were the only ones who cared to fish. None of this bothers me: I see fishing as having a future and bird watching as having an even bigger future and no conflict between the two. Indeed, there is a certain benefit to having a hand in both sports.

Fish need water and so do birds and while some species of birds are sometimes found far from water the better concentrations and diversity are found along permanently flowing streams. One of the best days I ever had fishing involved birds. In the Gila country where I fish, I'll take any fish that takes my fly or bait and puts up a struggle; my favorite species is the one I just caught. With birds I'm a lot fussier. I see dozens of birds every time I go fishing but only take note of a few. But their allure never fades.

Great blue herons always get me for their size and grace; it's "great" to watch one catch a fish and then lift off with its prize secured midst such an easy reliance on air. And the Mexican black hawk is notable. A large raptor, they are coal-black predators with a white tail-stripe, a notable wing span almost as broad as wide, and a set of yellow legs and talons seeming to belong to a still larger raptor, as one crosses overhead imparting a whirr of wings and carrying a reluctant and quite unlucky bullfrog, snake, or fish. Officially called Common Black Hawk, they are not common but seem to symbolize our rare southwestern rivers. But there are two other birds that will really have me talking about them when I get home.

Well the time I remember didn't offer any special anticipation at the start. I geared up with the usual 4-weight fly rod. I don't recall what fly I used and I headed upstream. I hiked for an hour, started fishing, and from the start was catching small bass – 7 to 10 inches. Not bad, but I was pleased rather than thrilled.

I got to a certain pool that had been a honey hole in the past. I worked it pretty hard and got nothing larger than all those ones along the way that I'd been letting go. I'd just decided to quit – not for the day but to go on up to a piece of shade to have lunch – when I saw the bird. Even a dolt like me, who doesn't count himself amongst those 55 million named "bird watchers," can spot and name a vermillion flycatcher. Vermillion is a special color, especially in sunlight out along a wilderness stream. Juxtaposed with the bird's coal black highlights and, well, for several seconds that little flycatcher made me forget all about fishing. It was like he was illuminated from within. Then he was gone.

I found a log in the shade to sit on to eat my sandwich and drink some lemonade. A Bullocks oriole flew from across the stream and landed on a branch, close enough that I could have tossed him a crust of bread. The orange-yellow color of this oriole has to be seen to be believed, but I was close enough to believe it, and again this bird's primary colors are made the more vivid set off by black feathers in just the right places. For those several seconds that bird made me forget all about my lunch. Then he was gone.

I fished hard through the afternoon, wanting at least just one fish of size. I changed flies but again I can't recall what it was I changed to. But the change worked and I hooked one.

This was a nice fish and he had a big pool to show his stuff. He soon jumped, it was a bronze bass as I figured, and I mean he cleared the water. He would run and he would jump and he would bore deep and pump the rod. I'd like to say he was that 20-inch smallmouth I have always wanted from the Gila but he might have been more like 18; they always look bigger when they jump.

It took a while but I got him to the bank. He was barely held in the lip and I easily removed the hook. I reached to hold him into the current for revival, but it wasn't necessary. He had plenty left, and the getaway when he flapped his tail left splotches of mud and river water all over my dark glasses. I didn't even see where he went. But it was back in the river where he belonged. I wasn't going to keep him anyway and since I had touched him, well, to me it was a catch.

I don't recall anything of note on the hike back to the truck – no big or brightly colored birds, no big-leaping fish. But it had already been a day plum full of memories.

Did the fly catcher or the oriole equal that big-leaping bass? Rare and beautiful as they were, I'd have to say no. Strictly speaking, I'm an angler, not a birdwatcher; and as such, it appears I'm a minority, possibly a fading one. But I can tell you there may be some pleasant surprises that have nothing to do with fishing when you're out along the stream with rod and reel.

Fishing Within the Classic-Romantic Split

There are several books I like to read one more time every few years. Or at least I will reread substantial parts of them. Thoreau's *Walden* is one; then Leopold's *Sand County Almanac*; and Harold Blaisdell's *Philosophical Fishermen*. Finally, I can't resist a rerun of that metaphysical trip, *Zen and the Art of Motorcycle Maintenance* by Robert Pirsig. Although I haven't been a cycle rider for many years, I'm rereading *Zen and the Art....* now, as I enter the last/best months of this year's fishing season. And it comes to me that Pirsig's motorcycle book can make me, and you, a better fisherman.

Oversimplifying a bit, Pirsig's 400+ pages concern the classic-romantic split that plagues both our society and our individual lives. As example, we'll consider the split over what to do with New Mexico's undammed Gila River.

The classic mind sees the river and its waters as a means to expanded, subsidized agriculture, or as a type of fuel to spur subdivision and growth. Certain individuals will have visions of getting rich off the river diversion; a dam is needed.

The romantic says, "Nothing doing!" To the romantic, the river and its waters mean birds, fish, butterflies, sycamores turning colors in the fall, pleasures like angling and river running. To the classicist, the river is "useful," a source of potential power, seductive growth, and maybe money. To the romantic, it is a source of inspiration and aesthetic pleasures.

Pirsig uses the motorcycle as his metaphor to explain a similar dichotomy. Motorcycle riding, he says, is pure romanticism; motorcycle maintenance draws on ones' classic understanding of, and interest in, the use and function of the machine. Basically a classicist, Pirsig sees the good sense in doing most of the mechanical maintenance on his cycle, a plebian model, and he enjoys the work. His companions on the trip keep their more expensive, more "attractive" cycle in beautiful condition, but have all their cycle work done at the shop; they are helpless when something goes wrong on the road. To them, motorcycle maintenance spoils the romance of cycle riding, renders it unattractive.

Pirsig sees this split as a metaphor for society's ills (how does one get and spend – be practical and consumptive – without being ugly or destructive in the process?) and the book gathers as a creative force as the author reveals he once went literally mad trying to resolve the philosophical dilemma. I haven't room here to use fishing as a metaphor to resolve society's ills, but Pirsig's explained split between surface appearances (the romanticism of motorcycle riding) and underlying form (the classicism of motorcycle maintenance) comes up every time we take rod, reel, line, and hook to the water.

Fishing itself, and especially catching a fish, is pure romanticism. The maintenance of doing all the things necessary to achieve this romantic pleasure is the classic understanding in fishing. It would seem that, in this sport (as in motorcycle riding), the romanticists would have all the fun. But not if you're a classicist.

I've known fly fisherman that spend far more time in tying their flies than in fishing them. I've known bass fishers who spend more time fussing over their boats and gear – changing line, buying and sorting and showing off lures of one kind or another, lubricating reels and experimenting with terminal tackle, fussing over expensive gear and technology, like depth finders – than they do casting to cover.

Ever watch one of those pro bass tournaments on TV? They crank those fish in like so many old tennis shoes. There are exceptions of course, and all those guys do know how to catch fish, but they are – most of them – classicists, more concerned with efficiency than any amenity involved in being connected to a tight, lively line. In what has evolved since time of Isaac Walton as a romantic sport, for few anymore fish commercially, or as a cheap way to gather protein, they have decided that fishing must "pay."

That fly tier too, is often very good on the water, even if he spends more time at the vise. By nature he's meticulous, precise; he does the little things right that often make the difference in fooling over-fished, spooky trout.

And even the bait fisher, often ridiculed in the modern sporting press, can benefit from the classic approach about a myriad of creepy/crawlers; bait that lives in or near the waters and the fish. As Harold Blaisdell points out in *The Philosophical Fisherman*, bait fishing often requires a more precise, natural presentation than that required of an attractant lure or fly.

Myself, I'm a romanticist. When I had a motorcycle I didn't know how to maintain it, or fix it, and didn't care to learn. But after reading Pirsig, and were I to once again own a bike, I think I'd take the trouble to learn a thing or two about cycle trouble, mechanics, and keeping myself mobile on the road. And I'd try to save a few bucks that would otherwise go to the cycle shop.

Fishing? I'm a romantic once again; I'll never possess the meticulous precision, with either gear or presentation, to be better than average. But I like to fish and love catching them. So I've become enough of a classicist that I'm now a better angler than I was. My gear is not so bad as when I didn't know enough to care, I'm more careful about my knots, I've learned to hunt streams rather than stumble along from pool to run. And through persistence, and keeping line in the water, I've missed enough big fish that I lose fewer of them now, either at the hook-up or, once connected, wearing them down on medium tackle.

210

I also have an advantage over many other anglers; unlike the purists who are stuck on one species or method, any fish that takes my hook and fights to be free pleases me almost equally well. My favorite fish is the one running my line. And I'm not that particular how I get them on the hook. I love fly fishing – nymphs, dry flies, and streamers; each one provides its own pleasure and calls for its own technique. But in the end I won't hesitate, usually toward evening on the hike back to the truck, to add a live hellgrammite to the mix and perhaps catch the best fish of the day, preferably a catfish, which I have no qualms about keeping for the fry pan.

The classic-romantic split? In *Zen and the Art of Motorcycle Maintenance* Robert Pirsig succeeded brilliantly in showing us how to profit from both modes of understanding, whether the subject is motorcycles or public policy; "an understanding," as he says, "of what it is to be a part of the natural world, and not an enemy of it."

Similarly, the angler can bridge the classic-romantic gap, become a better fisherman, and enjoy the sport all the more.,

Drawing by Fred Barraza.

211

Fishing with the Kid

It all happened in less than a year. Last summer on our wilderness campout he was 12 years old, still a kid of just middling size for his age, and he acted like he knew he still had a lot to learn.

This spring he turned 13, he's sprouted to 5' 10" and now literally looks me in the eye. And there's hardly a thing he doesn't know. Some "Kid"!

Only in the realm of hunting and fishing does he readily defer to me; odd, in that I am the quintessential non-expert outdoors, only earning high grades for enthusiasm. Maybe he's just being nice.

Our first campout of the summer is still a week away. But we've recently had some interesting day trips of the blast and cast variety. I thought some reminiscence of my outdoor life with The Kid might be of interest.

I wrote a few weeks ago of finding a nice tributary of the Gila River where there swam a goodly number of trout. My report as I recall totaled 12 to 14 rainbows with a couple in the 15-inch range. Even before I got home I thought, "This would be the perfect place to take The Kid for a day's fishing."

The Kid likes action, is an impatient fisherman, but a week can make a big difference in a falling stream. The heat had reduced the flow to less than half, the water warmed, and I'm sure others were catching, and maybe keeping, some of the same fish I had caught and released a week earlier. Instead of 12 to 14 fish by one person, we managed 5 fish between us. But I was pleased The Kid caught one more than me. He never complained the action was slow. And he got the biggest one

There was a deep run of fast water. I told him to stand upstream in the flow and strip out line. "Strip fast," I said, "so your fly drifts down through that chute on a slack line."

He did it right and at the bottom of the chute his nymph got a terrific whack. He gigged him and fought him with some skill up through the fast water and he beached a 14-inch rainbow that made the whole day for both of us. The trout was hooked deep so we wrapped him in a wet bandana and the next night at supper I said, "No, you eat him all yourself; you out-fished your old man." I also contemplated that a year earlier he probably would have tried to horse the fish in that fast water and lost him to a broken tippet. The Kid was learning some of the subtleties of hooking and playing fish.

Another week of heat and drought. The Gila was down to 12 cfs, but I knew a few deep, green pools would remain. I told The Kid, "Say Buddy, let's go someplace where we can fish with flies or bait. We might catch a trout, or a bass, or a carp, or a catfish." We both knew it would a hot day afield but The Kid was game and we got an early start.

I caught one small rainbow on a fly but in the first hour that was it – Bud didn't even get a hit. So we changed rigs, still using fly rods but baited up with worms. Things picked up. At least for me.

I got something to play with my worm and by luck struck at the right time. I hooked a powerful fish that made some nice runs where he spun the handle on the reel and in the end the carp I expected turned out to be a 17-inch Sonora sucker. Once again I had forgotten about and underestimated this Gila native.

I caught some hellgrammites and rigged one up for The Kid and told him, "One of these will change your luck." We fished them without sinkers, like live flies, and The Kid fished his well, letting it rest on the bottom in the slow catfish/carp/sucker pools and drifting it like a fly in current where one might expect a bass or trout. But again it only worked for me as I caught a rainbow about 15 inches long. Then the heat and drought shut the fishing down.

We were tired hikers when we finally gave in and trooped up the bank to the truck. Here we met another angler, resting in the shade.

"This stretch is fished out," he said, "Everybody I met says so."

I thought it was more the heat and low water and he seemed surprised we'd gotten three pretty good fish. The Kid seemed not much discouraged the luck was all mine this time. And he really perked up when we stopped on the way home for a coke float, enough that he would ask: "Dad, when are we going rabbit hunting?

June is not hunting season except there is no closed season on jackrabbits. I had bought The Kid a 20 gauge Remington 870 pump for his birthday. He'd busted a few clay pigeons but wanted to try live game. So early one morning we went rabbit hunting.

It gets hot on the desert near Deming, New Mexico. Mid-June! But I knew of a coulee, semi-open, with yucca and mesquite and catclaw – a briar patch with some grassland openings – just hopping with big hares. In an hour and a half we had six and The Kid rolled five of them with his new 870 pump. An 8 lb. jack is a trophy to a kid with a new gun and I showed him how to filet the meat off the back legs for jackrabbit *posole*. I worked the knife rapidly and we left in a sweat for home.

The Kid is learning: to cast, to catch, to release the catch most of but not all of the time, and to shoot. He knows how to take the good days with those where the game is unaccountably elusive and superior. He's gracious when he wins, and philosophical when the luck goes another's way. And if he's not taller than his father's plebian 5' 10" right now, he will be by the time this story makes the press!

213

Flies for all Seasons

Flies are part of the fun of fly fishing. To some people I think they are even more interesting than the fish or the fishing. I can understand that, to a point.

Each fly is different, many are beautiful, like a tiny jewel, some so much so that you almost hate to cast them out there for fear they might be never seen again. And, on the other hand, each is an invitation to fantasy; you can look at an individual fly and wonder what it might catch next time it hits the water.

Still, one can get lost in fly selection; there are so many options. I like flies, especially the pretty ones, but to keep things manageable I put in my fly box a relative few styles that ought to work most anywhere. Here's my choice for a few flies for all seasons.

First, to cover the possibilities, you need some that sink and some that float; some that imitate and some that attract. And as we'll see, there may be some overlap at times.

The Wooly Bugger should be in any fly box and of course it's a sinker. Black ones imitate hellgrammites or leeches, brown ones imitate crawfish, and green ones could well be a bullfrog tadpole to a fish. Dead drift them and they are imitators, but jig them and they become attractors. Use one with a bead head and you can get down deep without a split shot, and I think the bead itself can act as an extra attraction to the fish. They come in all sizes but are famous for enticing the bigger bass or trout. All said, a dandy fly.

Another relatively large fly for larger fish is the Marabou Minnow. It does rather take on a minnow-like movement with a little help from you and they come in colors to imitate most minnows you find in your local waters. But really, I'd say color seldom matters. Fish go for the marabou more as a moving minnow lure rather than precise imitation. All those flowing feathers in flight stimulate fish to strike; it simply works.

Is the Pistol Pete a fly or a lure? It casts like a fly, once you get the hang of it, but that spin propeller makes it a spinner too, as though it belonged to a spinning rod. The spinner works even on a dead drift, but more so when you jig it or simply strip it in. Whatever, it is an attractor fly that comes in all colors, usually on a #6 or #10 hook. Purists won't use them but, no purist, they sure work for me.

One could name nymphs in the hundreds but who could name a better one than the Prince Nymph? Where the above are all big, attractor-type flies that sink the Prince Nymph is usually on a #12 to #16 hook and is perfect for small trout in small streams (not that big ones won't hit it). It must be the white wings, that make it appear an emerger, that time and again allows it to out-fish otherwise similar nymphs. I usually try an upstream cast and dead drift, then, if that fails, twitch it back upstream. It works both ways.

Surface flies always start with the Adams, not flashy at all yet it fools fish precisely because it imitates sufficiently well a variety of mayflies, *et al.* And by "and others" I mean a great variety as the Adams is the one dry fly that so often works when there is no hatch on. This is often the case on the Gila streams so always have an Adams in your fly box.

To give the same fly some flash, which sometimes works better, use the Parachute Adams. It is simply the bland Adams with a white furl on top to increase visibility. I think the well known Royal Wulff works for the same reason and is also a good addition. I regained my interest in dry fly fishing with the Parachute Adams, fishing for rainbows and browns a few years ago on the headwaters of the Little Colorado River of Arizona.

Most trout on most streams are familiar with the caddis fly hatch. The Elk Hair Caddis in the standard tan color is often best though various shades work. Not that you need a hatch. Again, on the Gila streams, a heavy hatch that truly activates a heavy trout rise is unusual. Simply use the elk hair when the trout are hungry, which is most of the time.

The Elk Hair Caddis, Adams, Parachute Adams and Royal Wulff should have you covered for dry flies. There are a couple of others that float that you will also want though they hardly resemble dry flies.

Dave's Hopper has become a standard grasshopper pattern and as summer wears on hoppers multiply, get bigger, and some of them land in the water. Trout and bass, and others, allow few to escape. When you see live hoppers on the bank assume a Dave's Hopper will work in the water. Lay it out up-current and watch the drift, at the ready.

Finally, you ought to have a few "popping bugs." These float, some fish hit them when they land, but the "gurgle" the bug puts on the surface when you pop it is what activates the quarry. These are commonly used to fly fish for pan fish but don't think they won't work on a calm evening on a local stream for trout or bass.

Well, that's an easily acquired handful of flies for most anything you might encounter in the streams of New Mexico or Arizona. You're covered. It doesn't mean you'll score every time, but run through this list and catch nothing and the problem is likely something other than the fly!

Tricked by a Fish?

Game fish are hard to figure. Compared to mammals or birds, or even reptiles and amphibians, they can only be regarded as primitive (in the beginning, we all came from the sea). On the intelligence scale, they can only be regarded as dumb. Nobody ever taught tricks to a fish, yet fish trick us all the time.

One measure of intelligence is memory and the memory of a fish is very short. Up along the San Juan River near Farmington fisherman line the waters and catch the same fish over and over again. We know they do because this is largely a catch and release water and many of the fish caught show the pricks and cut marks of previous hooks. Compare this to a coyote caught in a trap who gets away. You will have the devil of a time ever catching him again. Coyotes catch on; fish don't.

Yet I'm sure the guides along the San Juan would tell you that the trout there are very "smart." Only certain flies will work. And the one that works today may be ignored tomorrow, depending on what the fish are feeding on. Further, the fly must be tied precisely to effectively imitate the real one in the water, and the presentation of the fly must be correct in order to fool the fish. Cast the wrong fly, or cast the right fly the wrong way, or let any fly drag the least bit unnaturally in or on the water and you may go all day without a strike, though you can see trout feeding in the water and more skilled anglers at your elbow are catching them left and right.

For all of that, San Juan fishing in the "Quality Waters" seemed somewhat simplistic to me the one time I tried it. I had a San Juan veteran angler in the boat with me and he knew his stuff as in less than two hours I hooked three nice fish and the biggest, about 18 inches, was a colorful, thick-bodied rainbow. The fly was a tiny midge-like thing on a #22 hook that would be hell for me to tie on the tippet even with reading glasses. And up the line a couple of feet was a "strike indicator" which is a rarified term for a bobber and he said: "Cast it to that seam in the current over there and watch the indicator (bobber)." Well that was good advice too and the big one took the bobber (indicator) right under and it proved a wonderful fish. Yet I don't know how smart he was to fall for a rig that, excepting for the artificial bait, was rather like what we used as kids to catch bluegills.

The paradox is further illustrated by a trip I made a few years back to a Gila forest stream – Sapillo Creek. My partner, Stephen O'Day, and I were both fishing nymphs. Mine was a Prince nymph, a fly of well-earned effectiveness that roughly imitates a number of nymph species. A nymph sinks and the idea is to cast the nymph upstream on a light tippet in such a way that it will float down with the current almost as if it was the real thing. I say almost because no fisherman can ever completely eliminate the fact that his fly is attached to a line, however fine. Still, a lot of trout have been fooled by Prince nymphs.

But these weren't. I'd lay it up to my own poor skills but O'Day is pretty good and he couldn't get a hit either. Then, at the next pool, as my nymph once again finished its float downstream without a take, I twitched it back up through the current. A trout whacked it straightaway. Over the rest of the day I was able to hook trout by this method, while the drifting nymph continued to fail. Keep in mind that a nymph jigging its way rapidly upstream is unnatural. Real nymphs don't do that. Ultimately, these trout proved catchable on this day. But were they smart or dumb?

As Harold Blaisdell has pointed out in his wonderful book, *The Philosophical Fisherman*, all fishing is either imitative or provocative in nature. Knowing the difference, and which works best in a given situation, can improve your catch.

Most San Juan fishermen try to fool the trout with an imitative approach. Trout are vulnerable to a good imitation presented "naturally." This makes sense, but fish are not only vulnerable to a proper imitation of something they normally eat. They are also vulnerable to provocative lures and flies that look and behave like nothing that lives in water.

Suppose up on the San Juan you were to toss a red and white dardevle over the water and drag it back in across the current. I'd bet a six-pack a big trout would belt it a good one. Yet what is a trout thinking when he whacks a dardevle? Some would say the fish is hungry and thinks the lure is a minnow. This is nonsense.

A dardevle does not resemble any minnow; it does not resemble anything that lives in fresh water. Yet the lure continues to catch millions of fish yearly, including trout that will turn up their nose at a fly that, to us, looks like a perfect imitation. Lures, and many wet flies and streamers, are essentially provocative in nature; they are attractors that somehow stimulate an angry, emotional response in fish that need have no connection to hunger or imitation of real food.

It is often said that imitative fishing, as with dry flies, is more difficult and challenging than fishing with lures or with flies that are fished as attractors. This has led many a fly fisher to "graduate" to dry fly fishing only, and to turn up his nose at any fly fishing that is not imitative.

And then there's bait fishing. It, too, is imitative in form, and I think in the hands of a master also exhibits more skill than just tossing lures and reeling them in.

So some would say that when I jigged my nymph and caught a trout I was cheating. Maybeso. But I want to catch one, if only for the pleasure of letting him go. I can't give up easily. We've pretty well established that fish aren't very smart, and what does that make the fisherman who gets tricked by a fish?

The Chance to Ruin My Life for Sport!

I was stuck in Albuquerque a while back with nothing to do. I'd had a meeting the day before, had another one tomorrow, but was stuck this day with empty time in what for me is a large city teeming with boredom. So I hit a good used bookstore and for $5 found a worn paperback title I figured would get me through the empty hours back at the motel: *Trout Bum* by John Gierach.

I knew the author to be a readable and entertaining fishing writer but what caught my eye, and stimulated this column, was the book's subtitle: "Fly Fishing as a Way of Life." It got me to thinking…when does an outdoor pursuit graduate from a diversion, to a hobby, to "a way of life"? Or maybe even a compulsion? Are there values attached to these levels of interest? Benefits? Psychological dangers?

Diversions are easy. These are occasional outings and you can take them or leave them alone. I'm this way with bird hunting and predator calling. I'll go a time or two each year if the opportunity is right. Often it takes a friend to suggest it and I'll tag along. If I have some luck I'll enjoy it more than anticipated yet still, somehow, the activity doesn't quite catch on. The next season I'll bird hunt or call predators again maybe one to three times and be much more active with other pursuits. And here's a key reading – I don't day-dream much about bird hunting or predator calling.

When you start day-dreaming a lot about an outdoor sport – fantasizing about it when you should be tending to business and earning money – then you've got a hobby or avocation. With a hobby you'll go on your own if no one is available; you may even prefer it that way. You'll want to be out there more than a few days a year and you'll start reading, and collecting, books on the subject. You won't give up your spouse or your job for a hobby, but if they start to conflict seriously with your sport you might well day-dream of the day you can give one or both the boot. If they don't beat you to it. You know what I mean.

My hunting hobby is chasing jackrabbits with coursing hounds; I was captured by this pursuit in 1969 and have been at it every year since. Other hobbies can come and go however. Fly fishing, especially for smallmouth bass, grabbed me for a time as a teenager – circa 1959 – then I dropped it for 30 years before Stephen O'Day nudged me back, at least part way, into the sport. For a while, when I had a good cur dog and access to lots of squirrels, I was a hobbyist during New Mexico's squirrel season; I filled the season up. Now it's an occasional thing and some years I don't go at all.

John Gierach is a "trout bum" and I'll take his word for it that he pursues fly fishing as "a way of life." More so than a hobby or avocation, this is some serious outdoor sport; one's interest in "a way of life" does

218

not wax and wane; you're hooked, day and night. Here is Gierach in *Trout Bum* in a chapter called "Small Streams."

"The fisher of small streams can come home tired, maybe with sore knees or a bunged elbow for a souvenir. He will have covered some ground. Back at home he might feel a little old, especially if it's an early trip taken while his physical edge is still dull from the winter, but then he'll remember how far he went, all the pretty brook trout, and he'll feel like a kid.

"That night he'll sleep like a kid too, drifting off on the comforting wings of egotism – a man with, he tells himself, an aptitude for rugged country, honestly bushed."

He adds that as a trout bum, "You know that six miles in this country can be a momentous bushwhack...the farther off the beaten path it is the better. Only a maniac would hike miles of steep, brushy stream to fish that one good hundred-yard run. That's the point."

I agree. From reading *Trout Bum,* and some of Gierach's other collections of fishing essays, it is apparent that the author fishes hard all but the dead of winter, often making long trips away from home to find and fish new or famous streams. During that relatively brief winter reprieve he ties flies like mad, having gone through several full fly boxes the rest of the year. So he only breaks from fishing to get ready for more fishing, and fortunately for us, to write about it.

One can find admiration in that sort of commitment to sport. One can also find costs. Gierach refers obliquely to two ex-wives who apparently didn't accommodate the lifestyle too well. There is no reference to children; the responsibilities of even one of which can cut into your schedule of outdoor pursuits, not to mention other avocations.

In the book, *An Outside Chance*, another writer of the outdoors, Thomas McGuane, recalls meeting a sporting artist in the field who is carrying both a shotgun and a fly rod.

"What are you doing?" he asks the artist.

"Trout fishing and duck hunting."

The author comments: "I feel like a man who has been laid off to be only trout fishing." Elsewhere, with a touch of envy tilted to the artist, he adds: 'This would be a man who has ruined his life for sport."

And then there was the late Jason Lucas, post World War II outdoor scribe of the *Hook & Bullet* press who used to brag that he fished literally every day (365 times!) of the year, including Christmas. He revolutionized bass fishing at the time, only to miss seeing it revolutionized again, several times over, after he was gone.

And here's myself from *Tales of the Chase,* when I gave myself over to the hounds: "I became a dog man. That's more than just owning a dog, or going hunting with a dog, or saying 'I love dogs.' A dog man (especially a houndman) has more than one dog. Sometimes a lot more.

219

He's breeding dogs, raising puppies, he's buying and selling dogs and he'll do some trading. He's dog poor......"

Although I am more fanatical about hunting my hounds than fishing I think it is generally easier to fish as a way of life than hunt. Hunting for the most part has seasons and bag limits; those for big game are almost invariably limited to one "take" per year and a short season – a week or so for deer; maybe five days for elk, etc. Even the quail shoot is a mere three months in New Mexico. But you can legally, and effectively, fish all year......at least where I live.

For myself, I think I will not qualify as a "trout bum" any time soon, or make fly fishing "a way of life." For one thing, I'm not that good at it. I also like bait and spin fishing – even running trotlines – and fish other than trout. I do get out a good deal with hound and rod & reel – more than most – and I can read Gierach with a touch of envy. I also daydream about running dogs, guns, all kinds of fish and fishing, and things I'd tremble to detail, when I'm not actually afield; enough mental self indulgence for any man. And I have and enjoy a family and a homestead and this writing thing. It's a touchy business to get the right balance; I don't want to ruin my life for sport – but if you one day meet some ol' boy afield with a fast hound in the slips on one hand and a fly rod in the other, you'll know I've found it.

Fly Fishing in Hemingway's Footsteps

Fly fishing has a literature. More so than bait fishing, or spin fishing with lures, fly fishing has an aura that over the years has attracted fine, or at least well-known, writers to the sport. Indeed, so well connected is fly fishing with its own literature that it is beyond me to say if the aura is there from the fishing itself, of if it was created by the writer's works. Without the wordsmiths, is fly fishing really any different, or better, or more alluring than, say, worm dunking?

In *The Joys of Trout*, Arnold Gingrich, certainly one of the better of these wordsmiths, listed "Fifty Books for a Fly Fisherman." From the list, most any fly fisher would recognize these authors: Dame Juliana Berners; Izaak Walton; Sir Humphrey Davey; Wm. Scrope; A.J. McClane; Lee Wulff; Roderick Haig-Brown; Nick Lyons. I would add to that list more recent writers like Thomas McGuane and John Gierach. That's a very short selection of all the lofty names of those fly casters who, over the centuries, have expertly penned fishing tales and literate exposition to the delight of numberless generations of anglers who would "live" the pursuit vicariously. No wonder an aura illuminates the sport!

Notably, the Gingrich list does not include the name of Ernest Hemingway. This is likely because, although he wrote about fly fishing in portions of works, "Hem" never focused an entire book on the sport. Yet few would argue that the two must recognizable scenes in the history of fly fishing literature were penned by the young American expatriate, Ernest Hemingway, living in Paris in the 1920s and trying to write "truly." If you're literate, and fish, you know I'm talking about the fly fishing trip into Spain's Irati river from *The Sun Also Rises*; and, the monumental short story, "Big Two-Hearted River."

A close look at these two works puts the fly fishing aura in a whole new light. Here's what Hemingway's Jake Barnes did that early morning before the long hike to the Irati:

"I hunted around the shed behind the inn and found a sort of mattock, and went down toward the stream to try and dig some worms for bait. The stream was clear and shallow but did not look trouty. On the grassy bank where it was damp I drove the mattock into the earth and loosened a chunk of sod. There were worms underneath. They slid out of sight as I lifted the sod and I dug carefully and got a good many."

At the river, it is clear that the anglers are both using fly rods. But Jake's friend Bill ties on a McGinty and heads downstream. Jake has his worms.

"As I baited up, a trout shot up out of the white water into the falls…another trout jumped at the falls, making the same lovely arc and disappearing into the water that was thundering down. I put on a good sized sinker and dropped the bait into the white water close to the edge of

221

the timbers of the dam. I did not feel the first trout strike. When I started to pull up I felt that I had one and brought him, fighting and bending the rod almost double, out of the boiling water at the foot of the falls and swung him up onto the dam...in a little while I had six...they were beautifully colored and firm and hard from the cold water."

When Bill comes back he has four of his own, slightly larger than Jake's, caught on the McGinty.

The entirety of the fishing takes several pages. It is beautifully written in the Hemingway minimalist style and thus a famous scene to this day, and the protagonist Jake Barnes, the author's alter ego, caught all his on worms he dug himself early that morning in the moist earth behind the inn. Both used a fly rod and Bill was clearly fly fishing, but was Jake Barnes? Neither seems to care; it was good fishing and they kept their fish to eat later at the inn and the author described everything "truly."

In "Big Two-Hearted River" he is Nick Adams and he uses grasshoppers for bait. Of course he catches them himself, in the early morning, while the hoppers are still dormant with the cold. He is very accurate in this description, and in the way he hooks the hoppers under the chin and down through the thorax and the way the hoppers grab the hook and spit their brown juice on it, not liking being impaled. Then he fishes:

"Nick swung the rod back over his shoulder and forward, and the line, curving forward, laid the grasshopper down on one of the deep channels in the weeds. A trout struck and Nick hooked him.... Nick worked the trout, plunging, the rod bending alive, out of the danger of the weeds into the open river. Holding the rod, pumping alive against the current, Nick brought the trout in."

There is more to this story than fishing of course (Nick fears to fish the swamp because the fishing there would be "tragic"), but in the end even today's fly fishermen, more sophisticated in gear and technique and eschewing bait, can't get enough of it; we've all read it. Nick, using a fly rod, caught the trout on a grasshopper he caught himself and he kept the fish.

Two weeks ago I caught a nice 13" rainbow on a parachute Adams; except that there was no hatch to match it was a classic catch. He took it on the surface and he jumped five times! It was my only catch of the day, the whole experience was restorative, and I was not disappointed by having but a single fish for a day's work.

Last week I went to what looked like better water. Lows flows were augmented somewhat by a series of beaver dams that created deep pools. It was a lovely spring day where you want a flannel shirt when you start out and then you want to take it off and put it in your pack before noon. You sweat walking and fishing upstream and the intermittent breezes dry you off. Yet through the morning I caught nothing, nor saw or felt a fish.

Early afternoon I caught up with the biologists who had been electro-shocking the water ahead of me. Their fish sampling, needed from time to time, provides valuable information for management; the fish recover, but they're sure not going to feed after being whacked by that current.

"Dave," I said, "I think I just figured out why I haven't been catching any fish."

"Yeah; you need to get ahead of us," he said.

I was on a schedule and running out of time. But I knew that now that I was ahead of the equipment I had a chance. I removed my wooly bugger and put on a #8 hook. I got some live hellgrammites from under some rocks along the shore. When the time came I hooked each one carefully through the collar.

Lofting long, curving casts I looped each hellgrammite in turn into the pools above the dams and let them drift with the current. I landed three rainbows, touched a fourth before he got off; the biggest jumped twice, and fought with the tenacity of a Gila River bass. I don't keep many trout but the best one went 15 inches and showed pink flesh at home sautéed in a pan.

Was it fly fishing? I make no claims. I know I felt a certain aura, catching my own bait, fooling the fish, and feeling the fish fighting the rod and the current. I have tried to describe the whole experience 'truly," and hiking out with a trout in the bag I was, it seemed, fishing very much in Hemingway's footsteps.

Full Creel, Empty Creel

Anymore, most of us keep but few of the fish we catch. And when we do keep one, we no longer haul it home in one of those quaint wicker baskets known as a creel. So the full creel, or empty one, is mostly metaphor these days. But it seems a useful metaphor at that, based on what I've seen lately along our local streams.

I went to a reach of water that seldom lets me down. On an earlier trip this summer I'd caught, if I remember right, 7 trout and a bass, the fish coming about equally spaced – one an hour – through the day. I thought it was odd about the bass, since they usually outnumber the trout in that section, but I didn't hike out complaining of 7 rainbows 10 to 14 inches long. And the bass was pretty good sized too.

This time, fishing the same stretch, I got into the bass right away. They were all unimpressive in size – nothing so much as ten inches – but they were lively and I'd get a fish or two at every stop. There were other reasons too, for enjoying the day.

We've had good rains this summer and it showed. The stream flow was merely normal, but that's good after the long drought, and the surge in vegetation had seep willow and black-eyed Susans and Indian paintbrush and so much else choked up against the banks; in places the sawgrass was up to your hips.

Sometimes it was hard to get off the trail and down to the bank to check out the pools and better runs. But I didn't mind. Bees and butterflies were everywhere and this was the riparian jungle nature in her better years offers a free-flowing stream. Plus the jungle keeps the riff-raff out.

There's a sharp turn in this watercourse I always look forward to. Just above the turn there's a log across the flow. If you can drift your fly in under that log just right there's usually a trout in there. Not always big, but you can about count on it. Just below the turn is the depth of the pool. There's a pocket back there – a "V" in the rocks – and if you can put your fly in there just right it's near certain a bronze bass will smack it. He's not always big but, again, you can about count on it. I don't want to count the times I haven't put my fly in under that log, or back in that pocket, just right, but this day I would have no reason to kick myself.

In under that log went the beadhead wooly bugger and out came the trout, over a foot long; I gigged him and he was seemingly well hooked. Close to the bank he got loose. I was inspired anyway and went downstream a few steps and cast to that pocket in the rocks.

Incredible, I dropped the fly right into the "V". I didn't even have time to jig it and I was into a bass. He was all over that pool, never jumped, but worked me over good. I didn't lose this one and lying in the

224

shallows he was the spread of my 9-inch hand, twice. I've caught bigger bronze bass, but not by much on a fly.

By noon I was eating a good sandwich in warm sun sitting on a log with a dozen bass and two trout brought to the bank. All the bass but one were small. But that 18-incher was a hummer and, metaphorically, my creel was nearly full. I thought: if I catch another trout, and he has some size and looks like a stocker, I'm going to take him home and fry him up in butter.

I got two more small bass hiking out, and then I came to that pool with the log just above the turn in the stream. Of course I can't say for sure he was the same fish but at 13" he was about the right size and pale coloration told me this was a stocker rainbow. I put him in the "basket," now full.

A day like that can have you thinking of yourself as a master of craft. In my case, it was all just a tease. My next outing, all I carried out was a story to tell.

It was problematical from the git-go. I got to the river and it was murky – almost muddy – from recent rains. I used a pistol pete in several colors, hoping the flash would draw a strike. By noon I was eating a good sandwich in warm sun sitting on a log and I'd yet to get a hit. I'm not above catching bait by way of catching a fish, and I did have an excuse – that water was pretty dirty.

I caught a hellgrammite, changed to 9 lb. tippet, and put the bait in a slow pool where I knew carp would be lurking in the murk. Of course carp don't need to see it to find it. One did find the hellgrammite and soon I had a big fish on going downstream fast.

I never saw him; it could have been a catfish. But it ran like a carp and in that part of the river they will average two feet and 30" or better is not unusual. That's a challenge on a 4 wt. rod but, still, I should have got him in. It was the reel that let me down.

His second run was so fast, I was slow getting my palm on the reel. And I should have had the drag tighter. He spun me into a backlash; the fly line looped and caught itself. Unable to loosen any line, I knew he would break me off or break the rod. Oddly, it was the fly line itself, not the tippet, that cut him loose.

Well, I guess it really wasn't the reel's fault. I kicked myself more than once hiking back to the truck. No one need feel guilty about killing a carp, I know how to cook them, and I would have eaten this fish too.

But my creel was empty.

Does the Gila Hold a Record Bass?

The New Mexico state record smallmouth bass was 24" long, weighed 7 lbs., 3 ozs., and was caught just a few years ago at Ute Lake (the world record of 10 lbs., 14 ozs., caught at Dale Hollow Lake, TN, has stood since 1969). Yet there is evidence that the biggest bronze bass in New Mexico may be swimming in the usually meager flow of our own Gila River. I came close to such a fish just last week myself. And anglers I trust report they may have already caught the state record smallmouth from the Gila but, sporting chaps they are, they released the fish with a cursory measurement and no certified weight.

How can the Gila River, a stream you can walk across most of the year without getting your knees wet, grow such trophy bass? And while the state's largest smallmouth may well reside in the Gila River system, why is it unlikely to make the record books ahead of the bass in big reservoirs like Ute, Conchas, Navaho, or Elephant Butte? Therein reside some tales.

The smallmouth bass is not native to the Deep South or west of the Continental Divide which means it's not native to the Gila River. But the species *(Micropterus dolomieui)* has been widely stocked nation-wide. New Mexico Department of Game & Fish records show that the agency released smallmouth bass into the Gila River twice in the 1940s. They must have liked the habitat for natural reproduction took over straight-away. By 1953, one of the agency's first electro-shock surveys showed the bass already well established from the Gila forks area all the way down to the Gila Middle Box Canyon.

They've been there ever since. Blow-out floods and ash flows periodically knock their numbers down, but some bass always survive and they bounce back quickly. I've been fishing for them in the Gila for almost 30 years and for a long time I thought the stories I was hearing of "twenty-inch smallmouth" and "record bass" were so much stuff and feathers. I wasn't catching any such fish, on bait, flies, or lures.

Oh, I caught some nice fish. On one trip through the heart of the wilderness Stephen O'Day and I hiked and fished four days on the river. We must have caught nearly 100 bass between us. But only a half dozen or so were over a foot long and the biggest one was maybe 15 inches. Where were these trophy Gila bass I kept hearing about but never saw? I was suspicious – we all know how fishermen lie. You would think at least a picture of one of these trophies would survive?

Then one day, fishing alone, I tossed a black wooly bugger into a distant pocket of water between two boulders and, unaccountably, I caught a bronze bass 18 inches long. At least that's what the span of my hand (two spans, nine inches each) told me. Of course, I'm a fisherman too; I was alone, took no photo, lacked a ruler or a scale...so maybe I was lying too. But I felt him on the line, saw him in the shallows, and not only made a cursory measurement; I held him in my hand as I removed the fly and let him go. For me, that was a trophy bass.

I began to pay more attention to the fish tales I was hearing, considering the source, the location (if they'd reveal it), fly, bait or lure, and method of measure (length and or weight). Most of the anglers, I decided, were like me – they wanted to catch big bass, didn't want to kill one to prove anything, and were making truthful estimates based on a look, or the span of a hand, or a mark on the rod. I heard several estimates of "at least twenty inches," a couple at "twenty-two inches" One guy was convinced his stretched to "twenty three!" and another said: "Two feet long!"

The only weight record I got was from an agency fisheries biologist who told me they had electro-fished a 5.5 lb smallmouth from out of tiny Beaver Creek back in the 1980s. Otherwise, claims of 20-inch bass or better came from all three forks and the main Gila from Grapevine Campground down through the Middle Box, though the West Fork and Middle Box appeared to have fewer bass, the one dominated by trout, the other by catfish. If even half these assessments were true, it would appear there were indeed trophy bass in the Gila and possibly a record fish. Though a slim flow, the Gila clearly produces a fertile food base for fish; if it grows catfish and carp in excess of thirty inches, why not bass in excess of twenty?

In 2007 I caught a 20" smallmouth from the Gila using a worm while fishing for catfish in water too murky for a fly. Then, last month, fishing with local angling author Rex Johnson, I hooked a similar fish on a hellgrammite imitation. "That's a 20-inch bass!" Rex said as the fish appeared in the shallows before breaking me off. It seemed I was getting the hang of big bass.

And so, just last week, I caught a bigger one. My son was with me and using his span of hand he said, "Twenty-three inches, Dad!" I suggested the fish was over 20" but probably not over 22" long. We did have a camera which doesn't prove any measurement but does tell us it was a nice fish, the biggest Gila bass in my record book, and that we didn't make it up. He struck a beadhead brown wooly bugger and took10 minutes to land on a 4-weight rod and 4 lb. tippet.

To his credit, the Ute Lake angler kept his record fish alive in a live-well till it was certified and released. That option is not available to the wilderness bass of the Gila drainage. If you carry your Gila trophy out for certification you may as well eat it; it's not going back in the stream. If the state record bronze bass lives in the Gila and I catch him, I'll likely take my pleasure in the experience – both the catch and the release – and enjoy the debate of speculation when I tell people I let him go. I'd better have a ruler though, and a camera, so I can prove I didn't make it all up.

Gila Trout Inspires Anglers Old and New

It would seem a stretch of logic that there are trout here at all. The Gila River mountains of southwest New Mexico are isolated and surrounded by desert – how did they come to raise their own unique salmonid, the Gila trout *(Oncorhynchus gilae)?* Well, many millennia ago the climate was cooler and the water more ample. The Gila ran all the way to the Colorado back then, within the historical range of the rainbow trout, including the West Coast mountains and their rivers that drained to the Pacific. Our Gila trout must have shared some ancestry with these rainbows as even today they will readily interbreed and produce fertile offspring. But the climate changed.

Waters receded, became warmer, and the fish that would become known as Gila trout was left isolated in the remaining cool water of the Gila mountains where, over many millennia, they would take on their own "look" and behavioral traits sufficient that later biologists would declare them a separate species. But before the biologists there were the anecdotal jottings of settlers who variously called these fish "speckled" or "mountain" trout. One of these was an erstwhile British officer turned frontier rancher named Captain William French.

French was that rare gem among frontiersman in that he was literate and left a very readable memoir of the times: *Recollections of a Western Ranchman.* In the 1880s he made an extended jaunt into the upper West Fork of the Gila River where he documented the presence of two species that were already in trouble, though in the case of the trout the Captain could hardly be expected to know it. But his first encounter was with the rare Merriam's elk.

To this day in southwest New Mexico there are locals who will tell you that the idea of elk in the historic Gila is a hoax; the 20th century introduction of elk into the region put "exotic" big game where they were never meant to be. French remembers differently.

"The next day," he wrote, "we went on to Elk Mountain and actually ran into the herd of elk. There were eleven head of them. From what I could see of them, they appeared to be all does or cow elk which I believe is more correct. This was the only bunch of wild elk I ever saw in New Mexico. A few years later they were all killed by prospectors and others. I never heard of any heads or antlers being preserved.

"From there we drifted over to the West Fork of the Gila where we camped for several days. It was there that we found use for our fishing tackle for it was swarming with mountain trout."

French reports that they caught their dinner with "tackle" and using grasshoppers for bait (as Hemingway would do, famously, in another story) but he and his partner, Ed Erway, soon came up with a better plan.

228

"The water was very low and we herded them into a pool which was several feet deep. We then blocked the entrance, so they could not get out. They were so numerous we succeeded in scooping them out with our hats. It would have been more successful if we could only have kept them in our hats till we secured them. Most of them jumped out and finally most of the rocks were so slippery we both slipped into about five feet of water and got thoroughly soaked."

Great sport, that! French could not know that within 15 years these isolate native gems would face the beginnings of a steady stocking by individuals and agencies of rainbow trout that would crossbreed and "genetically swamp" the native species to virtual extinction. By the 1950s identifiable Gila trout were reduced to at best a half dozen seminal streams and no more than 20 miles of water. The New Mexico Department of Game & Fish, with help from the U.S. Fish & Wildlife Service and Gila National Forest, began a restoration program that wasn't always popular.

Streams were closed to fishing as piscicides were used to eliminate non-native species and people complained about the loss of fish and angling opportunity. In the early 1990s advancing DNA analysis revealed that Gila trout thought 100% pure were tainted with a few degrees of rainbow gene introgression and had to go. Some anglers complained, including me; trout that for all the world looked and behaved like pure-strain Gilas were poisoned by the bucketful. Ash flows from forest fires wiped out entire streams to the dismay of all. But the agencies were persistent and by 2006 some sixty miles of stream had been renovated and the species was downlisted from Federally endangered to threatened, allowing the State Game Commission to open a few streams to legal Gila trout fishing for the first time in decades. In the summer of 2007, Greg McReynolds and I journeyed to Black Canyon Creek to see if this "new" fish was worth all the fuss.

The day drizzled, the creek was low and clear, and at the first good pool we could see these yellow-flanked trout fining beneath an undercut bank. Greg's dry fly was ignored. Thinking them spooked, I nonetheless tossed in a beadhead nymph. As it drifted and sank a trout came casually out from cover and just as casually inhaled the fly. Once I tightened up he went nuts. Lacking the discrimination of the cagey brown, or the leap of the rainbow, he was nonetheless the hardest fighting trout for his size (about 11 inches) I can recall, all the while flashing those yellow-bronze flanks, decorated with black speckles, in his lengthy, desperate, athletic attempt to shed the hook. In the end, I shed the hook for him; as he swam off I felt he had vindicated his race and fifty years of species renovation conducted by fits and starts.

In the end we only caught about seven between us, up to 13 inches long, but each giving meaning and substance to the fly fisher's ultimate quest for "wild trout." Naïve, unsophisticated, these trout all fought like freedom was in their blood and that capture was a disgrace to be avoided with every possible effort of muscle and fin.

Problems remain. Over 20 miles of the upper West Fork of the Gila have been treated with poison multiple times; this would bring Gila trout range in New Mexico close to 100 stream miles but getting all the non-native browns removed is still incomplete. Even after a successful renovation of a stream reach a few rainbows may slip back in by hook or by crook and this can compromise the 100% purity standard of the Gila stock demanded by the agencies. We need about 150 miles of Gila trout stream habitat, including several Arizona streams, to achieve a delisting from "threatened" under ESA to full State management. It won't be easy and there is no consensus among the public regarding either the methods or the goals.

Still, the Gila trout has earned some defenders now that a measure of legal fishing has been achieved. Overstocks of hatchery Gila trout are being released in The Forks area of the Gila, among other streams. If you can "swamp" a species close to oblivion perhaps you can also "swamp" it back to prominence. And starting July 1st, 2008 a portion of Mogollon Creek will open to Gila trout fishing. Like Black Canyon, it will be strictly catch and release, artificials only, single barbless hooks, and you need to get the free Gila trout fishing permit. Check the Fishing Proclamation for all the details. I was certainly impressed with the Gila trout as a game fish; they were born and raised for pursuit with a #12 Prince nymph and about a 4-weight rod. As for herding them into a pool and scooping them out with your hat, I'd suggest you confine that pursuit of these speckled beauties to a reading of Captain French and his *Recollections*!

"Going Dry"

It's been apparent to me for some time that I don't fly fish "right;" that is, the right way. My breaks from orthodoxy and propriety are myriad but, principally, I usually fish flies below the surface.

Fly fishing tradition was largely formed centuries ago in Europe, especially the United Kingdom, and this tradition was taken up and scarcely modified in our northeastern states. By that tradition, a fly is selected to match a specific insect hatch coming off the surface. You cast a matching dry fly upstream and try for a dead drift to fool the rising trout.

Sounds good to me, but when was the last time you saw an organized rise on a Gila Forest stream? It happens, but if you limited your fishing to rising trout us locals would spend most of our angling days simply watching water, adrift with unfulfilled possibilities.

So, like you, I drift nymphs and wooly buggers and streamers and other wet flies of various sizes and hues under water and elicit a feeding response from trout that, by appearances, aren't even hungry. In this line of logic I am comforted by some old lore that may or may not be true that says something like 90% of a trout's feeding is below the surface. Still, tradition holds a certain allure to the fly-fisher; even the maverick feels its pull and tug and occasional reprimand for taking too many trout from "the deep" instead of "on the rise." And so the other day I went fishing having made a vow that I would only take them with a dry fly – "going dry," call it..

I started off by losing seven dollars to the Federal Government. It's come to be that the Forest Service wants a parking fee – three dollars a day in this case – to leave your vehicle at certain recreation areas and trailheads. I always forget about this and, sure enough, I arrived at the trailhead with a ten dollar bill. There was no person nor place nearby to make change. I was left with the choice of stiffing the Forest Service (my first impulse) and risk a ticket, or, leaving ten dollars in the numbered envelope when they only asked for three!

Having paid my taxes last April, even three dollars seems like a gouge on public land; still, I parted with a ten-spot without much hope that my government would put the extra seven bucks to good use.

Upstream, at the first pool, I chose a Parachute Adams. This is simply the world's most lauded dry fly with a tuft of white hair added to increase buoyancy and make it easier to see. Typically, there was no hatch in progress but I could see trout holding and wavering in the pools.

I went for the upstream, dead-drift, approach. I'm not practiced at this and I'm sure it showed. Yet the fish kept rising and bumping my fly. I couldn't hook them and blamed myself, thinking I lacked the reflexes to hook fish on the surface. Eventually, the trout bumped it enough that my dry fly got wet and started to sink.

The usual suggestion is to periodically false cast to dry the fly. This was not possible along the confines of this tight little stream. So I let the fly sink and they bumped it under water and I still couldn't hook them. Buggers were "striking short" and I broke for lunch. It was a pretty spot and a good sandwich but it was eating me up that I'd paid ten bucks to the government to prove to myself I couldn't catch trout on a dry fly. Grim.

After lunch I debated changing flies, maybe even giving up and going with a nymph. But it wasn't that they wouldn't hit the Adams, and when it was wet my Adams was rather like a nymph anyway. I put some floatant on the same fly and went back to the surface.

A small rainbow hybrid took that floating Adams on the first pass. He hit it so hard he hooked himself. I landed him, turned him loose, and after that I could hardly miss. I got most of them on the dead drift though I'm sure many of my presentations were flawed. Often, they hit it anyway.

At the end of each drift I would twitch the fly, or even skitter it back upstream. This is against traditional dry fly dogma, but it often worked.

I also fished some of the pools from upstream. Sometimes, this was the only cast available. I'd make a roll cast down into the pool and feed some slack out, hoping for that dead drift. This, too, is nontraditional but it worked, including on the only fish of the day that exceeded a foot in length.

Traditional or not, I was dry fly fishing. It was fun to see the fly, see the fish attack, and watch the swirl and see the belly-flash as the fish took the fly down. In spite of myself, I must have caught twenty trout. When I finally got back to the parking lot, still empty of people or cars, I felt not so bad about losing seven dollars to the Forest Service.

Things got more interesting when I got home. In my bookshop I have on sale a first edition of Leonard Wright's classic, *Fishing the Dry Fly as a Living Insect – An Unorthodox Approach.* This was a revelation.

Wright agrees that the upstream dead-drift approach is best when there is a hatch underway. But he says the dead drift approach is not the best for dry flies when fishing for reluctant trout. Then, the fish must be convinced the bug is alive. Wright does this with a twitch technique that is more sophisticated than what I employed but fulfills the same purpose, to fish the dry fly as a living insect.

Wright also has a chapter on why it is sometimes best to fish the dry fly from upstream down. He explained in detail, from long experience, what I had just discovered that day by indirection. I thought, I'm not so dumb after all!

232

In the end it was just neat that I had learned something useful on the water that day, and that my knowledge was largely self-discovered, then confirmed, by the estimable Leonard Wright.

Also, since I gave the Forest Service seven dollars too much, I figure I've got two days built up where I can park at that trailhead for free. I wonder what my chances are of getting away with that?

A Hard Hike to the Waterfall

It used to be one of my favorite trout streams. It must have been about 1989 that Stephen O'Day and I first went in there and made a three-day camp. I had fly-fished as a teenager but this was my first bit of stream casting with the long rod in many years.

O'Day said, "I've always done well here. They're wild rainbows, or rainbow-Gila hybrids, though most are not big, and the best fishing is at the end of the hike at the waterfall."

The stream is in a steep canyon and I remember we had to scramble up and down banks when we'd see a good pool. The trail up the canyon hadn't been maintained for many years and it would appear and disappear and when it would disappear we would have to bushwhack and that's always a pain carrying a fly rod.

But there were trout there and the stream was lucid and often you could see them and sight-cast to individual fish and that's always fun. I spent a fair amount of time with my fly caught in the bushes but O'Day said that's part of the game and even he got hung up a time or two himself.

As we worked our way upstream, towards that distant, hoped-for waterfall, the pools got better and we left the maybeso path we'd been on, went down into the canyon and climbed the boulders and slash and tried all the better pools and runs. O'Day did better than me of course but even I caught a few trout on flies and was beginning to recall that I once knew how to fly fish.

The waterfall arrived, finally. It would be music to anyone's ears and it made a large plunge pool full of trout at the bottom of the drop. O'Day rigged me up with a tiny black ant and I cast – not badly – and got two pretty ones before the rest of them got spooked. It was a beautiful spot to fish and have lunch and then we hiked back to camp.

Over the years O'Day and I did about as well on several other trips there and I did all right on a hike or two alone, always ending at the waterfall. You could do it all in a day and make it back to the truck before dark if you got an early start.

Then about four years ago things started to get tough. I went in for a day trip with my son Bud. He was about seven and too young to fly fish much and mostly just sort of tagged along. I was surprised he made it all the way to the waterfall and back without much complaint. But the fishing was poor.

A drought had left long stretches of the stream dry and only at the upper end did we find any trout. There weren't many and I think I caught two or three and considered myself lucky for that. The waterfall was just a trickle and the meager pool below held no trout that we could see or catch. It was still a pretty spot for lunch but I was alarmed by the stress on the fish with the lack of water and wondered what the future might hold.

This year began with a long drought that actually began back in '05 and ended finally with the recent flush monsoon season that went on for two and a half months. This past weekend I said, "Bud, let's go make the hike to the waterfall. You've got your own fly rod now and there's sure to be plenty of water in the stream."

It was my first trip in there since four years before and with the recent monsoons there was plenty of water all right. Not too much though, and it was clear enough to see fish, if we could find any.

We couldn't. I suspected trouble when we first scrambled down a bank above a perfect habitat for trout. A nice flow made a deep pool up against a big boulder and there was a tree there you could hide behind while you made your cast.

Bud had tied on a large black gnat and I added a tiny split shot to make sure it got down in this pool that must have been 6 feet deep. We snuck up on the pool and Bud hid behind the tree and looped a good roll cast right up against the boulder in the deep spot and just off the main current. Perfect. But nothing hit, nor flashed nor followed on this and repeated casts and there were apparently no fish in this picture-perfect pool.

We eventually got right down in the canyon and cast to many fine trout habitats – pools and runs where you could just see trout if only they'd been there.

We made the waterfall, finally, and the pool looked like a small pond with the ample cascade throwing oxygen into the nicest place for trout you would ever hope to see. Bud worked it well upstream and down; he had that looping roll cast with the small split shot down pat. But as to fish, this locale like the others was dry.

We had lunch at this pretty place and I don't think Bud was as disappointed as I. Talking half to myself I tried to explain it, though it was pure speculation.

"Bud," I said, "this monsoon season we've just had has made this stream look real good. But we had a nine-month drought before and it dried up the stream and killed all the fish. This stream runs down to other streams that still hold trout but they haven't had time to repopulate this one and so we're left with no fish stories to tell. I suppose it could just be we didn't fish very good but we always catch fish here and we didn't even see a trout."

It's a hard hike to the waterfall and back to the truck in one day when you know you've been skunked. I was still looking for something positive on the way out. As we passed a pool we'd worked pretty hard that morning I found it. Here I had tried to cast my fly, a Pistol Pete, around a boulder into the best lie in the pool. I wasn't quite making it. Now, on the way out, I was getting into position to try again.

Bud said, "Dad, I think I see a better way to fish this pool."

He crossed the creek, upstream, scrambled around another big boulder and got in good position to drop that black gnat right into the honey hole and all without showing himself to the fish. Of course there still weren't any fish in there and we still got skunked. But he's only eleven and as a father I was beaming as we climbed the rough trail out of the canyon.

"Bud," I said, "you're on the road to catching lots of fish."

Seeking Wild Trout in Old Mexico

Grand obsessions can lead one to glory and a lifetime of satisfactions.
Or drive one to drink. Rex Johnson's grand obsession – perhaps only
entirely appreciated by a fellow angler – has played out rather well. You
can share it now in book form: *The Quiet Mountains – A Ten-Year
Search for the Last Wild Trout of Mexico's Sierra Madre Occidental*
(University of New Mexico Press, hardcover, 10 x 8 1/2, 216 pgs.
$45.00).

About ten years ago, Johnson of Silver City, New Mexico had a trout
experience in tiny Cow Creek of the Gila Wilderness. This experience
was something of an epiphany and would eventually lead him south.

Baffled by a large wild rainbow in Cow Creek, that would defer to
the smaller trout in the pool whenever presented a fly, Johnson
proceeded to catch all the small trout in the pool and move them
upstream. He then was ready for the big one:

"Its path had been cleared. It came all the way up to the top, to look
more closely at the fly. Now, this time, it didn't chase after the fly; it
didn't even seem to swim. It just drifted effortlessly upwards, as though
it were being buoyed, moving only its two pectoral fins like little wings,
or oars, to keep balance, until it was right up on the fly. The creamy
white of its mouth and throat opened, and it took the fly."

Incredibly, Johnson had caught a wild trout nearly 18 inches long in
a creek he could step across. The act was a kind of perfection, made the
more momentous by its implausibility, and led him to speculate on trout
even further south, at the southern tip of their implausible range, in Old
Mexico. Those first Mexico mountains were visible from the ridge above
Cow Creek.

There would follow nearly ten years of haphazard travel to various
streams of the Sierra Madre. Johnson stumbles upon many adventures
there, sometimes foolishly but always lived and reported in good grace
and humor, such as brushes with bandits, *narcos,* unrequited love and
lost companions. The ultimate goal, the wild, native trout of the Rio
Bavispe, is finally found, surviving implausibly in greatly degraded
habitats. Still, Johnson gets into some good fish:

"This is a good pool. I bet there are more. I go back up, repeat the
same drift, and another one pulls the rod down. This one is even bigger.
It takes two or three minutes before I can see it. Sixteen or more, thick
and strong. Hard to believe. I see the red band, the pale yellow belly. It is
very plump, with a tiny head. A female probably. As I reach for the
nymph it breaks the line. Now I have only one of the good nymphs left."

A remarkable experience, enriched for the author by the sight of two
Sierra Madre otters who shared the stream with the trout. Johnson reports
that the native trout of the Bavispe are essentially rainbows distinguished

not only by the above colors but a yellow throat slash as well. A singular trout, in lots of trouble.

Not only are the streams going bad due to unregulated grazing, logging, dam building and irrigation, imported hatchery rainbows are cross-breeding the natives out of existence. Curiously, these imports do not arrive in a misguided attempt to improve the fishing, as is often the case north of the border, but to be raised in ponds and tanks for food, like catfish farms! Some get loose, and while they don't survive long in the harsh streams, they last long enough to muck up the gene pool of the native trout of the Bavispe watershed. Sound familiar?

Johnson goes into a long harangue, well thought out, regarding how the native Apache trout of Arizona – a close relative of both the Gila trout and the Bavispe trout – has been turned into a domesticated fish at the Alchesay hatchery in Arizona, a poor degenerate of the original Apache trout of wild streams. But this new trout is designed to satisfy all the put-and-take anglers of this world. Johnson fears the same for the Bavispe and Gila trout:

"Scientific breeding, after all, is pretty crude. One could not conceive of the trout, one can only mess around with it…. The Bavispe trout came from no one knows where, certainly not from the regional fish hatchery, but from nature, from God, and they have been in the same river not for one hundred years, when the first *blancos* came into the Sierra Madre, but for anywhere from three to ten million years. Time is more intelligent than even the finest experts at the nearest second-rate or even first-rate university. The Bavispe trout is time-tested. One might say, at the risk of sounding trite, that it is highly evolved."

In the end the author is fatalistic, yet eloquent, over the passing:

"One thing is certain, and that is that none of this can last very much longer. The Bavispe trout are scarce and becoming scarcer; all the finest things are leaving us, we have all proven ourselves so completely undeserving. The third millennium is here. There is no change in sight, no second coming. Yet all these things considered, if I do return, I'll be sure to go down into the Gavilan Box, then ten or twenty miles further down…all the way, and there we *compañeros* shall meet again where the cows can't possibly follow….

"…I'll be there, at least, I'll be there to look for the sycamores, and the hidden side canyons far bigger than Laborcita, with drinkable water and, who knows, maybe if I still deserve anything in this world, I'll find a seventeen-inch Bavispe trout, the very last one, deep in the Sierra Madre Occidental, beneath a cloudy, black mountain lit by insects and made of all the stuff that all our different dreams are made of."

Dog Days, Low Water, and Big Fish

There is a tendency during the dog days of summer to get lazy, find excuses to stay indoors with the "AC," or at most just putter around the yard when you've got time off. Not us.

We descended into the canyon, all downhill, but it was already hot and that old familiar sweat patch began to form underneath our backpacks. The hound carried a pack as well and panted profusely though he's tough as a boot and was not over-stressed. At the confluence, the river was almost painfully low but still the water and shade provided a certain relief. We were off in the Wilderness for four days of fishing and camping in the dog days of summer.

Dog days? The phrase I discovered goes back to Roman times. They identified and named the two dog constellations, *Canis major* and *Canis minor*. *Canis major* includes Sirius, a star so bright in the night sky the Romans thought it helped the sun heat the earth (not so according to modern astronomy). Sirius is readily visible in the cooler months but "rises" with our Sun in summer and during this period "disappears;" the sun "brights" it out. But the Romans believed the 20 days either side of the conjunction of Sirius and the Sun contributed to the peak of mid-summer heat; thus the "dog days" of summer, roughly July 3rd to August 11th.

Bud and I (and I believe we can add Archie, the hound, to this) have decided the Romans may have been on to something. We went in July 6th, stayed four days, and each day was warmer than the last. We hiked downstream a couple of miles. The long holiday weekend had passed and we would see no one else throughout this outing. We could have gone further downstream and I wish now we had but by noon that sweat patch under my pack had drenched my whole shirt. When we arrived under a big sycamore with shade, a flat sandy patch for the tent, and a fishing hole nearby, I said, "Camp!"

We each had a 4-wt fly rod and this was a run of water where bronze bass and several kinds of trout might be found. But we had been fly fishing for trout and bass all summer. And we'd been catching some. Between us we had hardly caught a catfish or carp this season. As we set up camp we both decided we'd focus on trying to catch fish 20" long, or better.

"There's got to be a big flathead (catfish) in one of these pools." I said.

"Channel cats too," Bud said. "And I saw some big carp on the way in. How long will our worms last?"

"If we keep them in the shade, a couple of days," I said.

"We can always catch some hellgrammites when the worms run out, Dad."

239

"Yeah, and if we get desperate we can stoop to using flies."

The irony of two fly fishers opting for bait on a fishing trip, and "stooping" to using flies only as a last choice that they might keep fishing, well, it was not lost even on a 14-year-old kid. "I don't think we'll need any flies," he said.

This showed experience and confidence a father likes to see. The bait-fisher camping out in the wilderness needs to know not only how to catch fish but how to catch the bait that will catch fish. Bud was familiar with both wooly worms and garden hackle and, like me, liked a variety of fishing. By the time the tent went up we were both itching to try something live in those pools that, despite the near-record low flows, remained a dark green and deep enough to hide fish – even big ones – from our Polarized lenses.

We deferred to the heat however, until the pool too was shaded, and then after a supper of grilled pork steaks Bud caught a 21" Sonora sucker. We had a measuring tape this time – no estimating with our hands – and as we crawled into the tent that night I said, "That's pretty good, Buddy, when you can get a fish over twenty inches in the pool right by camp."

"I'll bet there's some bigger ones just upstream," he said

The next morning we went up there, a nice backwash pool that was large enough for a big catfish or carp. We might have camped there had there been any shade. By now we had caught a few hellgrammites and it was fun to speculate as to which would produce a trophy, the natural bait from the river or the "Canadian" night-crawlers from the outdoor store in town.

There wasn't much to choose from as I caught a 25-inch flathead on a hellgrammite and Bud got a 25-inch carp on a worm. We saved mine for supper, more than enough for us and the pack dog. Buddy's was the thicker, heavier fish however, and the stronger in resistance, though on a 4-weight rod it took a while to wear both fish down. Those were the best though not the only fish of the day and again we gave the afternoon to the sun and the heat and hid out in the shade with a nap..

The next morning, downriver, we found a pool that would "float a battleship," according to Buddy. I wish we could have fished it at night and I thought we'd do better but we each managed a 20-inch catfish, him a channel cat and me another flathead. On the way back, from a small pocket of water, I got a 22-inch flathead, just right for supper, and I said, "We'll stringer him and haul him out tomorrow for a family meal."

That evening Bud rounded out his game list with a 15-inch smallmouth, again right at camp. It was the largest of perhaps a half dozen bass on the trip along with three trout. And okay, maybe some of them – like Bud's bass at camp – were caught on flies. We're not bragging on it; we are eclectic and versatile in our fishing and throwing a few flies at smallmouth bass and trout is ok, even on a catfish trip. And

240

come to think of it, one of those trout was a brown, nicely colored with the bright markings of that species. Brown trout have not been stocked in the Gila drainage in something like forty years. So this was a wild trout and I got him on a black wooly bugger that did a good job of looking like a real, live hellgrammite and out of the same pool where I had caught a 25-inch flathead catfish two days before. Needless to say, the flathead wasn't a hatchery stocker, either. There may be another stretch of water where these two species of gamefish co-habit but I can't name it.

The next morning we hiked out, 4-hours in the heat and dodging two big harmless rattlesnakes along the way…harmless because we dodged them. We hadn't beaten the heat of the dog days of summer. Nor had we added any water to a stream in drought. But we'd learned to live with it all, as is, and make it worthwhile, with memories of a hand-full of fish that went twenty inches, or better.

Spanish Mackerel, and Kings, on My Mind

In the fall of the year they come south along Florida's west coast, swimming in packs like wolves of the sea, following migrating baitfish none of which can swim as fast as their streamlined pursuers. Few fish can. By mid-October the first of them were showing up in gulf waters in and around Tampa Bay, luck for us as we were visiting relatives in the area. Some mackerel, I was aware, can be found in these waters year round, but we had stumbled into a rush.

I could recall the Spanish mackerel from an earlier trip to the area. By chance I had caught a few while fishing off a pier, using thawed shrimp and a light weight spinning rod rigged for bait. Even at a mere 18 to 20 inches they worked that rod, slim as a pike and similar teeth, but faster; they came up finally and flopped on the planks, an iridescent silver blue below, on the flanks, shading into a darker blue-green above, along the spine, with bronze spots highlighted here and there.

"You catch one of those at five pounds," someone said, "and you're in for it."

I could believe it. And I would learn that the Spanish is not the trophy mackerel, topping out at an uncommon 20 lbs or so and always averaging less than ten. No, the trophy mackerel is the king mackerel, same physique, teeth, speed, and fight, but averaging twice the size and the big ones weigh 50 lbs. and more.

A mackerel story appeared in the local paper our first day in Florida. Now I was no longer thinking about getting back to New Mexico to baitfish for catfish or fly fish for trout and bass. Palm trees lined the streets, I would be fishing salt water, and I had Spanish mackerel, and kings, on my mind.

We started our mackerel hunt bank fishing off a break wall near Clearwater. We couldn't get our son to leave the pool so Cherie and I went without him. We cast thawed shrimp and cut squid and caught pinfish, grunts, and Cherie caught a flounder. No mackerel. And nothing very big. But we'd been fishing.

And we weren't worried about suffering from the vagaries of bank fishing. Our good relations had arranged a charter with a friend who was reputedly one of the best guides in the area. When I asked what his specialty was, I was told: "This time of year...mackerel." The anticipation was awesome. Bud was in no more of a mood to get up 5 a.m. than to leave the pool the day before. But we rousted him out of bed and arrived at the marina in the dark. We met Captain Brad Foster and his deckhand Brian, it took a little while for them to ready the boat and load up some gear, then we started away at no-wake speed out of the cove and headed for the open gulf. It was still dark.

242

It was a warming sun and breezy, putting the boat into a steady roll in the ocean swells, by the time we fed out the lines to troll for mackerel. We were trailing various spoons and jigs to entice these fish, the rigs were solid with stout rods and star drag reels, and notable were the 60 lb test shock leaders that attached just above the lures.

"You don't know what you might hook up with out here," Brian said, explaining the solid rigs. "We could see a 50 lb king or redfish, and if the mackerel start cutting those leaders we'll switch to wire."

The mackerel did not cut through the 60 lb monofilament leader but they hit the lures a belt and fought fast and hard for their size. The smaller of the Spanish mackerel were soon over powered and were simply cranked in to the boat, but the larger Spanish were in the 5 lb range and could run the drag some and swim off at swift angles from the angler. The action was sporadically fast and slow and depended in large measure on the birds. Brad was watching for diving gulls and pelicans.

"They're dropping to the water for baitfish," Brad said. "It's likely mackerel that are driving the baitfish to the surface. So you find birds dropping down for feed near the surface and you find mackerel underneath."

Indeed we did. And one of them ran quite a bit of line before I could begin to gain control, tire the fish, and bring him to the gaff. It was a king mackerel and I guessed he was close to 30" long.

Then Cherie hooked a bigger one. He cramped her arms after a while so Bud took over and wore the fish down. He was foul-hooked just in front of the dorsal fin, one explanation for his prolonged fight, the other being he was the best fish of the morning.

We came in at noon with 22 mackerel, mostly Spanish but also a half dozen kings. Brad filleted a few of the larger fish for us and we took the fresh meat across the street to the café where they will cook up what you have just caught as you like it. So we had blackened mackerel with fries and slaw. It was as good a fish as I have ever eaten and only Bud did not get the added pleasure of a cold beer.

I'm back in New Mexico now, hiking the streams fly fishing for trout and bass and bait fishing for catfish, enjoying the Indian summer and hoping for one more trophy before freeze-up. But whenever I go to Florida I will have Spanish mackerel, and kings, on my mind.

Making It Good with a Big Fish

Bud and I hadn't done well the last two times we'd fished the Gila.
This was last summer but the memories stay with you when you get
skunked just like they do when you beach a trophy, you just recall them
with gloom instead of animation. Last summer we'd sweated through
what had to be the hottest day of the year for one channel cat too small to
keep or eat; then, fly fishing, fought the brush of a tributary for hours to
find there were no trout in the stream. I work through all that, but when
Bud got a free day from school this spring I worried that he would, with
vivid recall, be sour on fishing and tell his father, "Well Dad, no thanks."
Instead he said, "OK; sure."

Just days before I had fly-fished the river, successfully, in spite of
muddy waters. I bragged on it in this column and I told Bud all about that
16-inch rainbow I inelegantly brought to hand. "He lost his dark glasses
on that fish," I heard him tell a friend, "and didn't even care."

But it had rained again since then and we would be fishing 40 miles
downstream – more silt. "Bud," I said, "we'd really be pushing it
catching a trout or bass on a fly in this water. But a catfish or carp can
find a bait in any kind of water. We'll take some nightcrawlers, and we
can always catch some hellgrammites if the worms don't work. Let's
gear up for big fish."

"OK, Dad, as long as we don't spend all our time sitting on the
bank."

"We'll move every 15 or 20 minutes until we find them. And the
biggest pool in that section, you've never been there but it should hold
fish. We'll fish upstream to the big pool before we turn back."

A destination like that will get any fisherman going, especially a kid,
and Bud is becoming a cast and move angler. So am I, some days. Other
days, or nights, I can just as happily doze by a line for hours in sedentary
and undirected contemplations. Waiting for luck. Apparently, it's not a
family trait. I can't see Bud as happy for long fishing in the manner of
Huck and Jim.

On the way out we went over the different kinds of fish this kid had
caught from the Gila Forest: rainbow trout, cutthroat trout, brown trout,
smallmouth bass, carp, channel catfish, roundtail chub, Sonora sucker.

"Ever catch a flathead catfish?"

"I don't think so."

"Biggest fish in the river."

"Oh?"

I let that sink in.

We left the trailhead at a good hour and hiked to a nice pool that
funneled into a deep, murky run. I had plenty of night crawlers kept cool
and lively in an insulated sack with an ice pack. It's really important to

have those crawlers fat and squirmy when they hit the water. I gave Bud the run and I took the pool and 15 minutes later we were ready to move on.

A second pool was futile as well and already Bud was hammering me about, "When are we going to get to the big pool?"

"We've got time," I said; "try here." We'd come to a long, deep pond in the river where, when the water is clear, you can see the carp in the slow current.

I got Bud a fresh worm and right away something started playing with it…little taps like a small fish. Then it just ran off with his bait. His drag was loose or he would have lost the rod. He tightened down and set the hook and he was in a battle with a good fish. Bud had an old Zebco Rhino spinning rod that was plenty stout for most any Gila fish and I had restrung it the day before with new 8 lb. test. There would be no excuses.

"Make him work the drag and don't point the rod at the fish and you got him," I said.

He did well and wore him down and eventually beached a 22-inch carp, nothing special for the Gila but a nice fish and Bud said, "Well, we didn't get skunked this time…when do we get to the big pool?"

He took it well when we were stopped short. The trail hit a narrows in the river – fast and deep – and we just couldn't cross.

"How far are we from the big pool?

"A quarter mile maybe."

"That's all?

"Yup."

"Well, next time, Dad."

Now he was consoling me!

But there are always other pools and many hidden holes along the Gila and we stopped by one on the way back.

"Work that deep backwash there," I said, "and I'll work the run below. And bait your own hook this time"

He did, but quickly grew bored with my backwash pool. So, on his own, he nicely cast his worm well downstream to a deep quiet spot by a cliff-face.

"Not a bad idea," I thought, and soon he was into a fish. It came easily at first but then made a long run and I reeled in and splashed ashore to help. It fought like the carp, only longer because it was bigger, and Bud made him work the rod and the drag and finally beached a flathead catfish 26" long.

"Don't let go of him!" he said.

"I won't."

"He looks freaky."

Well, they do look primitive, with that massive head and mouth. Built like a linebacker, I could see this one would easily go 10 lbs. I don't keep many but after some pictures to prove we didn't make it all up

I put this cat in the fish sack. Nothing eats better than a wild flathead from good water

We had plenty of day left but not blue sky. The rains came, not heavily, but there soon was lightning in the air and you don't stand in a river waving a stick in a lightning storm. It sent us on a direct hike back to the truck.

On the way home I wanted to tell Bud that days like this get bigger in a son's mind as he grows older. But he's too young to hear that now; you have to get to be a father to catch on to how important a big fish can be when you're just a kid.

A Story of Wet Flies in Muddy Waters

"I spent the early nineties fishing the Gila Country," Rex Johnson said, "and wrote *Fly Fishing in Southern New Mexico* (with Ron Smorynski). I fished across the state line in the late nineties and wrote *Arizona Trout*. Then it was *The Quiet Mountains* (his book about fly fishing the Sierra Madre of Mexico). Now I'm back in the Gila and I can't imagine a better place for year-round fly fishing…if somebody doesn't screw it up."

On the way to the East Fork of the Gila we talked about the chances that somebody *would* screw it up. Like maybe the New Mexico Interstate Stream Commission with their plan for yearly diversion and consumption of 14,000 acre feet of water from the Gila system. And whoever botched it on the upper end of the stream we planned to fish.

"You wouldn't believe it," Rex said. "Somebody used thousands of old tires to try to control erosion below old Wall Lake, and when the high water came last summer it all gave way. I was up there last week and the East Fork is strewn with tires from Taylor Creek to Diamond Creek. Trash tires in the Gila Wilderness! Some of them made it all the way to the mainstem of the Gila, thirty miles downstream. One ol' boy who lives up there told us the silt load that came down afterwards killed thousands of fish. That would include roundtail chub, a state endangered species."

Sure enough, when we got to the forks the East Fork was murky while the Middle Fork was clear. But I told Rex I had recently fished the Middle Fork and wanted to try something new. We took the fishing of the East Fork's muddy waters with flies as a challenge and headed upstream.

We didn't cast a fly till we got well up into the Forest Service lands, a one hour hike. The stream cleared a bit up there but we were still worried the fish wouldn't be seeing the fly. Rex had a large, non-descript black nymph with a bead head. He still added a split shot to make sure the fly bumped the bottom from time to time. I tied on a black Pistol Pete, thinking the flair of the spinner would attract fish in the muddy water, as well as sink the fly. I was confident I had the better plan but two hours later Rex had three trout and I had none. Further, one of his was a rainbow pushing 16 inches, fat and well muscled – a really nice fish – and I was starting to feel the pain of an "empty creel" (not that we were keeping any of them).

Obviously, getting to the bottom was part of it and I switched to a big fuzzy-green wooly bugger with a heavy bead head and promptly caught a bronze bass about a foot long. At least I wasn't skunked and the fish not only fought well, as you'd expect of a wilderness bass, he gave me back some confidence, an important element of success.

247

It was tricky though. The depth of the pools and runs was a constant mystery because you couldn't see three inches into the water. We were casting blind, guessing at the water by the way it moved. It was surprising we were having any luck at all. Then I caught a fair sized chub, and a bigger fish, a Sonora sucker, proving "rough fish" can find an artificial in the murk as well. We weren't getting a lot of hits but enough to keep us pushing upstream where maybe another 16-inch rainbow would use its good underwater vision and make another mistake. One thing in our favor; as murky as it was, and deep, we didn't have to worry about sneaking up on them.

Rex had another trout on for a while, saw it, a brown, before it flipped off. The same thing happened to me, only it looked like a bass. "I count those," Rex said. "I call it a 'long release.'" Normally, I don't count them unless I touch them. But Rex is more fly fisher than I will ever be and "long release" can certainly raise your score. So I go along with "long release" when I fish with Rex and by that reckoning I now had four fish and he had five.

Then he got the best bass, too. It fought like a bull terrier and Rex followed it into the pool, too far as it turned out; his attempts to keep that smallmouth on the tether soon led him in up to the arm pits, sliding down-slope ever deeper, and he was now trying harder to back out to dry ground than to land the fish. Eventually he managed both. Rex has always been a trout man but I like to think I had something to do with his more recent enthusiasm for the Gila's bronze bass.

We were miles from the truck and headed back. On the way I drifted that wooly bugger into a deep run in under a fallen tree. I got a take and hooked a fish that seemed to fight harder the longer I had him on. And Rex would tell me later I had him on "a long time." At one point I saw his tail and knew I had a good rainbow. I beached him finally, bent over a boulder to lift him one handed and show Rex. You need two hands for a 16-inch fish but we both got a good look before he flipped out of my hand and off the hook. He looked like a twin of Rex's fat, muscled trout. I also fell over that boulder in the process, wet to the chin, and dropped my dark glasses in the river, the reason I always buy cheap ones.

At the Buckhorn Saloon several hours later we totaled up two beers, buffalo burgers, and about 15 fish between us, wet clothes and one pair of lost sunglasses. On balance, we couldn't imagine that anyone else in the bar could possibly have had that much fun. We vowed to find out who was responsible for the tires upstream; even in wild country, someone was always trying to screw it up. Still, we'd done all right; and it may not ever happen again, but I considered it's not everyone can hold his own fishing with Rex Johnson while catching 4 species of wild fish on wet flies in muddy waters.

A Quizzical Look at Nymph Fishing

Any day now I hope to have a spring fishing story to tell. Of course you may be way ahead of me on this and are already out there, hiking and casting along the waters. More power to you.

But I'm waiting, like most of you, for that warm spell that will raise the temperature of the stream, activate the fish and their feeding, and give some better chance for success. So far, it hasn't been quite warm enough – not for me anyway – but we can still talk fishing. Today, to fire us up for that first outing, I will consider some thoughts on fishing with nymphs.

Dry fly fishing is generally named as more popular than nymph or streamer fishing; it certainly gets more press and at least appears to have a far larger following. Yet countless fishing writers over the years have told us that a trout (and presumably other species) does 90% of its feeding below the surface. These are for the most part the same experts who extol the dry fly approach and certify its popularity. I don't know how they quantify these figures but for the sake of this story I'm going to accept both assumptions as approximately true.

It's an anomaly: fish feed below the surface, yet the dry fly, which floats, gets the most use and, presumably, catches the most fish. I can think of two reasons why this may well be the case.

First, watching a fish take a fly off the surface has always held a special appeal in fly fishing lore (for many purists it's the only way to fish a fly). Second, it's easier to catch a trout on top than down in the deep.

Take a typical fly fisher and give him an afternoon on the water. He arrives in the heat of the day and, predictably, there's no hatch on and no fish rising. He's no purist so he ties on a nymph. The fish are deep, in the cooler waters, so can't be seen, but our man knows the 90% rule and the likely spot for feeders who aren't rising – the feed trough provided by the tail end of some fast, deep water.

Not being a nymph fisherman he likely makes several mistakes. He doesn't use a beadhead, or split shot, so doesn't get down deep where the fish are. When he does get a strike he misses it because he can't see the fish or his fly; being a dry fly expert he's not used to watching the line as an indicator of a take. He misses other hits because he leaves too much slack in the line; the fish takes the phony fly, then spits it out in disgust and our angler never knows he had a bite. He'd be skunked if not for the predictable hatch that appears in the last hour before darkness.

Suddenly some of the nymphs are rising in a metamorphism; trout are feeding on the surface as aquatic insects transform into flies, settle momentarily on the surface, then attempt to fly away. Our angler can see the hatch. He can see these fish. He can see his fly floating on the stream;

when his own fly is taken he can see that too and he tightens up, connects, and has a fish on. He catches more trout in an hour, fishing a hatch on the surface, than in a whole afternoon of that confounded nymph fishing.

Fish may feed 90% below the surface but, down below, it can be hell to catch one on an artificial fly, especially a nymph imitation, which the invisible trout gently "takes" rather than striking with force as with an attractor fly or lure, like a streamer, spinner, or spoon. How do you take better advantage of that 90% feeding pattern and turn the frustration of nymph fishing into a hooked fish?

I'm no expert but I recently read some notations on the subject from two of the best: John Gierach and Taylor Streit.

Gierach mentions the importance of watching for the fish. Often, he notes, even in the deeper runs, there is a barely perceptible flare or flash when the trout takes the sunken fly. If you see that, even if the line doesn't move, gently but immediately strike the fish. He mentions what should be obvious: keep as little slack in the line as possible, while still allowing a drag-free drift, so you'll see the line check at the take. But a lot of it, he says (and I like this explanation) is intuition. Do it a lot, learn to watch the line and the water at depth, "and you'll get the hang of it."

Streit also stresses that "just right" slack in the line while acknowledging that he's known very few fly fishers who can consistently detect the faint signs of a take on a nymph and strike quick enough to hook the fish. He includes himself among those found wanting. So he uses a strike indicator. He concedes that this is a bobber by any other name, but they do help one detect the take on a nymph. And he says the key to effective use of the indicator is to place it as close to the fly as possible so long as you still get the nymph to the desired depth.

On trout, I'm mostly a nymph fisherman myself. I'm intrigued by having the lure and the fish down out of sight, looking for the flash at the take, watching the line for that "check" when the fish stops the drift of the fly. It doesn't bother me that I usually don't see the fish till after he's hooked; the revelation is belated, that's enticing, and I can always fondly hope that the cryptic fish will turn up bigger than expected.

One time on the Gila River I was using, for me, an unusually long leader – about nine or maybe ten feet. I cast a bead-head prince nymph upstream and tried to keep an almost-tight line as I followed the invisible fly in its travel downstream with the current. With the end of the fly line right below me, I caught the faint flash of a fish on a deep roll downstream at the bottom end of the pool. The line never moved. Almost too late I struck, realizing that flash had to be a trout on the take; I had forgotten about that long leader and where it put the fly! Though a bit slow, and undeserving, I had enough dumb luck that I still gigged that fish.

It was a wild rainbow, as I judged by the way he jumped, and he was all over the pool till his last jump and maneuver left him tangling the line in some sunken slash. Held by the brush, I got him in my hand and guessed 15 inches before I turned him loose.

Would he have provided more excitement or satisfaction if taken on the surface? I can't see how.

Nymph fishing is neglected in the literature and lore of fly fishing, and underrated as a skill. I rarely use a strike indicator and, by golly, usually manage to catch some in spite of myself. But Lord knows how many fish, unbeknownst to me, take my sunken drifting fly, then spit it out in disgust to swim away all the wiser, never to be fooled again.

Slot Limits for Trophy Bass, Lengthy Trout, Big Blues

Perhaps it's a rite of passage.......at different times in my fishing life I've been a trout snob – where nothing but trout would draw my interest or praise – a bass snob, and just to be contrary, a catfish snob. Each time it was an above average specimen of its kind that turned my head in a new direction – a 22 " smallmouth on a brown wooly bugger from a wilderness stream; a 19" Gila trout on a Pistol Pete, a 47 lb blue cat on cut bait, a real brute from the deep South.. And while I like them all about the same now, I'm looking at two management techniques that could produce even larger fish: slot limits, and selective harvest.

Often employed to improve a bass fishery, the idea of the slot limit is either to protect, or harvest, the fish within a particular size range in order to improve fish numbers, or fish size, or fish "recruitment" (reproduction and growth to reproductive age). Or better yet all three in a given pond, lake, or stream.

Most states have some sort of slot limit for bass on at least some of their lakes or rivers but here in New Mexico we do not have slot limits for any of our sport species. We do have "quality waters" which are almost invariably trout waters like the San Juan River where it's all catch-and-release and artificials only. This does yield big trout but there may be a still better way for still bigger trout under slot limits and creative harvest. Meanwhile, the statewide bass regulation allows you to keep 5 bass per day (10 in possession) with a minimum size limit of 12" for smallmouth bass (14" at Ute Lake) and 14" for largemouth bass statewide. This protects the younger fish but means the bigger bass – up to 5 per day – may be killed. One wonders if some sort of slot limit might leave us with more big bass?

And catfish..........ever hear of a catfish quality water? Keep reading!

I fish the Gila River often for smallmouth bass. By my experience, the river is full of 6-9 inch smallmouth, indicating good recruitment. There is the occasional lunker bronze bass – 16+ inches. When I catch one that size I let it go, but anecdotal evidence tells me that many of our local anglers will keep and eat a big Gila bass. There's nothing to stop anglers at The Butte from killing and eating a bunch of trophy-size largemouth bass either. How might a slot limit affect bass size and numbers in Elephant Butte or the Gila River? The first thing to know is that there is both a *protective* slot limit and a *keeper* slot limit and they can have markedly different results.

An example of a protective slot would be: you must release all bass within the slot (say 12" – 16") but you can keep 5 bass below or above the slot (less than 12" or more than 16"). An example of a keeper slot would be roughly the opposite: you can keep 5 bass between 12 – 16 inches but must release all bass less than 12 or more than 16 inches.

The protective slot doesn't strike me as the way to go in the Gila or Elephant Butte. It might yield more bass of medium size but many anglers would tend to keep the trophies. Big bass – 18" and up – would become scarce.

A keeper slot makes more sense for the "big game" angler. One place a keeper slot is being tried is the Winnibigoshish chain of lakes in Minnesota. There, a limit of walleyes between 12 and 17 inches may be kept, but smaller and larger fish must be released. A recent report says that the Minnesota state fisheries people are finding the yield of 19+-inch walleyes going from 20% to 40% of the take under the keeper slot.

And it seems that large fish will produce even larger fish. A study from the State University of New York at Stony Point was reported a few years back by Bob Marshall in *Field & Stream*.

"Researchers worked with three tanks of Atlantic silversides (a minnow-sized fish averaging about 6" long)," Marshall wrote. "They removed the largest 90% from one tank, the smallest 90% from another tank, and a random selection from the third. After four fish generations the average weight in the group where the largest fish were removed was 1.05 grams, compared to 3.17 grams in the random selection and a whooping 6.47 grams in the tank where only the smallest fish were removed."

Thus, it would seem that the protection of trophy-size silversides, or bass, coupled with the removal or harvest of smaller individuals would yield even bigger silversides, or bass, in subsequent generations.

It has worked this way on the Red River of the North that splits North Dakota and Minnesota on the way to Manitoba. There, native channel catfish up to 40 lbs. were discovered some decades ago. But anglers "discovered" the fishery, it got popular, and they were keeping these trophies. The average fish size went way down, What to do?

The two states got together and said: "You can keep 3 catfish/day but only one of these can exceed 24 inches." In Manitoba, *none* of the keepers could exceed 24". With this simple regulation in place average catfish size began to climb year by year and this river is now the number one destination in North America for trophy channel cats. Although the fish mature at almost a glacial pace in that cold climate, some once again reach 40 lbs.+ thanks to a creative harvest.

Following this lead on the Gila, we could remove the bag limit on smaller bass (under 12") but rule you can only keep one/day over 16 inches. Why remove the bag limit on the smaller bass? Because they are not native west of the Continental Divide and in places compete with natives like spike dace et al, for survival. The result? Fewer bass (to help the native fish) but more lunkers (to please the anglers).

For trout in the Gila River we could do something similar – establish a population of wild Gila trout, protect those above 16", remove

253

rainbows, let the browns fend for themselves (they don't really need a bag limit anyway).

Where might we set up such "quality waters" for bass or trout? The 7 miles of the Gila River between the Turkey Creek confluence and Mogollon Creek confluence, a lovely stretch of bass habitat with white water, deep blue-green pools, no vehicular traffic (a defacto wilderness). For trout we could consider the Gila West Fork from the wilderness boundary upstream to White Creek Falls – almost 20 miles of good trout water.

But the most spectacular gains in size and trophy status thru the creative harvest with slot limits could be with a New Mexico native that few of our residents have ever caught or even seen – the big Blue Catfish. And I can reveal there appears to be an exciting change in catfish demographics in New Mexico.

"Along about 2003," Eric Mammoser of New Mexico Game & Fish in Las Cruces told me, "we began to see more blue catfish in our electro-fishing surveys, and it seemed to coincide with lower water levels in the two reservoirs (Elephant Butte and Caballo)." Mammoser couldn't say if the low water levels were a real factor or, more likely, just coincidence but the takeover by blue cats from the formerly plentiful channel catfish was dramatic.

"By 2007 our surveys were turning up more blues than channel cats," Mammoser said, "and by last fall (2013) we counted 50 channel cats and 452 blues electro-fishing at night at The Butte in coves and flats in 3 to 10 feet of water." He added, "They come in there, in the shallows, at night to feed." And he said the big ones were up around "forty pounds; but they get bigger than that........the state record is 54 pounds."

While the record channel cat is impressive at 58 lbs. (Santee-Cooper Lake, South Carolina), and the flathead catfish record of 123 lbs is from a farm pond in Kansas, the blue cat record is 143 lbs. from Buggs Island Lake in Virginia. Keep in mind that Virginia didn't have any blue catfish until an introduction in the 1970s. Now the Potomac River running right thru the nation's capital is growing 100 lb. fish! Virginia has a simple limitation on blue cat: per license, only one blue cat/day over 32 inches may be kept. And the record is broken every few years!

The trend in fishing is away from the goal of a stringer full of dead fish and towards the capture of a trophy fish that is returned to the waters. Based on what I've seen so far, a keeper slot or that simple variation as on the Red River would work best for The Butte. And the Gila River, where natural reproduction and recruitment of bass doesn't seem to be a problem, might be the best place for an experimental look at a slot limit, or size regulation, that could reduce the population of bass in the river, and still produce more trophy bass.

We Finished Strong on Florida "Redfish"

As a fisherman, Bill Crown doesn't have much patience. If he doesn't get some action in a given spot in 10 minutes of so he moves on. I have perhaps too much patience – or maybe I'm just lazy – and thus am inclined to work an area harder and question all that moving around. But in the end, this day, hopping about worked out well.

It was a family holiday to visit in-laws near Clearwater Bay in Florida and the principal in-law was good enough to line us up for a day's fishing with neighbor, tax accountant, and veteran angler Bill Crown. I know close to nothing about salt water fishing; we arrived at first light at the marina and Bill welcomed Bud and I aboard.

"Snook, redfish; that's what we're after," he said. "But you never know what you'll run into out there."

First, he took us for a ride, out to the outer reaches of the bay; the 20 foot craft, built for fishing inshore salt water, had a 150-horse Mercury outboard and ran like a scalded cat. Kids love that and young Bud had a smile all the way out as we removed our hats to keep them from blowing away in the 40 mph breeze.

Bill called them "sardines" though they looked like 5-inch smelt to me. He let Bud run the boat at very low throttle while he threw the cast net. I enjoyed watching him throw it; I've done it myself with a smaller net. And Bud liked the responsibility of wheel and throttle and gear; casting close in to a small island Bill soon had the live-well swimming with sardines. Catching your own bait is as much a part of fishing, and as much fun, in the ocean as along New Mexico's Gila River. We then began to work our way back towards the marina, fishing the flats off small islands for "snook and redfish."

Bill didn't have much patience when none showed up. I caught a small black drum and had a good bluefish on till his mouthful of teeth cut the line. Bill landed a nice bluefish. We all caught a slender, graceful fish of a pound or two called a ladyfish that fought well and jumped. We were casting those sardines live with no sinker with spinning rods that let you feel the fish. But in Bill's mind we were striking out.

Bud and I were still happy though. It was a good day with an easy breeze and a hazy sun; everything was new and birds were everywhere and we were catching fish. Plus those speedy runs to the next stop were always lively; I'll never be bored in boats that run that fast.

It wasn't long and we were fishing spots back in close to the marina. When they didn't produce snook or redfish either, Bill said: "If I knew it would be this slow I would have rigged us all with wire leaders and stayed with those bluefish way out there."

They were lively all right, those bluefish, and hit with the passion of a predator with a mouthful of teeth. But we were hopping about and had long since moved on from the bluefish flats.

We came to the least likely place in a long morning. At least it seemed so to me. We ended up fishing some flats off a breakwall by the 7th hole of the Bellaire Country Club, close enough to the marina Bud and I could have swam back to the car in a pinch.

Bill put out the anchor and we cast towards the breakwall. At first, it wasn't even good for a ladyfish. Then Bill noticed something.

"There's something chasing those mullet over the oyster bar just downwind of us," he said.

I looked and some sort of baitfish was surfacing over a shallow area that I took to be the oyster bar. Bill did the smart thing and simply let out enough anchor rope to put us within casting distance of the frightened baitfish. We would now try to find out what was chasing them.

I was proud of Buddy. He got up on the casting deck and threw those sardines with that spinning rod as far as either me or Bill. They began to hit right away and Bill said, "redfish!"

Bill hooked the first one and handed the rod to Bud. He landed it. Redfish can run from a foot long to 40 or 50 lbs. but you can only keep one apiece and the "slot" is 18 to 27 inches. Bud got the first keeper, though we let it go, anticipating bigger fish.

Also called "channel bass," redfish are in fact a saltwater drum; they seldom jump but fight with speed and a bulldog tenacity. We all got one or more over two feet and Bud got the biggest. He hooked it himself on his own cast and here's how the fight went.

The fish was running the drag and circling the boat. When he got to the front he went under the anchor rope. Following Bill's instructions, Bud fed the rod under the rope and picked up on the fish. Then when the fish circled back he did that anchor rope trick again, just like a veteran. He wore him down with a tight line, a well-set drag, and patience, and then Bill hauled the fish aboard. I thought, "That kid's becoming a fisherman."

The feed shut down as abruptly as it had begun. By then we had each caught several with one each in the livewell for grilling that night; redfish are renown as an eating fish. Hopping about, fishing here and there, had paid off at our last stand. In the end it was redfish on bait and spinning gear that let you feel the fish. Bud and I, from arid New Mexico, are still rookies in the saltwater fishing games. But with redfish and Bill Crown we had started at the top.

Trophy Hunting Wild Trout and Bronze Bass

I knew I was in for it when I saw O'Day take that spinning rod out of its case. I commented in a recent column that Stephen O'Day is a deadly stream fisher with a spinning rod, light, open-faced reel, light line, and the right spinner. He'll fly fish, but I really think he prefers a spin-cast rig. And with that light line, that would about match a 3x (6 lb) tippet, and the way he sneaks up on the pools, he's not totally unlike myself, the hopeful fly caster, trying to catch the same fish in a Gila forest stream.

True, it didn't help him last time we were out. He caught nothing before he quit and went home, while I managed a single trout before salvaging the day by switching to bait and catching several stout suckers and a chub. But this time we were on different water and I knew that, given a stream with fish, O'Day and that spin rig could lose count of their catches.

This time of year there's no sense being out along the waters at 7 a.m.; the air's too cold for the fisher and the water's too cold for the fish to bite. But it was a day that warmed fast and along about 11 a.m. I caught two rainbows out of the first deep run while O'Day was still rigging up his rod. Then, upstream, I caught two more out of the first deep pool and one of them was about 16 inches long. I was using a Pistol Pete and O'Day, still empty, was complaining about his spinners.

"I've got a little box of Rooster Tails and left them home," he said. "I don't think a Mepps is what they want today. Darned if I didn't leave those Rooster Tails home!"

It was a lovely day of warming air, cloudless sky, and just enough breeze to keep it from getting hot. The cottonwoods and sycamores were wonderfully colored. The fishing slowed for a time but we kept moving and I picked up another rainbow and O'Day broke through with a 15-inch fish that he said "looks like a walleye." He held it up and it was a roundtail chub.

"He wasn't fast but pulled some," O'Day said. He turned him loose and complained some more about not having his Rooster Tails. "Somehow, I left them home," he said for what I hoped would be the last time. I wasn't convinced it was the Rooster Tails anyway; this was a fly fisher's day.

Well upstream now, I drifted that Pistol Pete down a deep run and, when the line came taut, let it swing through the current of a fast pool. At the end of the swing I got a terrific hit.

"That's a trout!" O'Day said. He was downstream, where the fish was headed, and could already see I was into a fish I could brag on, if I could land him.

I started downstream myself, keeping a tight line and hoping I'd tied good knots. It was an impressive flurry by a fish but soon enough he

257

tired and I could see his size and colors in the shallows. He was the biggest trout I'd worn down all year. And with the red-magenta stripe, that went along the lateral line from the tail right up to the gill plates, was no hatchery stocker. I beached him and, measuring with the span of my hand, he was at least 17 and maybe 18 inches long. O'Day was generous in praise and we stopped for lunch.

"Here's a Rooster Tail," he said, drawing that particular lure from a mass of spinners, "but look at that puke-green blade."

Between bites of a sandwich he used his knife to scrape the paint from the blade, changing it from puke-green to flashing silver. He now had the weapon he wanted all along. And the next pool is where I made my mistake.

I knew the pool and got there first but left it to O'Day; poor thing, he was still waiting on his first "good" fish. Casting that Rooster Tail gently and from a distance, he promptly hooked and landed a bronze bass that was at least 17 and perhaps 18 inches long. He outfought my big rainbow, jumped twice, though he couldn't match my fish in colors. O'Day was on the board with a trophy and from then on he couldn't be stopped.

We hiked back to the trucks not long before dark, a little bushed but exalted with results. My Pistol Pete lost its allure in the afternoon but I still finished with a half dozen trout, including a 16-incher and a bragging fish with all the colors of the rainbow and pushing 18 inches. Plus a couple of pretty good bass.

O'Day, as predicted, outfished me in the end with that spin-cast outfit and Rooster Tail. He landed 10 or 12 bass (I told you he might lose count), 2 nice rainbows, and a big chub. One of his bass carried bragging rights and, favoring that species in wilderness streams, I wished I'd caught it myself. O'Day, who prefers trout, was a little jealous of my rainbow.

Of course neither fish was as big as a Sonoran sucker I caught two weeks earlier. But a 20" sucker, no matter how tough, is just a fun fish. He's not magic. For that you need to successfully hunt big wild trout and lengthy bronze bass born and raised in a wilderness stream.

Squawfish on the Fly

Well, actually, they don't call it a squawfish any more. Fishery science now calls it the Colorado pike-minnow. The new name *is* a better fit, not because of political correctness, but because the fish is a minnow and is pike-like; long and lean with predatory instincts and the potential to reach 50 lbs., or better. My skills as a fly fisher are average at best but I count myself among the elite because I have caught a squawfish (pike-minnow) on the fly.

Indeed, I caught two of them fly fishing and one on bait – a live hellgrammite – from the Verde River of Arizona. It was May, circa 2000, and a half dozen of us put in at the Childs Power Station and headed for Horseshoe Dam 45 miles downstream. We took ten days to do it.

That's a nice way to travel by canoe, a leisurely float, when you have time to lay over a couple of days here and there at a good camp. The Verde runs clean and clear and turquoise blue through the Mazatzal Wilderness in this reach; it's challenging water in an open canoe; I swamped twice but nothing serious. And we fished.

I was the only fly fisher in the group and, as usual, I also fished bait. Altogether, we put an impressive mix of fish on the bank: smallmouth bass, largemouth bass, channel catfish, flathead catfish, and carp. No lunkers, but some nice ones and more than we could eat or keep, though we ate a good many – fish fried, fish soup, fish in foil, fish on the grill – and then about the third day out I caught something I didn't know what to do with.

I tossed a black wooly bugger into a run, expecting a bronze bass; I got a good hit from what looked and struggled like a foul-hooked snake or eel in the water. I got him in and it was a fish, lean but healthy looking, about 16 inches. I thought…a roundtail chub? Then I saw, and felt, the teeth. I had a squawfish, a federally endangered species. I knew then what *not* to do; keep it, or throw it up on the bank! The fly loosened easily and a rare fish swam away.

Down river, over the next several days, I would catch two more, one on a pistol Pete, and one, like I said, on a hellgrammite. They were all about the same size and each felt like a whiplash on the end of the line. Then we met up with Arizona Game & Fish. They were rafting, and doing a fish survey; they would electro-shock a section, take data on everything that surfaced, then throw all the non-native fish – bass, catfish, carp, including some real lunkers – up on the bank. They also took wildlife data from us.

We told them we'd seen otters (re-introduced to the Verde) and I mentioned I'd caught three squawfish. They lit up and one fellow took down all the details – where, when, size, fly, lure or bait, etc. He said the pike-minnow and razorback sucker were principal native fish of the

Verde and the lower Colorado River watershed; Arizona Game & Fish and U.S. Fish & Wildlife Service were engaged in a recovery program in the drainage for native fish that included removal of competing non-native species. He said the Colorado pike-minnow had great potential as a game fish and they were happy to have the evidence that they would take a fly. I wished them luck.

They'll need it! Mind you, I'd be the first to say that I can think of nothing better as a fisherman than to catch a 50 lb. pike-minnow, or even a five lb. pike-minnow, on a fly. But I probably won't ever catch another, of any size. That's because the species has become increasingly scarce in the new millennia, despite frequent re-introductions and vigorous control of competing non-natives, in the Colorado River watershed. One who recognizes the reality of the native fish dilemma is fishery scientist Gordon Mueller, Ph.D., of the U.S. Geologic Survey

In a long, fascinating article – "Lost: A Desert River and Its Native Fish" – Mueller details the slow but ineluctable decline and loss of the Colorado pike-minnow and other natives to dams and other human modifications of riverine habitats, and to the eventual domination of these natives by non-native, predatory sport fish. He also recognizes the implausibility of system-wide native fish recovery in main-stem rivers like the Verde, Gila, Salt, San Juan and the Colorado itself; the dams are not coming down. And the non-natives are ubiquitous; experience has shown we lack the technology, money, labor, and political gravitas to rid these major rivers of popular sport fish such as bass and catfish, according to Mueller

The Verde River is a case in point. After my canoe trip I followed the fortunes of the pike-minnow there. I learned that re-introductions began in 1991 with some 10,000 fingerling pike-minnow. There followed other releases, some of larger juvenile fish, over the next ten years and augmented by removal campaigns against non-natives. By 2002, fish surveys by Arizona Game & Fish of the Childs to Horseshoe reach turned up less than 100 pike-minnow, all stockers and no recruitment. The non-natives remained in force and the recovery effort is in limbo.

Mueller thinks our efforts for native fish recovery should be directed toward establishing "refugeium populations" in smaller headwater streams and other limited locales where habitats and competing non-natives can be better controlled. I'd support that. Mueller's "Lost River" piece has historical photos of pike-minnow that remind one of big muskellunge. This fish can inspire anglers; catch one on a fly and join the elite.

Trout and Otters: Victory at the Stream

Whenever some conservation group, leading environmentalist, or journalist declares victory on a given environmental issue I always take a second look. For it's usually not in fact a victory but more a holding of the line; e.g., we stopped the dam, the road, the oil drilling in a pristine grassland, or, at least temporarily, the extinction of a species. Only rarely does "winning" in the environmental wars involve an actual gain, a recovery of something lost. Yet that is just what has happened along the Gila River in the past month.

In mid-August the U.S. Fish & Wildlife Service accepted the proposed downlisting of the Gila trout from endangered to threatened, thus acknowledging real gains in the fish's range and population and allowing for the possibility of limited fishing for the species as early as next year.

Then on August 24th the State Game Commission voted to reintroduce the river otter to a portion of the Gila River, and to the Rio Grande Gorge near Taos, by the fall of 2007, thereby returning to the wild a delightful predator last seen in our state in a trap along the Gila in 1953. Both actions were part of the overall philosophy of native species recovery in New Mexico and both may be viewed as real victories at the stream.

The Gila trout recovery program was the more controversial. Identified as a separate species in the 1950s, numerous attempts at recovery were thwarted by combinations of bad weather, bad luck, and, in the view of some of us, bad management. The Gila trout is of course the native trout of the Gila/San Francisco drainage, closely related to the rainbow but rendered distinct in color pattern and other traits by millions of years of geographic isolation.

Around the turn of the century (1900) introductions of rainbow trout began to hybridize the distinct Gila strain out of existence. Many rainbow introductions from hatcheries were made into numerous Gila forest streams, the sole Gila hatchery was abandoned, and the local strain was genetically "swamped" out of existence in all but portions of a half-dozen upper headwater streams. Just in time, some anglers and biologists got worried. By the 1960s plans were underway to bring the species (I think it's a subspecies myself) back. It wasn't easy.

Rainbows and competing brown trout had to be removed, often with the controversial use of fish poison. Progress was made, population and range was gradually increased, and at one point in the late 1980s recovery seemed assured and a downlisting imminent. Black ash from forest fires wiped out the Gila stock of several key streams and the program was set back a decade or more.

261

Adding to the reversal of fortunes, increasingly sophisticated DNA genetic analysis, as applied by the wildlife agencies, began to declare entire populations of this fish, by all appearances pure Gila trout, as not "pure-strain," including the original "relic" population in Iron Creek. For a period of years the program was in retreat, some of the reversal self-imposed by the very biologists charged with its recovery as they poisoned Gila trout that were lacking a few percentage points of being "pure-strain."

But the agencies were persistent, new introductions from hatcheries were made, further ash flows and other natural disasters were evaded, "impurities" were for the time being forestalled. With the anticipated addition of 20+ miles of the upper West Fork to Gila trout recovery this fall, nearly 100 miles of stream may carry "pure-strain" Gila trout. A downlisting was justified, has been achieved; you could honestly call it a victory in the environmental wars.

This could be a fun fish, well worth the effort. More subtly colorful than a rainbow or a brown, the Gila is distinguished by a yellow to bronze coloration, belly to back, and often a yellow throat slash. One of the biologists told me recently a young population reached 9 inches in just two years in one small Gila stream and 14 to 15 inches in one of the larger runs.

Can the Gila trout strain be kept 100% pure (by the Federal requirement for acceptance as true Gila trout, even 1% introgression is a "hybrid" by rule and thus disqualified)? Would the agencies propose to re-poison a stream that showed a few points of genetic introgression of the rainbow strain? Can the competing browns be kept out? These are big questions, and possible debates, for a future column. For now we can be pleased by progress and prepare to fish the Gila's native trout in selected streams next year.

By contrast, bringing back the otter was relatively easy. A 10 to 25 lb. aquatic weasel, otters are endearingly playful and one of the few predators one could call "cute," even as adults. Vernon Bailey and other early naturalists described them as present, if not particularly common, in a number of the state's drainages, including the Gila/San Francisco. They eat some of the same fish that we anglers pursue, but reports from other states that have introduced otters show little or no decline in angler success; indeed, most of us fishers like the idea of having them around. And they love crawfish, currently present in plague proportions in portions of the Gila.

Studies by the New Mexico Department of Game & Fish over the past few years indicated a half-dozen river reaches that could possibly support 20 to 30 pairs of otters apiece, the upper Rio Grande and that portion of the Gila between the East Fork confluence and Mogollon Creek ranking highest. The public overwhelmingly approved and the

Game Commission voted unanimously to bring them back to these two river sections.

In a region, state, and nation all afflicted with rapid human population growth, aggrandizing industry and the machinations of man, a real victory in the natural world is rare. We should count our recent blessings in southwest New Mexico and strive all the harder to hold on to what we have left of the natural world.

Trout Lore: The Art of Drifting Worms

I some time ago largely gave up fly fishing when I go to the stream with Big Jon Finn. The over-size Scandinavian holds no truck with the effete sport of casting artificial flies and, frankly, my phony flies are seldom a match for his live wigglers.

The uninformed would call him a "worm dunker." The term is invariably delivered in pejorative tone but in the case of The Big Finn does not do justice to the art of drifting worms and other live bait for trout. I'm not the first to come to a late recognition and respect for this element of trout lore.

In that splendid angling volume, *The Philosophical Fisherman*, author Harold Blaisdell, a fly fisher by preference, lays out the truth, even if it hurts a little bit to admit it.

"If a fisherman has gone on to fly fishing after an apprenticeship in bait fishing," Blaisdell writes, "he can probably catch more fish on flies than a beginner can on bait. But let him revert to bait, if he is truly a master at the game, and I'll back him to outfish any fly fisherman over the long haul, or any spin fisherman for that matter."

Blaisdell goes on to relate an anecdote of fly fishing wherein he and his friend Pete, analogous to my buddy The Big Finn, were left stumped when visible trout and salmon were found in a run of water in the Maine wilderness. Despite repeated attempts by both men none of these fish would even cast an eye – let alone make a run – at an artificial fly or lure. Blaisdell, stubborn, stayed with his hardware and caught nothing all morning. His partner, Pete, meanwhile, switched to drifting live worms with a small split shot on light line. Blaisdell reported the melancholy (from his vantage) results.

"Pete continued to take fish after fish," he writes, "and it was obvious that the spot was teeming with trout and salmon, all apparently waiting in line to grab a sunken worm!"

Blaisdell delivers the hard conclusion which I believe any honest angler, experienced with both bait and artificials, will acknowledge.

"First," he writes, "there are times when it is virtually impossible to take fish on anything. Next, there are periods during which fish will respond to bait but will show almost no interest in flies, plugs or hardware. Finally, there are those interludes when they will hit both bait and artificials. In other words, there are times when fish will take bait and refuse artificials, but never a time when they will hit artificials and scorn bait."

I have read Blaisdell on flies and bait – he has much more to say on the subject than we have room for here – but sometimes forget his lessons. Like last week when Big Jon Finn and I went after trout and bass along a reach of the Gila River. Fishing alone, or with most anyone else,

I'd have fished with flies; efficiency is not always the goal and fishing flies is fun. But I didn't want The Big Finn to catch *all* the fish.

I had a 9-foot fly rod but was rigged with a sliding sinker, swivel and #8 Eagle Claw hook. Jon had a short (5 ½ ft) spinning rig, 4 lb test line, no sinker, and a #6 Gamakatsu Octopus style hook. We were both using night-crawlers and for this trip did not take time to hunt for live bait along the stream.

In the first hour we caught nothing, though some of the water looked good. I said, "They'll start to bite when the water warms with the day." I turned out pretty smart as this is just what happened. Jon caught a 12-inch brown. Soon he caught a 13-inch brown. Brown trout in the Gila have not been stocked in many years; these were wild trout and I was pleased when John let them go.

"We'll keep a rainbow (which are often stockers) if we catch one," I said.

But the next fish was another foot-long brown, with tan back, red spots on the sides, and yellow belly. Pretty fish. And I was pleased to have caught it myself. I had already noticed however that Jon and I were fishing the same baits differently.

With heavier line and sinker my worm would bounce along the bottom in strong current, sit on the bottom in weak current. Meanwhile, with 4 lb. test and no sinker, Jon's worm just drifted with the current, almost as if unattached. When I caught the next trout, a 13-inch rainbow that squirmed out of my hand before I could rap him on the head, I guessed it didn't make much difference how I was rigged. I was wrong. There is an art to trout fishing, even with worms.

Over the next several hours Jon caught 4 more trout, mostly browns and up to 14 inches long, while I came away empty with my heavier tackle. Worse, twice he took fish out of runs where I had just fished and failed. Suddenly I didn't want a rig that bounced along the bottom; I wanted a worm that fished like it just fell in the water. And I didn't like the way that sinker splashed at the end of a cast. I took it off and began to fish a free-floating worm.

Neither of us would land another fish the rest of the day. We would catch and release 7 trout between us, all a foot long or better, plus Jon kept one rainbow for supper. I did hook and lose two strong fish on the way back to the truck using my new free-drifting worm. Jon said I'd have gotten them to the bank if I had used the Gamakatsu "Octopus" hook. Well, maybe. But what was the principal lesson in trout lore offered for the day?

Simple: bait fishing for trout (or any other fish) goes better with a drag-free, natural presentation, just as fly fishing does, whether you're casting and drifting a worm, hellgrammite, grasshopper, minnow, or Prince nymph.

So, this day The Big Finn caught more fish than me. But I figure I still got the better of the deal. He will never learn fly fishing from me for he'll never cast a fly. But I will surely drift bait for trout another day, and I'll do better having fished with "a master at the game."

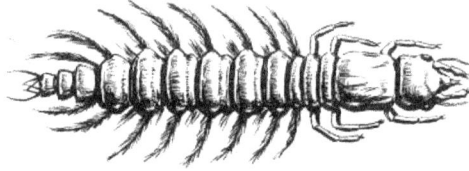

Twenty Inches is Big Bass, Small Carp

Size matters, as they say with a wink. But more to the point size is relative, as any fisherman knows who has ever stopped to think. Some fishermen don't stop to think, as they ably show by photos of themselves with a stringer full of sizeable trophies hung in bloody display. I've had days like that; I've caught them, kept one or two, yet felt no obligation to fill the freezer with the kind of fish you'd normally work a whole summer for. Most if not all of those fish are back in the water. Which ones? It depends, but on the Gila River I've found that 20 inches can be a line of demarcation, a size that matters.

There are times when I gear up for channel cat, or flathead catfish, or carp or even Sonoran sucker, and certainly one or more species of trout draw me to numerous days along the waters of the Gila drainage. But give me one day, and one fish to try for, and I'll hike miles to dapple the water with flies for the Gila's smallmouth bass. It has all the attributes of fly fishing for trout plus you hook into a harder fighting fish. And maybe a bigger one.

I've lost track of the Gila bronze bass I've caught in the 18-inch range, both with flies and bait. I can't give you the weights because I let all those big ones go, but the span of my hand is about 9 inches and I've caught a fair number of bass that went two spans, or thereabouts.

Those were nice fish and since 1982, when I first fished the Gila, far from common, for that's 25 years of fishing. More common over that 25 years were stories I'd hear of bigger bass, 20-inches or more. Some of these stories came from what I considered to be reliable fishermen, some not so reliable, but either way they were bass described as from 20 to 24 inches long that curiously never had a photo to go with them. At least I never saw one. Of course a photo is not a measuring stick – nor, precisely, is the span of my hand – but I looked longingly in the Gila's waters year after year for that mysterious 20-inch bass, thought I had him hooked on more than one occasion, yet once ashore the span of my hand always told me I was a little short of the goal, or maybe the myth.

I certainly wasn't expecting to reach that goal, or make real a myth, when I went to the Gila last week. It was my first outing on the river since October and I was merely shaking down – checking gear, getting the feel of rod and reel and fly and bait, the cast and drift, checking and reading the waters of cold spring run-off; and if I caught a few fish I would be ahead of myself and wasn't concerned about size. I wore my new hip boots but even at that didn't know if I'd be able to cross the river at 200 cfs .without topping out my waders or going over, swept away in an icy flow.

But I know this long pool that runs up against a cliff. I've caught bass, catfish, carp, sucker, even a rare trout, there. Under 100 cfs I can fish any of its swirling pools that lay up against the rocks on the far side but now I could see I'd be confined to the lower end where I could cross – maybe – on foot. I did make it across and worked a wooly bugger upstream and down, wherever it looked like the current might hold a bass. I spent an hour at the best spots, tried every angle, current, pool and drift. In truth I was just practicing my casting; the water was murky and cold and said, "Not likely with a fly."

I changed to a hook, split shot, and nightcrawler, and that quickly added catfish, carp, and sucker to the possibilities. I still fished it like a fly however, tossing the worm upstream into drifting currents and allowing a bit of slack as it drifted down into holding pools. I was clearly trying to give myself a chance at whatever species of fish might be in there.

On one drift I got a very tentative take and tightened up on a fish. We felt our connection at the same time and his response was a strong run, but not a swift one. He was invisible for some time in the murky water and I guessed a channel cat about two feet long. Then he rolled and I saw a bronze bass. He appeared to be in my 18-inch range and then he rolled twice more – almost a jump – and each time he looked bigger. He was strong but sluggish for the run-off was icy cold snowmelt; he was nowhere as swift and athletic as a summer smallmouth but he worked that rod into a deep bow for 10 minutes till I beached him – two spans and a good couple of inches more – a 20-inch bass!

The carp I caught and released later in the day wasn't much bigger; a disappointment, for along the Gila a two-foot carp is nothing and a 30-incher a real possibility. But he fought not unlike the bass and on a 6 wt. rod that's sport.

It's not a myth; there are 20-inch bass in the Gila. And those other anglers, no longer suspected liars and no doubt better fishers than I, were telling the truth. Most of them anyway. I realize I'd have had a better story, and a bigger brag, if I'd caught him on the wooly bugger instead of garden hackle. But in truth it took a live "fly" to get him to take. He was still 20-inches on a fly rod. And he's still in there. Maybe next time I'll catch him on an artificial. Even if I never see him again, I'll remember that bass long past a carp of equal spirit that was in fact a little bit bigger.

Poor carp. In fishing size matters, relatively speaking.

A Mixed Bag, A Long Life

With a lingering war going on in Afghanistan, constant bloody turmoil in the region, and "9/11" still on everyone's mind, Middle-Eastern life-ways are seldom praised in our time. Yet an old Arab proverb will always ring well with me: "Allah does not deduct from life a man's time spent fishing." Allowing for minor changes in language and syntax, and the sometime substitution of "hunting" for "fishing," it's apparent that what the British call "field sports" invite a universal brotherhood and philosophy of timeless pleasures unique to the pursuit of game and fish. But even with fishing there are days when you wonder if your time is well spent.

It had been weeks since I'd managed a full day on the stream, and when I finally grabbed one, I worried. Would the weather be good? Would the stream be too low in lingering drought, or high and muddy with recent monsoons? Would I be too late and find others had beat me to the best spots? Would I forget my lunch? A lot can go wrong even on your day off.

I was up with the chickens and made sure I was not too late. Once beyond the trailhead I entered the Gila Wilderness; I would see no one all day. The stream was indeed low but the fish would still be there, if somewhat harder to sneak up on. My sandwich was in my pack. It seemed there was no good reason not to make a day of it.

I caught a chub at the first pool. He was more than a foot long but there is a reason this fish is not on the "game" list. Well, two reasons. One is, the roundtail chub is scarce and "endangered" under New Mexico state law. The other is, though they will take a fly and strike hard, they invariably flag inside of a minute. Let's just say this fish had some size and was fun while he lasted.

Then I started missing fish. I think they call it "striking short." I'd get hits and they'd be on for a shake or two and then they'd come loose. I could see many of these fish and while some were small and could be anticipated as hard to hook, most of these looked like trout or bronze bass at least a foot long and I couldn't keep them on either. I switched from a #6 wooly bugger to a #10 wooly bugger and watched a bass that must have been 16-inches long come out from under a big rock and flash at my fly. He was on for two shakes then put it back in my face, as if spitting phony flies was an evasive technique he had learned at school.

It was now near noon. I'd covered miles of stream, was drenched in sweat, and I felt half starved. But I would not quit for lunch until I had a good fish to satisfy my mind. Would I go all day hungry?

At the next run I fooled a nice rainbow. He gave it a real belt, and when he surfaced the first time I could see the fly; he was hooked good. I determined to land him, then quit and relax for lunch, read the paper and listen to the waters gently ringing off canyon walls, my philosophy

269

restored. The bugger jumped and landed in a bit of slash that high water had sucked into the pool. He went under and wound the line in the branches of that slash and broke the tippet. A homily from Anglo culture goes: "The worst day fishing is better than the best day working." Or something like that. I was beginning to wonder.

It was mid-afternoon before I got something to eat. At a long deep run I cast upstream and used a split shot to bounce that wooly bugger along the bottom. I got a very tentative take but hooked the fish anyway and felt good weight. He was all over the pool, stayed deep, and kept going and going. Turned out to be a Sonoran sucker rather than the bass I expected, and would have preferred. But he was 20-inches long, had great spirit that he shared with me, and it takes a certain skill to catch a sucker fairly on a fly; i.e., not foul hooked. I now had reason enough to quit for lunch, read the paper, and listen for a time to a free flow gently ringing off canyon walls.

The reprieve was short, for the shade was now on the other side of the canyon and I was miles from the truck. I started on the return hike, fishing here and there. No longer were they all striking short, though most were small fish. But one, the only brown of the day, was easily a foot long. I landed him, too; things were looking up.

At the pool where the big bass spit back my fly I plotted my revenge. I cast from a distance, kept most of the slack out of the line, and the cross-current took the fly right by that big rock. He made a wake in his attack and struck so hard he snapped the fly off. Well, I'd had that fly on for half the day, had hooked and battled several bass and trout, a big sucker, and been hung up several times and worked the fly free, all on the same knot. It was my own foolish fault; even good knots fail over time. On the eve of retribution, my inattention had allowed one big bass to yank me deep into gloom twice in one day.

Things nearly got a whole lot worse. I sat on the end of a hollow log, got out a new wooly bugger, and heard a familiar buzzing rattle underneath my seat. I came up off that log like my pants were on fire. He could have hit me right in the back of the calf; it was certainly nice of him to give me a warning instead. I found a safer seat and hurriedly tied what I hoped was a pretty good knot.

Time was running out. Black clouds began to arrive, seemingly from all directions, perhaps because this stream can't ever go 100-yards in a straight line. In the last of the sun I made a proper cast, hooked and landed a 16-inch fish, thick, muscular and athletic, that jumped, then glistened all the colors of the rainbow when he lay finally in the shallows, defeated.

Released, the trout soon revived in the current. I revived in the rain on the hike back to the truck, knowing the Arabs had it all figured out, oh so long ago. Enough of this and I could live forever.

Country Sports II

HIGH-LONESOME BOOKS

"Published in the Greatest Country Out-of-Doors"

At **HIGH-LONESOME BOOKS** we have a great variety of titles for enthusiasts of the Southwest and the great Outdoors—new, used, and rare books of the following:

Southwest History

Wilderness Adventure

Natural History

Hunting

Sporting Dogs

Mountain Men

Fishing

Country Living

Environment

Our catalog is FREE for the asking. Write or call.

HIGH-LONESOME BOOKS
P. O. Box 878
Silver City, New Mexico
88062
575-388-3763
Orders@High-LonesomeBooks.com

Also, come visit our bookshop in the country
at High-Lonesome Road near Silver City or on-line at
www.High-LonesomeBooks.com

Country Sports II

www.ingramcontent.com/pod-product-compliance
Lightning Source LLC
Chambersburg PA
CBHW030639150426
42813CB00050B/212